Rainbow Edition

Reading Mastery VI
Skillbook

Siegfried Engelmann • Jean Osborn • Steve Osborn • Leslie Zoref

Macmillan/McGraw-Hill

Columbus, Ohio

SRA Macmillan/McGraw-Hill
8787 Orion Place
Columbus, OH 43240-4027
Printed in the United States of America.
ISBN 0-02-686415-0

  14 15 16 17   POH   08 07 06 05

Lesson 1

PART A   Word Lists

1	2	3	4	5
Ulysses	Hermes	advertise	**Vocabulary words**	**Vocabulary words**
chauffeur	freight	improve	box social	advanced
Athena	Odysseus	improvements	up and coming	batter
recipe	receipt	advertising	unkindly disposed	chauffeur
Zeus	Homer		for a spell	receipt
Odyssey			freight train	nutmeg

PART B   New Vocabulary

1. **box social**—A **box social** is a get-together. The people who come to the get-together bring their lunch in a box.

2. **up and coming**—Something that is growing fast or becoming very popular is **up and coming**. A singer who is becoming popular is an **up and coming** singer.
   - What do we call a business that is really growing fast?*

3. **unkindly disposed**—When you are **unkindly disposed** toward something, you don't like it.

4. **for a spell**—Here's another way of saying **for a while: for a spell.**
   a. What's another way of saying **She slept for a while?***
   b. What's another way of saying **They will rest for a while?***

5. **freight train**—A train that carries products, but not passengers, is called a **freight train.**
   - What do we call a train that carries products, but not passengers?*

6. **advanced**—Something that has moved forward is **advanced.** If somebody has ideas that are ahead of other people's ideas, that person has **advanced** ideas.
   - What would we call an operation that is far ahead of other operations?

7. **batter**—Cake and other things like cake are made from **batter.** When the **batter** is raw, it's soft and sticky.
   - What do we call that substance?*

8. **chauffeur**—A **chauffeur** is a person who drives a car for a wealthy person.
   - What do we call a person who drives a car for a wealthy person?*

9. **receipt**—**Receipt** is an old-fashioned word for **recipe.**

10. **nutmeg**—**Nutmeg** is a spice that is used in cooking.

PART C   Story Items

Write which character each statement describes. Choose from **Homer, Uncle Ulysses, the rich woman, Mr. Gabby,** or **the chauffeur.**

1. This character had a weakness for labor-saving devices.
2. This character was a relative of the shop owners.
3. This character knew a good recipe for doughnuts.
4. This character looked like a sandwich when he worked.
5. This character drove the rich woman around.

PART D   Writing Assignment

Write a paragraph about labor-saving devices. Be sure it answers the following questions:
- What is good about labor-saving devices?
- What is bad about labor-saving devices?
- How do you feel about labor-saving devices?
- Why do you feel that way?

Make your paragraph at least **four** sentences long.

Lesson 2

PART A   Word Lists

1	2	3	4
Aggy	Ithaca	theater	**Vocabulary words**
Odysseus	calamity	regular	hold the wire
pinochle	Zeus	sheriff	fat
Athena	gadget	tar	gadget
Polyphemus	Odyssey	tarnation	chute
chute	Hermes		divine
Poseidon			pinochle
			calamity

PART B   New Vocabulary

1. **hold the wire**—Hold the wire is another way of saying, "wait a minute" to somebody on the other end of the phone.

2. **fat**—People used to use **fat** to fry food. Today, most people use cooking oil instead of **fat.**

3. **gadget**—Another word for a **device** is a **gadget.**
   - What's another way of saying **He invented a very useful device?***

4. **chute**—A chute is a slide. Another word for a **coal slide** is a **coal chute.**

5. **divine**—Another word for **marvelous** is **divine.**
   a. What's another way of saying **I had a marvelous time?***
   b. What's another way of saying **Her party was simply marvelous?***

6. **pinochle**—**Pinochle** is a card game that is played with a special deck of cards.

7. **calamity**—Another word for **misfortune** is **calamity.**
   - What's another way of saying **She suffered through misfortune after misfortune?***

PART C　Story Items

1. Uncle Ulysses needs to get rid of all the doughnuts.
   a. How could he get rid of the doughnuts and make money at the same time?
      - By selling them
      - By giving them away
      - By burning them
   b. Do you think he'll be able to do that?
   c. Name another way he could get rid of the doughnuts.
   d. Who does he think will be mad at him?

2. Write which character each statement describes. Choose from **Mr. Gabby, Homer, Uncle Ulysses, the rich woman,** or **the chauffeur.**
   a. This character was married to Aunt Agnes.
   b. This character had a big fur coat.
   c. This character was a sandwich man.
   d. This character called his uncle at the barber shop.

PART D　Writing Assignment

Write a paragraph that advertises Homer's doughnuts. Be sure it answers the following questions:
- How do they taste?
- What ingredients are used?
- How are they made?
- Why should people buy them?

Make your paragraph at least **four** sentences long.

Lesson 3

PART A   Word Lists

1	2	3	4	5
skeptical	Poseidon	pinochle	Odysseus	**Vocabulary words**
Penelope	lyre	Zeus	bracelet	demand
Ithaca	citizens	cardboard	Hermes	create a market
Rupert	Circe	Odyssey	suspicious	enlarge
Iliad	merchandise	soda	Athena	hire
trident	Polythemus			citizens
				merchandise
				skeptical

PART B   New Vocabulary

1. **demand**—The **demand** for a product tells how many people want or demand that product. A large **demand** means a lot of people want to buy that product.

2. **create a market**—Here's another way of saying **create a demand**: **create a market**.
   - What's another way of saying **His invention created a demand for more telephones?***

3. **enlarge**—When you **enlarge** something, you make it bigger. Here's another way of saying **He made the circle bigger: He enlarged the circle.**
   a. What's another way of saying **He made the circle bigger?***
   b. What's another way of saying **They made the demand bigger?***

4. **hire**—When you **hire** somebody, you give that person a job.

5. **citizens**—**Citizens** are people who live in a place. The people who live in Emerald City are **citizens** of Emerald City.
   - What do we call the people who live in Centerburg?*

6. **merchandise**—When you **merchandise** a product, you carry out a plan for selling that product. When you carry out a plan for selling razors, you **merchandise** razors.
   a. What are you doing when you carry out a plan for selling razors?
   b. What are you doing when you carry out a plan for selling doughnuts?

7. **skeptical**—When you are very suspicious about something, you are **skeptical** about that thing.
   a. What's another way of saying **She was suspicious about his ability?***
   b. What's another way of saying **They were suspicious about his claims?***

PART C   Vocabulary Review

1	2
chauffeur	nutmeg
batter	advanced
calamity	

1. Another word for **misfortune** is
   _____.
2. Something that has moved forward
   is _____.
3. A person who drives a car for a
   wealthy person is a _____.

PART D   Story Items

1. **a.** Who would wear the signs
      advertising the doughnuts?
   b. Why was he called a sandwich
      man?
   c. Did his plan work?
   d. Where were most of the people in
      town?
2. The woman came back to the
   lunchroom.
   a. Why did she come back?
   b. Did they find the object they were
      looking for by moving the
      doughnuts around?
3. **a.** Who finally figured out what must
      have happened to the bracelet?
   b. Where was the bracelet?

4. Homer came up with a plan.
   a. How much of a reward did the
      woman offer for her bracelet?
   b. How could people find the bracelet?
5. As the machine made doughnuts, the
   supply and demand were not in
   balance.
   a. Which was greater, the supply of
      doughnuts or the demand for
      doughnuts?
   b. Homer made up new signs that
      told about the reward. Were these
      signs supposed to increase the
      supply of doughnuts or the demand
      for doughnuts?
   c. How many of the doughnuts did
      Homer and the others sell?
      ● All   ● Most   ● None
   d. Did anybody ever find the bracelet?
   e. Did that person get to keep the
      bracelet?
   f. How much money did the woman
      give that person?

PART E   Writing Assignment

Write a paragraph that explains what you
would do if you won a hundred dollars.
Be sure it answers the following questions:
● What are three things that you would
  like to do?
● Which of those things would you do
  and why?

Make your paragraph at least **four**
sentences long.

Lesson 4

PART A Word Lists

1	2	3	4
Apollo	Mount Olympus	Ithaca	**Vocabulary words**
Lochus	Hermes	Polyphemus	encounter
Circe	trident	Iliad	translate
Trojans	Athens	lyre	hinder
cyclops	Odyssey	Athena	disaster
Penelope	version	Poseidon	graze
Telemachus	Odysseus		tar
			fleece
			commotion

PART B New Vocabulary

1. **encounter**—When you **encounter** something, you come into contact with that thing. If you come into contact with misfortune, you **encounter** misfortune. If you come into contact with terrible mountains, you encounter terrible mountains.
   a. What's another way of saying **You come into contact with terrible mountains?***
   b. What's another way of saying **She came into contact with dangerous people?***

2. **translate**—When you tell a story in another language, you **translate** the story into that language. If you tell an English story in German, you **translate** it into German.
   ● What do you do if you tell the story in French?*

3. **hinder**—Some of the people helped her but others tried to **hinder** her.
   ● What could **hinder** mean?

4. **disaster**—A horrible event is a **disaster.**
   a. What's another way of saying **The flood was a horrible event?***
   b. What's another way of saying **The storm created many horrible events?***

5. **graze**—When animals eat grass they are **grazing.** If they are eating grass on the hills, they are **grazing** on the hills.
   ● What are they doing if they are eating grass in the valley?*

6. **tar**—Tar is a hard black substance that turns into a sticky mass when it is heated.

7. **fleece**—The fur of a sheep is called **fleece.**
   ● What do we call the fur of a sheep?*

8. **commotion**—A **commotion** is a disturbance.
   a. What's another way of saying **There was a great disturbance in the hall?***
   b. What's another way of saying **She created a terrible disturbance?***

PART C   Vocabulary Review

1	2
freight	merchandise
advanced	skeptical
gadget	

1. When you are very suspicious about something, you are _____ about that thing.
2. When you carry out a plan for selling a product, you _____ that product.
3. Another word for a **device** is a _____.

PART D   Story Items

1. a. What are the names of two of the oldest stories in the world?
   b. About how many years ago do the stories take place?
   c. Which person was one of the most important Greek kings?
   d. What was the name of the island he ruled?
2. a. Which story tells about a war?
   b. Which two armies fought in the war?
   c. At which city was the war fought?
   d. How long did the war last?
   e. Who won the war?
   f. That army won the war when they gave the other army a gift. What was that gift?
   g. What was inside?
   h. Who had the idea of tricking the Trojans?
3. The second story takes place right after the war.
   a. What is the name of that story?
   b. Who is the main character of that story?
   c. To which island does the main character try to go?
4. The stories were first told out loud.
   a. What was the name of the first person to tell the stories?
   b. What problem did that person have with his eyes?
   c. What musical instrument did that person play?
   d. Did that person know how to write?
   e. So how did the stories stay alive?
   f. About how many years went by before anyone wrote down the stories?
      ● 20   ● 200   ● 2000
   g. What language were the stories originally written in?
   h. The stories were told in the form of _____.
      ● a play   ● a picture   ● a poem
5. Write which god or goddess each statement describes. Choose from **Zeus, Poseidon, Hermes,** or **Athena.**
   a. This god was the messenger god.
   b. This god was the god of the sea.
   c. This god carried a lightning bolt.
   d. This god could make tidal waves.
   e. This goddess protected people who were in danger.
   f. This god was the chief god.
   g. This goddess showed people how to tame horses.
6. The gods had many powers.
   a. Could they control thunder and lightning?
   b. Could they control ocean storms?
   c. Could they control the way people acted?
   d. Who had to face dangers, Odysseus or the gods?

PART E   Writing Assignment

Which Greek god or goddess do you like the most? Write a paragraph that explains your answer. Be sure your paragraph answers the following questions:
- What do you like about that god or goddess?
- Why do you like that god or goddess more than the others?

Make your paragraph at least **five** sentences long.

Lesson 5

PART A   Word Lists

1
Telemachus
Calypso
Apollo
Scylla
Lochus

2
Poseidon
dairy
cyclops
lyre
Penelope

3
Athena
Circe
monstrous
Polyphemus

4
Vocabulary words
draw straws
fulfill
risk
bronze
pluck
departed
slay
mast

PART B   New Vocabulary

1. **draw straws**—People sometimes **draw straws** to see which person must do an unpleasant assignment. Here is how you **draw straws**. First, you present one straw to each person. All the straws are the same length, except for one. You cover the ends of the straws, so that nobody can see which straw is different from the others. Then each person draws one straw. The person that draws the odd straw is the loser.

2. **fulfill**—When something is **fulfilled,** that thing comes true. If a dream comes true, that dream is **fulfilled**.
   - What happens if a promise comes true?*

3. **risk**—When you take a chance, you take a **risk**.
   a. What's another way of saying **He took many chances when climbing the mountains?***
   b. What's another way of saying **Race drivers take chances?***

4. **bronze**—**Bronze** is a metal that is made by mixing copper and other metals.
   - What do we call the metal made from copper and some other metals?*

5. **pluck**—When you **pluck** a plant from the ground, you quickly remove it from the ground.
   - What are you doing when you quickly remove a plant from the ground?

6. **departed**—When you go from a place, you **depart** from that place.
   a. What's another way of saying **They went from the building?***
   b. What's another way of saying **They went from the forest?***

7. **slay**—Another word for **kill** is **slay**. What's another way of saying **They will kill their enemies?***

8. **mast**—The **mast** is the large pole that holds up the sails on a sailing ship.
   - What do we call the pole that holds up the sail?*

PART C Vocabulary Review

1	2	3
fleece	translate	freight
encounter	commotion	hinder
gadget	chauffeur	disaster

1. When you come into contact with something, you _____ that thing.
2. A terrible event is a _____.
3. The fur of a sheep is called _____.
4. Another word for **disturbance** is _____.
5. When you tell a story in another language, you _____ the story into that language.
6. Some of the people helped her, but others tried to _____ her.

PART D Story Items

1. a. What city was Odysseus leaving at the beginning of the story?
   b. How long had he been in that city?
      ● 10 hours ● 10 days ● 10 years
   c. What was the name of his home island?
   d. That island was a part of which country?
2. A great storm beat upon Odysseus's ship.
   a. In which direction did the storm blow the ship?
   b. Which land did the ship first come to?
   c. What was unusual about the faces of the people who lived there?
   d. What kinds of places did those people live in?
   e. What animals did those people take care of?
3. Odysseus went into a cave.
   a. How many men were with him?
   b. Name at least **two** things the men found in the cave.
   c. Who was the owner of the cave?
   d. What object did that character use to block the cave opening?
   e. Why couldn't Odysseus and his men move that object?
4. Polyphemus saw the men.
   a. Did Polyphemus care for the gods of Mount Olympus?
   b. Who was the only god that Polyphemus respected?
   c. That god was Polyphemus's _____.
      ● son ● father ● uncle
   d. What did Polyphemus do with two of the men?
   e. If Odysseus killed Polyphemus, he would still have a problem. What would that problem be?
   f. At first, Odysseus told Polyphemus that his name was _____.
5. Odysseus came up with a plan.
   a. What substance did he find?
   b. Where did Odysseus throw that substance?
   c. What did that substance do to Polyphemus's sight?
   d. When Polyphemus called for the other cyclops to help, he said that _____ had blinded him.
   e. What did the other cyclops do to help Polyphemus?
   f. Which god did Polyphemus call to?
   g. Where did Polyphemus lie down so that he could catch the men as they left the cave?
   h. Why didn't Polyphemus feel the men as they went by?
6. a. When he was far away, Odysseus told Polyphemus his real _____.
   b. How did Polyphemus try to hurt Odysseus after that?
   c. Which god heard Polyphemus?
   d. That god began to _____ against Odysseus.

PART E Writing Assignment

Write a paragraph that shows how cunning Odysseus is. Be sure it answers the following questions:
● What cunning statements did Odysseus make to Polyphemus?
● What cunning plans did Odysseus carry out?

Make your paragraph at least **five** sentences long.

Lesson 6

PART A Word Lists

1	2	3
cease	Penelope	**Vocabulary words**
Ino	mermaid	hideous
Sirens	companies	perish
Phacia	Lochus	mist
suitors	wisdom	sheltered
Calypso	Apollo	cease
hideous	Circe	deed
Scylla	Telemachus	wallow
perish		suitor

PART B New Vocabulary

1. **hideous**—Another word for **horrible** or **disgusting** is **hideous**. A horrible scene is a **hideous** scene.
   a. What's another way of saying **a horrible scene?***
   b. What's another way of saying **a disgusting monster?***

2. **perish**—When something dies, it **perishes**.
   a. What's another way of saying **Plants will die without water?***
   b. What's another way of saying **Without help, all the men will die?***

3. **mist**—A fine rain is called a **mist**.
   • What is a fine rain called?*

4. **sheltered**—If something is protected, that thing is **sheltered**. Something that is protected from the wind is **sheltered** from the wind.
   • What do we call something that is protected from the cold?

5. **cease**—Another word for **stop** is **cease**.
   a. What's another way of saying **The rain stopped?***
   b. What's another way of saying **Soon the battle will stop?***

6. **deed**—Another word for **an action** is **a deed**.
   a. What's another way of saying **Her actions were admirable?***
   b. What's another way of saying **His hideous actions were punished?***

7. **wallow**—When something **wallows**, it struggles in mud or water. Here's another way of saying **The ship struggled in the wild waters: The ship wallowed in the wild waters.**

8. **suitor**—A man who sets out to marry a woman is that woman's **suitor**.
   • What do we call a man who sets out to marry a woman?*

PART C Vocabulary Review

1	2	3
citizens	depart	slay
risk	hire	fulfilled
chute		

1. Another word for **kill** is _____.
2. When you go from a place, you _____ from that place.
3. When something comes true, that thing is _____.
4. When you take a chance, you take a _____.

PART D Story Items

1. The men came to another island.
   a. What was the name of the sorceress who lived there?
   b. Where did Lochus and half of the men go?
   c. What were the men changed into?
2. Odysseus went to the palace.
   a. Which god did Odysseus meet on the way?
   b. What did that god give to Odysseus?
   c. Whose power did that object protect Odysseus from?
   d. What did Odysseus make Circe do with the pigs?
3. Circe warned Odysseus about his journey.
   a. What did Circe warn Odysseus not to eat?
   b. If the men obeyed that warning, how many men would return to Ithaca?
      ● All ● One ● None ● 22
   c. If the men did not obey that warning, how many would return?
      ● All ● One ● None ● 22
   d. What would Odysseus find when he returned home?
   e. What would Odysseus have to plant in the ground before he could finally live in peace?
      ● An oar ● A tree ● Vegetables

4. Odysseus and his men sailed to a beautiful island.
   a. What was the name of the people who lived there?
   b. What sound did those people make?
   c. What happened to people who heard that sound?
   d. Why didn't Odysseus's men hear the sound?
5. a. Which person wanted to hear the sound?
   b. What did the men do to keep Odysseus from following the sound?
   c. What did the people seem to be offering Odysseus?

PART E Review Items

Write which character each statement describes. Choose from **Odysseus, Circe, Polyphemus, Poseidon, or a Siren.**
1. This character had only one eye.
2. This character changed men into pigs.
3. This character was the god of the sea.
4. This character sang songs that enchanted sailors.

PART F Writing Assignment

Pretend you are one of the Sirens. Write a paragraph that tells what you sing to Odysseus as he sails by. Be sure the paragraph answers the following questions:
● What do you offer him?
● How do you make your offer sound appealing?

Make your paragraph at least **five** sentences long. If you want, you can arrange your sentences into a song.

Lesson 7

PART A   Word Lists

1	2	3
Phacia	Calypso	**Vocabulary words**
perils	porpoises	in the midst
Ino	Telemachus	loom
tunic	scale	cherish
	scaly	perils
	Scylla	carpenter
		lurk

PART B   New Vocabulary

1. **in the midst**—When you're **in the midst** of something, you're in the middle of that thing.
   a. What's another way of saying **They were in the middle of an argument?***
   b. What's another way of saying **They were in the middle of a thick fog?***

2. **loom**—A **loom** is a large device that is used to weave cloth.
   • What do we call a large device that is used to weave cloth?*

3. **cherish**—Something that is valued very much is **cherished**.
   a. What's another way of saying **They valued her friendship?***
   b. What's another way of saying **I value his advice?***

4. **perils**—Another word for **danger** is **peril**.
   a. What's another way of saying **She experienced many dangers?***
   b. What's another way of saying **The soldiers are often in danger?***

5. **carpenter**—A **carpenter** is a skilled person who makes things from wood.
   • What do we call a skilled person who makes things from wood?*

6. **lurk**—When someone **lurks**, that person hides and waits to attack.
   • What is a person doing when that person hides and waits to attack?*

PART C   Vocabulary Review

1	2	3
cease	suitor	graze
deed	fleece	calamity
enlarge	fulfilled	hideous
perishes	encounter	skeptical

1. Another word for an **action** is a _deed_ .

2. Another word for **stop** is _cease_ .

3. When something dies, it _perishes_ .

4. Another word for **horrible** or **disgusting** is _hideous_ .

5. A man who sets out to marry a woman is that woman's _suitor_ .

6. Another word for **misfortune** is _calamity_ .

7. When you come into contact with something, you _encounter_ that thing.

8. When you are very suspicious about something, you are _skeptical_ about that thing.

9. When something comes true, that thing is _fulfilled_ .

PART D   Story Items

1. The sea narrowed between two high cliffs.
   a. What kind of pool was near the left cliff?
      - A calm pool
      - A shallow pool
      - A whirlpool
   b. What would happen to the ship if Odysseus went near that cliff?
   c. Name the creature that lived within the right cliff.
   d. How many heads did that creature have?
   e. What would be the worst thing that would happen to the men if Odysseus went near the cliff on the right?

2. After going through the narrows, Odysseus and his men came to a beautiful island.
   a. What animals were on the island?
   b. Which god did those animals belong to?
   c. Who would die if the men ate those animals?
   d. Name the person who would live.
   e. Who had told Odysseus about those animals?
   f. What did Odysseus make his men promise before they landed on the island?
   g. Which event forced the men to remain on the island?

3. a. What did the men decide to do while Odysseus slept?
   b. Did the men listen to Odysseus's warnings?
   c. What happened to the ship after it left the island?
   d. How many men drowned?
   e. How did Odysseus survive the storm after the ship sank?

4. Odysseus came to another island.
   a. What was the name of the woman who lived on that island?
   b. How did she treat Odysseus?
   c. How long did Odysseus stay in her cave?
   d. Why couldn't he leave the island?
5. Meanwhile, there was trouble in Ithaca.
   a. What was the name of Odysseus's wife?
   b. What was the name of Odysseus's son?
   c. What did his family believe that almost nobody else believed?
   d. What would happen to the man who married Odysseus's wife?
   e. What were the men who tried to marry Odysseus's wife called?
   f. How many of those men stayed at Odysseus's palace?
   g. Where did they spend their time?
6. a. Which goddess found out about the trouble in Ithaca?
   b. Which god did she talk to about Odysseus?
   c. Who did that god agree to help?
   d. Which god was still angry with Odysseus?

PART E   Writing Assignment

On each island that Odysseus visited, he found a new kind of monster or person. Which island do you think is the most frightening? Write a paragraph that explains your answer. Be sure the paragraph answers the following questions:
- What is on the island?
- What makes the island so frightening?

Make your paragraph at least **five** sentences long.

Lesson 8

PART A   Word Lists

1
Eumayus
Melanthius

2
tunic
farewell
Phacia
shadowy

3
Scylla
backwash
Ino
reins

4
Vocabulary words
canvas
launch
surf
savage
peering

PART B   New Vocabulary

1. **canvas**—Canvas is a strong cloth that is used for sails.
   - What do we call a strong cloth that is used for sails?*

2. **launch**—When you **launch** a ship, you put it in the water for the first time.
   - What do you do when you put a ship in the water for the first time?

3. **surf**—The **surf** is the waves near a shore.
   - What do we call the waves near a shore?*

4. **savage**—Things that are **savage** are wild and cruel. A wild and cruel beast is a **savage** beast.
   a. What's another way of saying **A wild and cruel beast?***
   b. What's another way of saying **Wild and cruel waves?***

5. **peering**—When you **peer** at something, you stare at that thing.
   a. What's another way of saying **She stared at the waves?***
   b. What's another way of saying **They stared from over the bushes?***

PART C   Vocabulary Review

1	2	3
mist	disaster	skeptical
commotion	slay	cease
lurks	hinder	fleece

1. A terrible event is a _____.
2. Some of the people helped her, but others tried to _____ her.
3. Another word for **stop** is _____.
4. When you are very suspicious about something, you are _____ about that thing.
5. Another word for **disturbance** is

   _____.

6. When a person hides and waits to attack, that person _____.

PART D   Story Items

1. a. What was the name of the person that Odysseus had been with for a long time?
   b. How many years had Odysseus been on her island?
   c. Who came to the island with an order to release Odysseus?
   d. Why was Calypso reluctant to let Odysseus go?
   e. But Calypso could not disobey the order of _____.

2. Odysseus had many strong feelings.
   a. Why was Odysseus sad on Calypso's island?
   b. What would he rather do, die on the sea or live forever on Calypso's island?
   c. Who was the one person he most wanted to see?
   d. What did he leave the island on?

3. Odysseus sailed for almost three weeks.
   a. Which god saw him?
   b. What had Odysseus done to that god's son?
   c. How did that god try to hurt Odysseus?
   d. Which goddess saved Odysseus?
   e. What object did she give to Odysseus to protect him?
   f. Name the island Odysseus came to at last.
   g. Was it easy for him to land there?
   h. What did he throw back into the water as soon as he landed?

4. a. As Odysseus slept on this island, a goddess helped him. Which goddess?
   b. This goddess gave a dream to a _____.
   c. The dream told that person to do something the next morning. What was that?

5. a. What woke Odysseus?
   b. Odysseus didn't dare to go near the girls because he wasn't wearing any _____.
   c. Describe how Odysseus's face looked.
   d. What did Odysseus ask the princess to give him?

PART E   Writing Assignment

If you were Odysseus, would you have left Calypso's island? Write a paragraph that explains your answer. Be sure the paragraph answers the following questions:
- What reasons would you have for staying?
- What reasons would you have for leaving?

Make your paragraph at least **five** sentences long.

Lesson 9

PART A   Word Lists

1
Antinous
Melanthius
Eumayus

2
Vocabulary words
flask
noble
minstrel

PART B   New Vocabulary

1. **flask**—A **flask** is a kind of bottle.
   - What do we call some bottles?*

2. **noble**—Somebody who is **noble** is proud and brave.
   - What do we call a person who is proud and brave?*

3. **minstrel**—The **minstrels** who lived at the time of Odysseus would read poetry, sing songs, and play the lyre.

PART C   Vocabulary Review

1	2	3
peer	launch	citizens
slay	cherished	peril

1. When you put a ship in the water for the first time, you _____ it.
2. Another word for **danger** is _____.
3. Something that is valued very much is _____.
4. When you stare at something, you _____ at that thing.

PART D   Story Items

1. a. Was the princess afraid of Odysseus?
   b. Odysseus went into the river to _____ himself.
   c. How did Athena make Odysseus look?
   d. What did the princess think she might do with Odysseus?
2. a. Did the princess want Odysseus to go with the girls when they reached the city?
   b. The princess was afraid that people would think that she had found somebody to be her _____.
   c. So what did Odysseus do when they reached the town gates?
   d. Which goddess did Odysseus meet when he entered the town?
   e. Did Odysseus recognize that goddess?
   f. What was the harbor full of?
3. a. Who did Odysseus meet at the palace?
   b. What did the queen notice about Odysseus's clothes?
   c. What did the king want Odysseus to do?
   d. Why couldn't Odysseus do that?
   e. What did the king finally promise to do for Odysseus?

PART E   Writing Assignment

Odysseus has visited several islands. Which islands would you most like to visit? Write a paragraph that explains your answer. Be sure the paragraph answers the following questions:
- What is on the island?
- Why would you like to visit the island?

Make your paragraph at least **five** sentences long.

Lesson 10

PART A   Word Lists

1
Argos
Antinous

2
Phacians
Eumayus
faithful
anchored
Melanthius
challenged

3
Vocabulary words
sow the seeds of doom
boar
lice
flee

PART B   New Vocabulary

1. **Sow the seeds of doom**—When you **sow the seeds of doom,** you do something that will cause death or something very horrible.

2. **boar**—A **boar** is a wild pig that has long tusks.

3. **lice**—Lice are insects that get in your hair if you don't keep yourself clean.

4. **flee**—When you **flee,** you move as fast as you can.
   - What's another way of saying **The boar will move as fast as it can from the lion?***

PART C   Vocabulary Review

1	2	3
bronze	noble	risk
minstrel	savage	cherished

1. A person living at the time of Odysseus who read poetry, sang songs, and played the lyre was called a _____.

2. Somebody who is proud and brave is _____.

3. Things that are wild and cruel are _____.

4. Something that is valued very much is _____.

PART D   Story Items

1. a. At the feast of Odysseus, what did the minstrel first sing about?
   b. Why did that song make Odysseus sad?
   c. What did Odysseus do to show his ability at sports?
   d. The princess was sad when she saw Odysseus again because she knew that he was already _____.
   e. The minstrel sang about a hero. Which person did he sing about?

2. When Odysseus was on the ship to Ithaca, he fell asleep.
   a. Did Odysseus know where he was when he woke up?
   b. What had the members of the crew placed all around Odysseus?
   c. Which person did Odysseus meet on the shore?
   d. Odysseus said that he was a _____.
   e. Why hadn't the goddess been able to help Odysseus on the sea?
   f. Athena changed Odysseus so that he looked like an old _____.

3. a. Which person did Odysseus go to see after he left Athena?
   b. What kind of animals did that person and his dogs herd?
   c. Which family had that person remained faithful to?
   d. Which person did Athena go find?

4. a. Odysseus told Eumayus that he was _____.
   b. Why did Odysseus tell that kind of story to Eumayus?
   c. Did Eumayus believe the story?

PART E   Writing Assignment

Pretend you are Odysseus telling his story to the Phacians. Pick your favorite part of his story, and then tell it as Odysseus would have. Start your story with the word "I." Be sure the story answers the following questions:
- Where were you?
- What happened?
- Why did you do what you did?

Make your story at least **ten** sentences long.

Lesson 11

PART A   Word Lists

1	2	3	4
courteous	Melanthius	Phacians	**Vocabulary words**
merely	breakfast	quarrel	revenge
Argos	Eumayus	Antinous	unearthly
		ivy	neglect
			custom

PART B   New Vocabulary

1. **revenge**—When you take **revenge** on someone, you get even with that person. Here's another way of saying **He got even with the robber: He took revenge on the robber.**
   - What's another way of saying **He got even with the robber?***

2. **unearthly**—Something that is **unearthly** is not like anything that you would find on this earth.

3. **neglect**—When you **neglect** something, you fail to take care of it.
   - What's another way of saying **She failed to take care of her dog?***

4. **custom**—A **custom** is a way of behaving that everybody follows.
   - What do we call a way of behaving that everybody follows?***

PART C   Vocabulary Review

1	2	3
bronze	peril	risk
mast	loom	perishes

1. When something dies, it _____.
2. When you take a chance, you take a _____.
3. Another word for **danger** is _____.

PART D   Story Items

1. Telemachus saw an eagle come out of the sky.
   a. What kind of bird did the eagle fly away with?
   b. Which goddess explained the meaning of that event to Telemachus?
   c. Which person was the eagle like?
   d. Name one way in which the eagle and that person were the same.
   e. Which people was the goose like?
   f. Name one way in which the goose and the people were the same.
   g. What would Odysseus do that was like what the eagle had done?

2. a. When Telemachus came to the hut, did he recognize Odysseus at first?
   b. Where did Telemachus tell the beggar to stay that night?

3. a. Eumayus's dogs suddenly began to whine because they saw _____.
   b. This goddess instructed Odysseus to tell _____ who he really was.
   c. How many suitors were at Odysseus's palace?
   d. Where did they leave their swords and armor?

4. a. How was Odysseus disguised the next morning, when he came to the palace?
   b. What did Melanthius do when he met Odysseus?
   c. What secret would Odysseus have given away if he had hurt Melanthius?

5. **a.** What was the name of the dog that Odysseus saw?
  b. Did the dog recognize Odysseus?
  c. How did that dog show that he knew Odysseus?
  d. What injury had Odysseus received when hunting with that dog?
  e. What finally happened to the dog as Odysseus watched?
  f. Where was Odysseus sitting at the end of the chapter?

6. Athena has helped Odysseus do some things, but Odysseus has done other things by himself. For each event, write **Athena** if she is responsible for the event. Write **Odysseus** if he is responsible for the event.
  a. Odysseus was disguised so cleverly that no one could recognize him.
  b. Odysseus told a clever story about how he came to Ithaca with all his riches.

c. Odysseus looked taller and fairer than he really was.
d. Odysseus threw a weight farther than any of the Phacians.

PART E   Writing Assignment

The event with the eagle and the goose had a special meaning because it showed what Odysseus might do to the suitors. Think of another event with two animals that might have the same special meaning. Write a paragraph that explains the event. Be sure the paragraph answers the following questions:

- How are the animals like Odysseus and the suitors?
- How could the meeting of these animals be like the meeting of Odysseus and the suitors?

Make your paragraph at least **five** sentences long.

Lesson 12

PART A   Word Lists

1	2
grind	**Vocabulary words**
Antinous	dusky
footstool	courteous
grinding	fawn
Argos	feeble
none	vow
nonetheless	supple
	uproar

PART B   New Vocabulary

1. dusky—Dusk is twilight. So, something **dusky** is like twilight. If the shadows were like twilight, the shadows were **dusky**.
  ● What's another way of saying **The shadows were like twilight?***

2. courteous—Another word for **polite** is **courteous**.
  ● What's another way of saying **She was very polite?***

3. fawn—A **fawn** is a young deer.

4. feeble—Something that is very weak is **feeble**.
  a. What's another way of saying **a very weak laugh?***
  b. What's another way of saying **a very weak person?***

5. vow—A **vow** is a serious promise. When you **vow** to do something, you promise to do it.
  ● What's another way of saying **She promised to work all day long?***

6. supple—Something that is **supple** is very easy to bend or flexible.
  ● What's another way of saying **The leather was easy to bend?***

7. uproar—A loud commotion is an **uproar**.

PART C Vocabulary Review

1	2
flee	enlarge
neglect	hideous
unearthly	boar
revenge	deed
custom	lice

1. When you get even with a person, you take _____ on that person.
2. When you fail to take care of something, you _____ it.
3. A way of behaving that everybody follows is a _____.
4. Something not like anything that you would find on this earth is _____.
5. When you make something bigger, you _____ that thing.
6. Another word for **horrible** or **disgusting** is _____.
7. Another word for an **action** is a _____.

PART D Story Items

1. a. What did the suitor Antinous do to Odysseus at the beginning of this chapter?
   b. What did the suitors do after sunset?
   c. Then who came to see Odysseus?
   d. Did Odysseus tell that person who he really was?
2. Odysseus told Penelope a story about himself.
   a. Odysseus described things that he had worn at one time. Name one of those things.
   b. Why do you think Odysseus told Penelope about those things?

3. a. Who began to wash Odysseus's feet?
   b. What did she see on Odysseus's leg?
   c. What did that prove to the nurse?
   d. Odysseus told the nurse to keep silent about what she knew because he didn't want the _____ to slay him.
4. a. Penelope had decided that she had to _____ one of the suitors.
   b. Which objects were to be used to test the suitors?
   c. To whom did those objects belong?
   d. To pass the test, a suitor would have to do these things: _____ the bow. _____ through holes in the _____.
5. The next morning, people began to arrive at the palace.
   a. What did Eumayus, Melanthius, and the other farmers bring for the suitors to eat?
   b. Which group of people came to eat?
   c. Which person threw something at Odysseus?
   d. How did the suitors react to that event?
   e. Why did Telemachus leave the room?
   f. Who gave a warning to the suitors at the end of the chapter?

PART E Writing Assignment

Do you think Odysseus should have told Penelope who he was? Write a paragraph that explains your answer. Be sure the paragraph answers the following questions:
- What reasons does Odysseus have for keeping his secret?
- What might happen if Penelope learns his secret?

Make your paragraph at least **five** sentences long.

Lesson 13

PART A   Word Lists

1	2	3
victorious	caution	**Vocabulary words**
reckoning	pillars	in vain
quiver	bedpost	day of reckoning
bewildered	lass	victorious
burro	lasso	quiver
orchard		bewildered
rodeo		nonetheless
		rodeo
		lasso

PART B   New Vocabulary

1. **in vain**—When you do something **in vain,** you do it without any success. If somebody is trying to run without success, that person is trying to run **in vain.**
   - If a person is trying to climb a hill without success, that person is _____.

2. **day of reckoning**—The **day of reckoning** is the time when people are repaid for their good deeds or their bad deeds.

3. **victorious**—A **victorious** person is one who wins.
   - What do we call a person who wins?

4. **quiver**—A **quiver** is a container that holds arrows.
   - What do we call a container that holds arrows?*

5. **bewildered**—Someone who is **bewildered** is very confused.
   - What's another way of saying **The boxer was confused?***

6. **nonetheless**—**Nonetheless** means **in spite of.**

7. **rodeo**—A **rodeo** is a show in which cowboys do dangerous things, such as riding wild horses.

8. **lasso**—A **lasso** is a rope that cowboys use to rope cattle.

PART C   Vocabulary Review

1	2	3
supple	hideous	enlarge
feeble	risk	courteous

1. Another word for **polite** is _____.
2. Something that is very weak is _____.

3. Something that is very easy to bend or flexible is _____.

PART D Story Items

1. Penelope and her servant brought in the bow and the axes.
   a. What would the suitors have to do with the bow?
   b. Where would the suitors have to shoot the arrow?
   c. What would Penelope do with whoever could do both things?
   d. Who came very close to stringing the bow?
   e. Were any of the suitors able to string the bow?

2. Odysseus talked to Eumayus and the cow farmer.
   a. Why did he show them the scar on his leg?
   b. Whose side were the two farmers on?
   c. Who had to place the bow in Odysseus's hands?
   d. How did the suitors react when Odysseus asked to string the bow?

3. a. Did Odysseus string the bow?
   b. What did he do with the arrow?
   c. Odysseus gave the suitors a choice. He told them to _____ or _____.
   d. Why couldn't the suitors find their weapons?
   e. What did Odysseus do that filled the suitors with fear?
   f. What did the suitors finally do?

4. a. Who ran to tell Penelope the news?
   b. Did Penelope believe the news at first?
   c. What kind of person did Penelope think the beggar might be?
   d. What did Odysseus have on his leg that proved who he was?

5. Penelope gave Odysseus a test.
   a. Where did Penelope ask the nurse to move the bed for Odysseus?
   b. Could the nurse have done that?
   c. What did the bed have for a bedpost?
   d. Name the only two people who knew that secret.
   e. That answer proved to Penelope that the beggar was _____.

6. Odysseus remembered what Circe had said.
   a. Odysseus was supposed to find people who did not recognize _____.
      ● his cloak ● his oar
      ● his scar
   b. What was Odysseus supposed to do with that object?

PART E Review Items

Some things proved that Odysseus was really Odysseus. Other things did not prove who he was, because those things could happen to anybody. Write **proof** for the things that proved who Odysseus really was. Write **no proof** for the things that could happen to anybody.
1. He knew about the bedpost.
2. He was from Ithaca.
3. The dog Argos recognized him.
4. He had been wandering for many years.
5. He knew how to sail a ship.
6. He had a unique scar on his leg.

PART F Writing Assignment

People who would not recognize an oar would not know about the sea. When Odysseus meets people who have never seen an oar, what do you think he might tell them about the sea and what the sea means? Write a paragraph that tells what Odysseus might say. Be sure the paragraph answers the following questions:
● How is the sea dangerous?
● How is the sea rewarding?
● How does Odysseus feel about the sea?

Make your paragraph at least **five** sentences long.

Lesson 14

PART A   Word Lists

1	2	3
Eleanor Clymer	designs	**Vocabulary words**
yucca	tourist	squash and gourds
mesa	sage	pottery
gourd	Louisa	mesa
corral		orchard
		burro
		corral
		yucca

PART B   New Vocabulary

1. **squash and gourds**—Squash and gourds are related vegetables. **Gourds** are not good to eat but **squash** is.

2. **pottery**—Dishes and pots made of clay are called **pottery.**
   - What do we call dishes and pots made of clay?*

3. **mesa**—A **mesa** is a large landform with steep sides and a large, flat top.
   - What do we call a large landform with steep sides and a large, flat top?*

4. **orchard**—An **orchard** is a farm that grows fruit trees or nut trees.

5. **burro**—A **donkey** is called a burro.
   - What's another word for **donkey?***

6. **corral**—A **corral** is a fenced area for horses or burros.
   - What do we call a fenced area for horses or burros?*

7. **yucca**—**Yucca** is the name of a plant that grows in the dessert.

PART C   Vocabulary Review

1	2
courteous	bewildered
hideous	in vain
nonetheless	

1. When you do something without any success, you do it _____.
2. Someone who is very confused is _____.
3. **In spite of** means _____.

PART D   Story Items

1. **a.** What was Kate's Indian name?
   b. Where did Kate go every summer?
   c. Which member of Kate's family lived in that place?
   d. How old is the village there?
   e. Name **two** reasons why it is hard to live in that village.
2. **a.** Which member of Kate's family made pottery?
   b. What material was the pottery made of?

3. Pretend you are making a pot.
   a. Which part do you use a flat piece of clay for?
   b. You use coils of clay to make the _____ of the pot.
   c. What do you use to smooth the clay?
   d. What kinds of things would you paint on the pot after it is dry?
   e. What do you do to make the pot hard?
4. This summer was different for Kate.
   a. Why didn't Kate's mother come to the mesa?
   b. Why was the ground so dry that summer?
5. Kate's grandmother had changed.
   a. What color was her hair before?
   b. What color was her hair now?
   c. How had her body changed?
   d. Had she planted a garden this year?
   e. How many pots had she made this year?

6. Kate lived in the town in the winter and on the mesa in the summer. Write whether each statement describes the **town** or **mesa**.
   a. Kate went to school there.
   b. The houses did not have running water.
   c. Some of the houses were built on top of other houses.
   d. The houses had electricity.
   e. Kate made pottery there.
   f. The houses were made of wood.

PART E   Writing Assignment

Pretend you live on the mesa. Write a paragraph that describes how you could save water. Be sure the paragraph answers the following questions:
- How could you use less water?
- How could you save the water you have?

Make your paragraph at least **five** sentences long.

Lesson 15

PART A   Word Lists

1	2
Kuka-Am	sight
metate	sightseer
juniper	grey
idle	greyish
	charcoal

3
Vocabulary words
idle
plaza
juniper

PART B   New Vocabulary

1. **idle**—When something is still and not working, it is **idle**.
   - What's another way of saying **Her hands were still and not working?***
2. **plaza**—A **plaza** is an open area surrounded by walls or buildings.
3. **juniper**—A **juniper** is a desert bush that has strong-smelling berries.

PART C   Vocabulary Review

1	2
day of reckoning	nonetheless
minstrel	custom
bewildered	in vain
supple	mesa

1. A way of behaving that everybody follows is called a _____.
2. Something that is very easy to bend or flexible is _____.
3. The time when people are repaid for their good deeds or their bad deeds is called the _____.
4. When you do something without any success, you do it _____.
5. A person living at the time of Odysseus who read poetry, sang songs and played the lyre is called a

_____.

PART D   Story Items

1. a. Where did Kate get water?
   b. What did she do with the metate?
   c. What did she do with the yucca brushes?
   d. What would she have liked to do to the walls?
   e. What did Grandmother do while Kate was working?
   f. Did Grandmother want to leave the mesa?
2. a. What kind of people came to the mesa nearly every day?
   b. How did Kate feel about those people?
   c. Name **two** things that made Kate feel that way.
   d. What would the people ask about buying?
   e. Why didn't the people buy anything from Grandmother?
   f. What material did Grandmother need?
      • Special clay   • Regular clay
      • Firewood
   g. Why didn't Grandmother use some other kind of clay?

3. a. What animals did Johnny play with?
   b. Who told Kate something about Grandmother?
   c. What happened to Grandmother when she went to get water?
   d. That event helped to explain why Grandmother had _____.
   e. Why was Kate afraid?
   f. Who did Kate want to send for?
   g. Why couldn't Kate send for that person?

PART E   Review Items

Grandmother had changed since last summer. Write whether each statement describes Grandmother during **this** summer or **last** summer.
1. She made pottery.
2. She spent a lot of time sitting in the sun.
3. Her arms were strong.
4. She worked in the garden.
5. She seemed very far away.
6. Her hair was gray.

PART F   Writing Assignment

Kate is worried about her grandmother. What would you do if you were in Kate's position? Write a paragraph that explains your answer. Be sure the paragraph answers the following question:
• What actions would you take if Grandmother became ill?

Make your paragraph at least **five** sentences long.

Lesson 16

PART A   Word Lists

1	2	3
ancestors	outspread	**Vocabulary words**
kachinas	polishing	cross
sympathize	guests	affair
cactus	clattering	ancestors
		ruins

PART B   New Vocabulary

1. **cross**—Cross is another word for **irritated**.
   - What's another way of saying **They were irritated in the morning?***

2. **affair**—Something that is your **affair** is your business.
   - What's another way of saying **That's his business?***

3. **ancestors**—A person's **ancestors** are the relatives of that person who lived many generations ago.
   - What do we call our relatives that lived many generations ago?*

4. **Ruins**—Ruins are the remains of buildings and other things made by people.

PART C   Story Items

1. a. Which animals were running around the plaza?
   b. Who had let them out?
2. The tourist girl didn't seem to be hot.
   a. What did her car have that might explain the way she looked?
   b. Name at least **three** ways that Kate was different from the tourist girl at that time.
   c. What did the tourist girl's mother want to buy from Grandmother?
   d. Why was the woman disappointed?
3. a. How did Johnny feel about the tourists?
   b. What did the man say might happen to Johnny?
4. Kate showed Johnny the special bowl.
   a. Who had the bowl belonged to?
   b. Where had the bowl been found?
   c. What had Grandmother learned from the bowl?
   d. What objects did Grandmother keep inside the bowl?
   e. What did she do with those objects?
   f. What did Johnny do by accident at the end of part 3.

5. Write whether each statement describes **Kate** or the **tourist girl.**
   a. She looked like she had just come out of a shower.
   b. She stared at the houses and scenery.
   c. She looked hot and dirty.
   d. She worked hard during the day.
   e. She did not like to be stared at.

PART D   Review Items

1. Pretend you are making a pot.
   a. Which part do you use a flat piece of clay for?
   b. You use coils of clay to make the _____ of the pot.
   c. What do you use to smooth the clay?
   d. What kinds of things would you paint on the pot after it is dry?
   e. What do you do to make the pot hard?

2. Write which Greek god or goddess
each statement describes. Choose from
Athena, Zeus, Poseidon, or **Hermes.**
  a. The chief god.
  b. The messenger god.
  c. The goddess of wisdom and work.
  d. The god of the sea.

PART E   Writing Assignment

Do you think that Kate would like to
trade places with the tourist girl? Write
a paragraph that explains your answer.

Be sure the paragraph answers the
following questions:
- Why might Kate envy the tourist girl's life?
- What does Kate like about her own life?
- Which life would Kate prefer?

Make your paragraph at least **five**
sentences long.

Lesson 17

Part A   Word Lists

1
waist
carrier
whipping
kachinas

2
Vocabulary words
hoe
sympathize

PART B   New Vocabulary

1. **hoe**—A **hoe** is a tool that is used to
break the earth.

2. **sympathize**—When you **sympathize**
with someone, you show sympathy
toward that person.

PART C   Vocabulary—Birds

Here are some birds you will read about
in today's lesson:

blue jay

mockingbird

hawk

bluebird

PART D Vocabulary Review

1	2	3
ancestors	minstrel	supple
idle	cross	in vain
custom		

1. Another word for **irritated** is

   _____.

2. A person's relatives who lived many generations ago are the person's

   _____.

3. When something is still and not working, that thing is _____.

4. Something that is very easy to bend or flexible is _____.

PART E Main Idea

Poseidon could make storms and earthquakes. He was the god of the sea. He carried a three-pointed staff, and he had a terrible temper. He once tried to overthrow Zeus, but he did not succeed. Many Greeks were afraid of Poseidon, because they believed that he caused shipwrecks and other disasters.

Write the main idea; then write three supporting details for the main idea. Use complete sentences to write the main idea and the supporting details. Write **1** in front of the main idea. Write **a, b, c** in front of the supporting details. Also, indent the supporting details.

PART F Story Items

1. a. What did Johnny break?
   b. Did Grandmother say anything angry?
2. Grandmother told a story about people who lived underground.
   a. What did those people go through to reach the earth?
   b. Which bird let them know about the place above?
   c. Why did the ants have thin waists?
   d. The spirit gave these people a magic ladder and a magic

      _____.
   e. Where did those people end up living?
      ● Forest ● Mesa ● City
3. Grandmother told Kate about the spirit who was responsible for guiding the people to their proper place.
   a. What was the name of that spirit?
   b. Why must you never kill that animal?
   c. What could you ask that spirit for?
   d. That spirit lives near a secret

      _____.
   e. If you see that spirit in her secret place, what should you leave for her?
   f. Then what should you do?
   g. What might happen if you stay?
4. a. Which character was missing in the morning?
   b. Who did Kate meet when she went out?
   c. What did those people tell her?
   d. What did Kate think that Johnny had done?
   e. Where did she think he had gone?

PART G Writing Assignment

Kate's grandmother told a story that explained why ants have thin waists. Write another story that explains why ants have thin waists. Be sure the paragraph answers the following question:
● What caused their thin waists?

Make your story at least **five** sentences long.

Lesson 18

PART A   Word List

hoofmarks
Spaniards
cloudburst
arch

PART B   Vocabulary—Plants

Here are some desert plants you will read about in today's lesson:

juniper

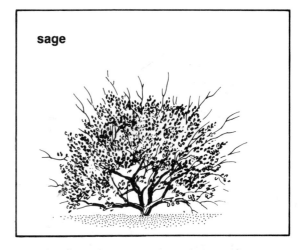

sage

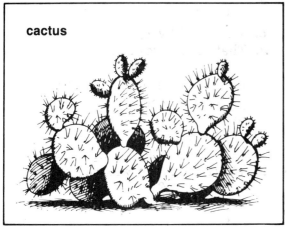

cactus

yucca

PART C   Main Idea

Odysseus told each man to select a large sheep, get under the sheep, and hold on to its fleece with his hands and feet. Then all the sheep went out through the cave doorway. Polyphemus felt the sheep, but he did not know that they were carrying out the men.

Write the main idea; then write three supporting details for the main idea. Use complete sentences to write the main idea and the supporting details. Write **1** in front of the main idea. Write **a, b, c** in front of the supporting details. Also, indent the supporting details.

PART D   Story Items

1. a. Who was Kate looking for at the beginning of part 5?
   b. Where did Kate go first?
   c. What signs did she look for?
2. a. What does "mesa" mean in Spanish?
   b. Why is that word used to describe where Kate lived?
   c. Name **two** plants that grow on the mesa.
   d. What were the valleys in the mesa called?
   e. Why did Kate use that name for the valleys?
   f. What place did Kate think that Johnny was looking for?
3. a. Who did Kate see in one of the valleys?
   b. Why did Kate start to hurry all of a sudden?
   c. What was the middle of the valley like after the storm hit?

4. a. What kind of hiding place did Johnny find?
   b. Johnny hoped to go to the ruins and find _____.
   c. Who had taken most of the bowls from the ruins?
   d. Did Johnny think they had taken all of them?
5. Write whether you would find each thing on top of the **mesa** or in a **wash.**
   a. A torrent of water
   b. A cornfield
   c. Burro corrals
   d. Good soil
   e. Houses
   f. Poor soil

PART E   Review Items

Grandmother had changed.

1. Her hair had turned _____.
   ● red   ● gray   ● black
2. She seemed very _____.
   ● far away   ● active   ● angry
3. Before, she had made bowls from
   _____.
   ● mud   ● regular clay   ● fine clay
4. Why didn't she want to make bowls any more?
5. What had happened to her special bowl?

PART F   Writing Assignment

As Kate walked along, she wondered if the old stories could be true. Do you think the old stories could be true? Write a paragraph that explains your answer.

Be sure the paragraph answers the following questions:
● What parts of the old stories are hard to believe?
● What parts of the old stories might be true?
● How do you feel about the old stories?

Make your paragraph at least **five** sentences long.

Lesson 19

PART A   Word Lists

1
dampness
buried
crumbled

2
Vocabulary words
rots
smudge

PART B   New Vocabulary

1. **rots**—When something **rots**, it becomes soft and falls apart.

2. **smudge**—A mark made from dirt is a **smudge**.

PART C   Vocabulary Review

1	2	3
cross	bewildered	juniper
hoe	ancestors	supple

1. Someone who is very confused is
   _____.

2. Another word for **irritated** is
   _____.

3. Your relatives who lived many generations ago are called your
   _____.

PART D   Main Idea

Athena made Odysseus's skin seem wrinkled and his hair thin and his eyes dull. She gave him dirty old rags for clothes. She also gave him a staff and a bag to hold scraps of food. There was not a man or a woman in Ithaca that would know that this humble beggar was really Odysseus.

Write the main idea; then write three supporting details for the main idea. Use complete sentences to write the main idea and the supporting details. Write **1** in front of the main idea. Write **a, b, c** in front of the supporting details. Also, indent the supporting details.

PART E   Story Items

1. a. What was coming out of the hole at the back of the shelter?
   b. What object did Johnny hope he could find in the hole?
   c. What animal did Kate notice near the hole?
   d. Who did Kate think that animal might be?
   e. What did Kate think that animal might do to Johnny?
   f. What kind of container did Johnny find in the cave?
   g. What was in the container?
2. a. What did Johnny and Kate carry in Johnny's shirt?
   b. What was the weather like when they left the cave?
   c. Would the crops grow better now that the soil was wet?
3. a. When Kate went back to the cave, who did she talk to?
   b. Kate told that person about the _____ she had the night before.
   c. What did Kate leave near the web?
   d. Louisa's _____ met Kate and Johnny when they returned to the village.
   e. Why was that person angry?
4. a. How did Grandmother look at first when Kate and Johnny came in?
   b. How did the clay make Grandmother feel?
   c. Did Grandmother know about the cave?
   d. When the woman was digging there before, how had the weather changed?
   e. Who was missing?
   f. Did the woman find that person?
   g. Why had the Indians never gone back there?
   h. Why did Grandmother think that finding clay was better than finding bowls?

PART F Vocabulary Items

Use the words in the box to fill in the blanks or replace the underlined words.

custom	orchard	lasso
irritated	unearthly	donkey
ruins	revenge	ancestors
hoe	rodeo	idle
	without any success	

1. They planted the _____ twenty years ago, and now the fruit trees are heavy with fruit every spring and summer.
2. When the <u>burro</u> sat down, she tried to coax it to get up, but it wouldn't budge.
3. Their <u>relatives who lived many generations ago</u> had hunted with bow and arrow.
4. He worked in a _____, riding bulls.
5. Her sister used to be active, but now she was <u>still and not working</u> during most of the day.
6. His _____ was too supple, so he waxed the rope until it was very stiff.
7. Although they worked very hard at digging the tunnel, their attempt to escape was <u>in vain.</u>
8. She was ill-tempered and <u>cross</u> most of the day.
9. At one time, the plaza had been very beautiful, but all that remained now were the _____.
10. She struck the hard ground with a _____, chipping off little bits of hard earth.

PART G Writing Assignment

Do you think that Kate believed in the old stories now? Write a paragraph that explains your answer. Be sure the paragraph answers the following question:
- What event might have changed Kate's mind about the stories?

Make your paragraph at least **five** sentences long.

Lesson 20

PART A Word Lists

1
dingy
wharf
quarry
obliged

2
metate
gourd
tansy
account

3
Vocabulary words
boarding house
obliged to somebody
quarry
crane
wharf

PART B New Vocabulary

1. **boarding house**—A **boarding house** is a place where you live that also provides your meals.
   - What do we call a place where you live that also provides your meals?*
2. **obliged to somebody**—When you are **obliged to somebody,** you are very grateful to that person for helping you.
3. **quarry**—A **quarry** is a place where sand or rock are dug from the ground.
4. **crane**—A **crane** is a large sea bird.
5. **wharf**—The place where ships dock is called a **wharf.**

PART C Main Idea

Kate began to work. She made a flat piece for the bottom. Then she put coils of clay on top of the flat part until she had built up a jar. Then she smoothed it with a stone and shaped it in beautiful curves. When it was dry, she painted it with lovely designs.

Write the main idea; then write four supporting details for the main idea. Use complete sentences to write the main idea and the supporting details. Write **1** in front of the main idea. Write **a, b, c, d** in front of the supporting details. Also, indent the supporting details.

PART D Story Items

1. **a.** What did Kate do to the clay on the metate?
   b. Why did Kate put wet cloths over the clay?
   c. What part of the bowl did Kate make a flat pancake for?
   d. What part of the bowl did Kate make clay rolls for?
   e. What did Grandmother do with the gourd shell?
   f. Why did they set the bowl in the shade instead of the sun?
2. Kate and Grandmother rubbed slip on the bowl when it was dry.
   a. What did the slip do?
   b. How did Kate polish the bowl?
   c. Who painted the design on the bowl?
   d. Where had he seen that design?
   e. Why did they build a fire?
   f. How did the completed bowl look?
3. Grandmother had changed.
   a. How had she felt earlier in the summer?
   b. How did she feel now?
   c. Who did she invite to the mesa?
   d. How did the family make money that summer?
4. **a.** Which visitor came back to the mesa one day?
   b. Why did that visitor have to move a lot?

c. Did that visitor want to live in a city?
   d. Did Kate still envy her?
5. **a.** When the bowl was finished, it looked just like another bowl. Which bowl was that?
   b. There was one bowl that was not for sale. Which bowl was that?

PART E Vocabulary Items

Use the words in the box to fill in the blanks or replace the underlined words.

bewildered	rotted	dusky
plaza	hoe	supple
smudge	vowed	ruins
neglect	ancestors	in vain

1. She tried to grab the door before it closed and locked, but her effort was <u>without any success</u>.
2. She had a high fever and her thoughts became very <u>confused</u>.
3. They searched through the _____ for things that might be valuable.
4. In the morning, people walked to and fro across the _____.
5. In the damp cellar, the newspapers <u>became soft and fell apart</u> into a mass of damp pulp.
6. They heated the bow and rubbed hot oil on it to make it more <u>flexible</u>.
7. She returned to the ruins to find out more about her _____.
8. He took a shovel and a _____ with him to the fields.
9. The _____ on her new white dress was very embarrassing to her.

PART F Writing Assignment

Write a paragraph that describes how to make a pottery bowl. Be sure the paragraph answers the following questions:
● What materials do you use?
● What steps do you follow?

Make your paragraph at least **five** sentences long.

Lesson 21

1	2	3	4
Nova Scotia	stoop	gurgle	**Vocabulary words**
obliged	pier	roughened	occupation
dingy	appetite	Massachusetts	craft
fiery	gangway	gurgling	strait
relevant		schooner	dingy
Charlottetown			curt
Trowbridge			

PART B   New Vocabulary

1. **occupation**—Another word for a **job** is an **occupation**.
   - What's another way of saying **She had a new job?***

2. **craft**—A boat or a ship is called a **craft**.
   - What's another way of saying **She went on a sailing boat?***

3. **strait**—A **strait** is a narrow body of water with land on either side.

4. **dingy**—Something that is very dirty, drab, and shabby is called **dingy**.

5. **curt**—Something that is very quick or short is **curt**.

PART C   Vocabulary Review

1	2
boarding house	smudge
quarry	rots
obliged to	wharf

1. When you are very grateful to a person for helping you, you are _____ that person.
2. A place where you live that also provides your meals is called a _____.
3. When something becomes soft and falls apart, that thing _____.

PART D   Relevant Information

You're going to figure out whether information is relevant to a fact. Here's the rule: *Information that helps explain a fact is relevant to the fact. Information that does not help explain a fact is not relevant to the fact.*
- What do we call information that helps explain a fact?Ⓐ
- What do we call information that doesn't help explain a fact?Ⓑ

Here's a fact: *The woman sharpened her pencil.* Here's information about what happened before she sharpened her pencil:
1. The woman had been writing a letter.
   a. Does that information help explain why the woman sharpened her pencil?Ⓒ
   b. So what do you know about that information?Ⓓ

2. The woman had red hair.
   a. Does that information help explain why the woman sharpened her pencil?Ⓔ
   b. So what do you know about that information?Ⓕ
3. The pencil had an eraser.
   a. Does that information help explain why the woman sharpened her pencil?Ⓖ
   b. So what do you know about that information?Ⓗ
4. The pencil's point was broken.
   a. Does that information help explain why the woman sharpened her pencil?Ⓘ
   b. So what do you know about that information?Ⓙ
- Write the answers for items 1 through 4. Remember to write **relevant** or **not relevant** for items 1b, 2b, 3b, and 4b.Ⓚ

PART E   Story Items

1. a. What was the name of the schooner in this story?
   b. In which city did the schooner begin its voyage?
   c. Where did the schooner stop to pick up cargo?
   d. What kind of cargo did the schooner pick up?
   e. To which city was the schooner supposed to take the cargo?
2. a. Before the schooner could sail, the wind had to blow from the
      _____.
   b. That wind is called a _____.
      - south wind   - east wind
      - west wind   - north wind
   c. About how long did it take the schooner to reach Nova Scotia?
      - 5 minutes   - 5 hours   - 5 days
3. a. What was the name of the boy who helped fasten the schooner to the wharf?
   b. About how old was that boy?

4. a. When would the schooner leave Nova Scotia for Boston?
   b. Which place did the boy take the narrator to?
   c. What was the condition of that place?
   d. Why didn't the mother offer to let the narrator stay in that place?
   e. What place did the mother recommend to the narrator?
   f. Who took the narrator to that place?

PART F   Outlining

Complete the following outline for *The Spider, the Cave, and the Pottery Bowl* by writing the supporting details.

Copy each main idea; then write three supporting details for each main idea. Use complete sentences to write the supporting details.

1. At the beginning of the story, Kate's grandmother was not normal.
   a. Tell what she did most of the time.
   b. Tell what she no longer made.
   c. Tell how she seemed to feel.
2. Kate and Johnny found some clay.
   a. Tell where the clay was.
   b. Tell what kind of clay it was.
   c. Tell which animal was near the clay.
3. Kate made a pot.
   a. Tell how she made the bottom.
   b. Tell how she made the sides.
   c. Tell how she smoothed it out.

PART G   Writing Assignment

If you could go anywhere, where would you like to spend your vacation? Write a paragraph that explains your answer. Be sure the paragraph answers the following question:
- What is so special about the place you chose?

Make your paragraph at least **five** sentences long.

Lesson 22

1	2	3
quaint	Nova Scotia	**Vocabulary words**
excursion	reluctance	predict
prow	heave	excursion
	circular	quaint
	predictions	vision
		evidently
		swells
		immense

PART B   New Vocabulary

1. **predict**—When you tell what will happen in the future, you **predict** the future.
   - What are you doing when you tell what will happen in the future?*

2. **excursion**—An **excursion** is a journey that brings you back to the place the journey started.
   - What do we call a journey that brings you back to the place the journey started?*

3. **quaint**—Something that is cute and old-fashioned is **quaint.**
   - What do we call something that is cute and old-fashioned?*

4. **vision**—When a person has a **vision**, that person sees something that is not there.

5. **evidently**—Another word for **apparently** is **evidently.**
   - What's another way of saying **She apparently fell down?***

6. **swells**—Large ocean waves are called **swells.**
   - What are large ocean waves called?*

7. **immense**—Something that is very large or vast is called **immense.**
   - What's another way of saying **a vast desert?***

PART C   Vocabulary Review

1	2
smudge	occupation
quarry	strait
curt	craft
dingy	obliged to

1. Something that is very quick or short is _____.
2. When you are very grateful to a person for helping you, you are _____ that person.
3. Something that is very dirty, drab, and shabby is called _____.
4. A narrow body of water with land on either side of it is called a _____.
5. Another word for a **job** is an

_____.

PART D   Story Items

1. When the narrator was staying in Nova Scotia, she discovered that Jake had predicted something before it actually happened.
   a. What event had Jake seen in his vision?
   b. Did the narrator believe at that time that Jake could see things before they actually happened?
2. a. What gift did Jake give the narrator?
   b. Jake told the narrator that a time would come when she would offer _____ dollars for a _____.
   c. Who did the narrator give the gift to?
3. The captain waited in the bay for a wind that would blow the ship to Boston.
   a. Which wind did he wait for?
      • A north wind   • A south wind
   b. As they waited in the bay, what approached?
   c. The captain assured the narrator that the oncoming vessel would _____.
   d. Why did that vessel make noises that were different from those made by the schooner?

PART E   Review Items

Pretend you are making a pot.
1. Which part do you use a flat piece of clay for?
2. You use coils of clay to make the _____ of the pot.
3. What do you use to smooth the clay?
4. Why do you bake the pot?

PART F   Outlining

Complete the following outline for *The Odyssey* by writing the supporting details.

Copy each main idea; then write three supporting details for each main idea.

Use complete sentences to write the supporting details.

1. Odysseus visited Circe.
   a. Tell what she did to some of the men.
   b. Tell what kind of meal she gave the men.
   c. Tell a warning she gave Odysseus.
2. Odysseus visited the Phacians.
   a. Tell who he met first.
   b. Tell how he showed his strength.
   c. Tell what they gave him.
3. Odysseus proved who he was.
   a. Tell what he did with an arrow.
   b. Tell what he had on his leg.
   c. Tell what secret he knew.

PART G   Relevant Information

Information that helps explain a fact is called **relevant**. Information that does not help explain a fact is called **not relevant**.
• Write **relevant** or **not relevant** for items 1 through 4.
• Fact: *The man purchased a needle and thread.*
1. He was wearing a green ring.
2. His shirt was missing a button.
3. One of his pockets had a hole in it.
4. His shoes were too tight.

PART H   Writing Assignment

Do you believe that people can predict the future? Write a paragraph that explains your answer. Be sure the paragraph answers the following questions:
• What evidence shows that people can predict the future?
• What evidence shows that people cannot predict the future?

Make your paragraph at least **five** sentences long.

Lesson 23

1	2	3
matzo	fasten	**Vocabulary words**
linoleum	prow	gaping hole
tenant	plunging	wrench off
mirage	fastenings	veer
thyme	frantically	plank
		lurches
		seaworthy
		cobblestones
		linoleum

PART B   New Vocabulary

1. **gaping hole**—A **gaping hole** is a wide open hole.
   - What is a wide open hole?*

2. **wrench off**—When you **wrench off** something, you twist it off.
   - What's another way of saying **He twisted off a small branch?***

3. **veer**—When you turn to one side, you **veer** to that side.
   - What's another way of saying **The truck suddenly turned?***

4. **plank**—A **plank** is a long board.

5. **lurches**—When something suddenly bounces or jolts, that thing **lurches.**
   - What's another way of saying **The car jolted?***

6. **seaworthy**—A craft that is **seaworthy** can stand up against the sea without sinking.

7. **cobblestones**—**Cobblestones** are round stones as big as your fist that were once used to pave city streets.

8. **linoleum**—Linoleum is a floor covering that used to be very popular for kitchens and bathrooms.

PART C   Vocabulary Review

1	2
immense	wharf
evidently	predict
curt	dingy
quaint	excursion

1. Something that is cute and old-fashioned is _____.
2. Something that is very large or vast is called _____.
3. A journey that brings you back to the place the journey started is an _____.
4. When you tell what will happen in the future, you _____ the future.
5. Another word for **apparently** is _____.

PART D Relevant Information

You're going to figure out whether information is relevant to a fact.

- What do we call information that helps explain a fact?Ⓐ
- What do we call information that doesn't help explain a fact?Ⓑ

Here's a fact: *The girl played a song on her trumpet.* Here's information about what had happened before.

1. She was in a brass band.
   a. What kind of information is that?Ⓒ
   b. How do you know?Ⓓ
2. She was giving a concert.
   a. What kind of information is that?Ⓔ
   b. How do you know?Ⓕ
3. The trumpet looked golden.
   a. What kind of information is that?Ⓖ
   b. How do you know?Ⓗ
4. The song was very old.
   a. What kind of information is that?Ⓘ
   b. How do you know?Ⓙ

- Write the answers for items 1 to 4. Remember to write **relevant** or **not relevant** for items 1a, 2a, 3a, and 4a.Ⓚ

PART E Story Items

1. a. What was approaching the schooner?
   b. When that vessel turned, the captain became excited because the vessel was coming _____.
   c. A few moments later, what happened?
   d. Which vessel was bigger?
   e. Which vessel seemed to walk over the other?
2. After the vessel drifted into darkness, the crew tried to save the schooner.
   a. What did the crew try to do to the hole?
   b. What happened to the lifeboat when it was lowered into the water?
   c. What had damaged the lifeboat?
   d. Who ordered the narrator to use a life preserver?
3. The narrator got into the life preserver and jumped into the water.
   a. What was the problem with the line attached to the life preserver?
   b. As the schooner sank, what happened to the narrator?
   c. What vivid thought did the narrator have at that moment?
4. When the narrator returned to the surface, something almost ran over her.
   a. What almost ran over her?
   b. The captain of the steamer had mistaken the _____ between the two ships.
5. The narrator wanted to have somebody else decide about Jake's powers. Who did the narrator say should do that?
   - The captain   - The reader
   - Jake

PART F Main Idea

The steamer came rushing down upon our left side. Our captain roared at the steamer, and all at once I could see people moving wildly on her deck. It veered again, and the schooner also changed its course. Both ships were trying to get away from each other, but it was too late. There was a tremendous crash, and I thought the steamer was actually walking over us.

Write the main idea; then write three supporting details for the main idea. Use complete sentences to write the main idea and the supporting details. Write **1** in front of the main idea. Write **a, b, c** in front of the supporting details. Also, indent the supporting details.

PART G Vocabulary Items

Use the words in the box to replace the underlined words.

irritated	hideous	hoe
die	ancestors	enlarged
curt	plaza	bewildered
dusky	supple	

1. The reporter saw many soldiers <u>perish</u> from hunger.
2. He was a remarkably agile and <u>flexible</u> dancer.
3. His sister's strange behavior <u>confused</u> him.
4. The children became <u>cross</u> when they felt hungry and tired.
5. Their <u>relatives who lived many generations ago</u> had lived near the North Pole.
6. Although King Kong was kind, most people thought he looked <u>disgusting</u>.
7. I did poorly on the test by <u>giving answers that were too short</u>.
8. The campers had the <u>trail</u> map made <u>bigger</u>, so it would be easier to read.

PART H Writing Assignment

How could you make up a test for Jake to see whether he really has the ability to predict things in the future? Write a paragraph that describes your test. Be sure the paragraph answers the following questions:

• How would your test show if Jake had special powers?
• How would your test show if Jake did not have special powers?

Make your paragraph at least **five** sentences long.

PART I Special Projects

1. (Individual Project) In *The Spider, the Cave, and the Pottery Bowl*, Johnny drew designs on the pots that Kate made. Find a book that shows Indian pottery designs. Study the designs, then draw some designs of your own. Draw your designs on paper. If you can, find an old pot and draw the designs on the pot. After you finish, show your designs to the class.

2. (Group Project) *The Voyage of the Northern Light* tells about two kinds of ships—steamers and schooners. There are many other kinds of boats and ships. Look in an encyclopedia and find out about at least ten other kinds of boats and ships. Then make a large chart with illustrations of different boats and ships. The chart should tell what each kind of boat or ship is used for, and how they are different from each other.

3. (Group Project) Make up a play based on the last part of *The Odyssey*. Start with the test of the bow and arrow. Then show Odysseus driving away the suitors. Finally, show Odysseus getting back together with Penelope. Figure out who will play each character. Then figure out what each character will say. You can use words from the book, or you can make up your own words. Students who do not play characters can work on costumes or sets. When you are ready, perform the play for the class.

Lesson 24

PART A Word Lists

1	2	3
De Marco	starvation	**Vocabulary words**
Adeline	busybody	dependable
Amelia	parsley	coop
Reinhardt	drenched	preen
Agatha	thyme	tenant
Callahan	matzo	twining
Grotowski		mirage
pumpernickel		outrage

PART B New Vocabulary

1. **dependable**—Something that always works without failing is **dependable.** Here's another way of saying **The washer always worked: The washer was dependable.**
   - What's another way of saying **The washer always worked?***

2. **coop**—A **coop** is a cage for small animals.

3. **preen**—When a bird **preens** itself, it uses its beak to fluff up its feathers.
   - What is a bird doing when it uses its beak to fluff up its feathers?

4. **tenant**—A person who rents space in a building is a **tenant.**
   - What do we call a person who rents space in a building?*

5. **twining**—Strings that weave in and out of each other are **twining.**
   - What kind of strings weave in and out of each other?*

6. **mirage**—A **mirage** is something that seems to be there, but is not really there at all.

7. **outrage**—Something that is an **outrage** is a great insult.
   - What's another way of saying **His statement was an insult?***

PART C Vocabulary Review

1	2	3
immense	veer	hoe
plant	lurches	seaworthy

1. A tool that is used to break the earth is called a _____.
2. Something that is very large or vast is called _____.
3. When something suddenly bounces or jolts, that thing _____.

PART D   Story Items

1. In Ireland around 1850, there was a terrible disaster.
   a. What happened?
   b. Where did many people start to go?
   c. Were those people rich or poor?
   d. What dream did many of them have?

2. a. From which country did Mrs. Dunn come?
   b. What was the name of the city she lived in before coming to the United States?
   c. What did she always dream of owning?
   d. What kind of place did the Dunns move into?

3. The neighbors warned the Dunns about Mr. Warfield.
   a. What did he own?
   b. What did the neighbors say about him?
   c. What job did Mr. Dunn find?
   d. After a year, the Dunns had saved
      _____.
      • nearly $15   • nearly $200
      • nearly $2000

4. Mrs. Dunn decided to start a farm.
   a. What was the first thing she purchased for her farm?
   b. In which room did the Dunns set up the coop for their chickens?
   c. Which part of the building did the Dunns use for their vegetable garden?
   d. Name at least **three** things that were growing in that place.

5. a. As Mr. Warfield approached the building, what dropped on his head?
   b. Where had it come from?
   c. At the end of the lesson, whose apartment was Mr. Warfield going to?
   d. What do you think he planned to tell the Dunns?

PART E   Main Idea

Mr. Dunn built large, deep boxes, filled them with earth, and planted seeds. Then he put the boxes on the fire escape outside the bedroom window. Soon, the fire escape was blooming with the green shoots of tomato plants, string beans, potatoes, onions, and parsley.

Write the main idea; then write three supporting details for the main idea. Use complete sentences to write the main idea and the supporting details. Write **1** in front of the main idea. Write **a, b, c** in front of the supporting details. Also, indent the supporting details.

PART F   Relevant Information

Write **relevant** or **not relevant** for each item.

• Fact: *The man went to the library.*

1. He was looking for a book.
2. He was forty-two years old.
3. He worked in an office.
4. He needed to look up things for a report he was writing.

PART G   Writing Assignment

If you had to grow a garden to make money, what things would you grow? Write a paragraph that tells what you would grow. Be sure the paragraph answers the following questions:
• Why would you grow those things?
• How would you sell the things you grew?

Make your paragraph at least **five** sentences long.

Lesson 25

PART A   Word Lists

1	2	3
lunatic asylum	chandelier	**Vocabulary words**
Foreign Legion	premises	lunatic asylum
Niagara Falls	Grotowski	nourishment
geraniums	Callahan	roosting
squat	relevant	dainty
	irrelevant	superb
		tamper

PART B   New Vocabulary

1. **lunatic asylum**—A **lunatic asylum** is a place where insane people are kept.

2. **nourishment**—The ingredients of food that help your body to work and grow are called **nourishment.**
   - What do we call the ingredients of food that help your body to work and grow?*

3. **roosting**—When birds sit on a branch or perch they are **roosting.**

4. **dainty**—Something that is very fine and delicate is **dainty.**
   - What's another way of saying **a delicate napkin?***

5. **superb**—**Superb** is another word for **super.** A super dinner is a **superb** dinner.
   - What's another way of saying **a super experience?***

6. **tamper**—When you meddle with something, you **tamper** with that thing.
   - What's another way of saying **He meddled with the machine?***

PART C   Vocabulary Review

1	2	3
twining	immense	outrage
veer	hoe	tenant
dependable	preen	

1. When you turn to one side, you _____ to that side.
2. Something that always works without failing is _____.
3. A person who rents space in a building is a _____.
4. Strings that weave in and out of each other are _____.
5. Something that is a great insult is an _____.

PART D   Relevant Information

Information that is not relevant is called **irrelevant.**

● What is the word for information that is not relevant?Ⓐ

So information that does not help explain a fact is **irrelevant** to the fact.

Here's a fact: *The boy fell off his bike.* Here's information about what happened before:

1. His bicycle had ten gears.
   Is that information relevant or irrelevant?Ⓑ
2. He had ridden into a pothole.
   Is that information relevant or irrelevant?Ⓒ
3.· He hadn't been looking at the road.
   Is that information relevant or irrelevant?Ⓓ
4. He was riding to the swimming pool.
   Is that information relevant or irrelevant?Ⓔ
● Write **relevant** or **irrelevant** for items 1 through 4.Ⓕ

PART E   Story Items

1. a. What problem was Mrs. Callahan complaining about?
   b. What did Mr. Warfield think was growing on the fire escape?
   c. Mrs. Callahan agreed to give Mr. Warfield _____ hours to fix the stove.
      ● 18   ● 28   ● 38
2. a. Mrs. Callahan was stalling Mr. Warfield so that Mrs. Dunn could
      _____.
   b. Mrs. Grotowski was angry because Mr. Warfield had failed to keep a promise. What had he promised to do to her apartment?
   c. On which day did Mr. Warfield say that he would fulfill his promise?

3. a. What were the Dunns trying to do as the other neighbors stalled Mr. Warfield?
   b. Who did Mr. Warfield think was making the chicken noises?
4. a. What did Mrs. Dunn hand Mr. Warfield through a crack in the door?
   b. What did Mr. Warfield want her to do?
   c. Name **two** excuses Mrs. Dunn gave for not letting Mr. Warfield in.
   d. What did Mr. Warfield see on the chandelier?

PART F   Outlining

Complete the following outline for *The Voyage of the Northern Light.* Copy each main idea; then write three supporting details for each main idea. Use complete sentences to write the supporting details.

1. Jake was a strange boy.
2. The narrator needed the pocketknife badly.

PART G   Writing Assignment

Pretend that Mrs. Dunn does not have money for the rent, but she has a lot of vegetables. Make up a conversation between Mrs. Dunn and Mr. Warfield. In the conversation, Mrs. Dunn is trying to talk Mr. Warfield into taking vegetables instead of the rent. Be sure the conversation answers the following questions:
● How does Mrs. Dunn try to convince Mr. Warfield to take the vegetables instead of the rent?
● How does Mr. Warfield feel about the vegetables?

Make your conversation at least **five** sentences long.

Lesson 26

PART A   Word Lists

1
Greenwich Village
Mr. Behrman
studio
pneumonia
gnarled

2
affectionately
geraniums
greenery

3
Vocabulary words
health hazard
stalk
squat
studio
pneumonia

PART B   New Vocabulary

1. **health hazard**—Something that is dangerous to your health is a **health hazard.**
   - Smoking is dangerous to your health. So what do we call smoking?*

2. **stalk**—When an animal **stalks** something, it tracks it and gets ready to attack.
   - What's another way of saying **The lion tracked the zebra?***

3. **squat**—Something that is **squat** is quite thick and stout.
   - What's another way of saying **She was thick and stout?***

4. **studio**—A **studio** is a large room where artists work.
   - What do we call a large room where artists work?*

5. **pneumonia**—Pneumonia is a disease that attacks the lungs and can be fatal.

PART C   Vocabulary Review

1	2	3
dainty	tenant	mirage
tamper	superb	outrage
nourishment		

1. Another word for **super** is _____.
2. Something that is very fine and delicate is _____.
3. The ingredients of food that help your body to work and grow are called _____.
4. When you meddle with something, you _____ with that thing.

PART D Story Items

1. **a.** What plants did many other people grow in their window boxes?
   b. Why didn't Mr. Warfield recognize the onion plants?
   c. What did Mrs. Dunn tell Mr. Warfield to pretend?
   d. Mrs. Dunn pretended that Mr. Warfield made an offer about using the _____ for a garden.
2. Mrs. Dunn said that Mr. Warfield was a man of action.
   a. The evidence supporting that statement involved the door. What evidence?
   b. What did Mr. Warfield finally say that he would permit Mrs. Dunn to do?
   c. What did the chicken on top of the chandelier think Mr. Warfield's hat was?
   d. The chicken was confused by the hat because it looked like a _____.
3. Write which character could have made each statement. Choose from **Mrs. Dunn** or **Mr. Warfield.**
   a. "Why don't you grow geraniums like everyone else?"
   b. "Those chickens are a health hazard!"
   c. "You were going to offer me the use of the roof."
   d. "I want one-tenth of everything you grow."
   e. "I shall grow the freshest vegetables in New York."

PART E Outlining

Complete the following outline for *Mrs. Dunn's Lovely, Lovely Farm.* Copy each main idea; then write three supporting details for each main idea. Use complete sentences to write the supporting details.

1. Mrs. Dunn had a farm in her apartment.
2. Mrs. Dunn and Mr. Warfield made a fair deal.

PART F Writing Assignment

Mrs. Dunn was very kind to Mr. Warfield, and she was able to make a deal with him. Make up a new ending for the story to show what would have happened if Mrs. Dunn had not been so kind. Be sure the new ending answers the following questions:
- What happened to Mrs. Dunn?
- Why did that happen?

Make your ending at last **five** sentences long.

Lesson 27

PART A   Word Lists

1
Persephone
Demeter
easel
idiotic
palette

2
Greenwich Village
Mr. Behrman
thermometer
mercury
skeleton

3
Vocabulary words
one chance in ten
swagger
accomplish
gnarled
decayed
broth
masterpieces

PART B   New Vocabulary

1. **one chance in ten**—Let's say that there are 10 people.
   a. If there is **one chance in ten** that somebody will get wet, how many people will get wet?*
   b. How many will stay dry?*
   c. If there is **one chance in ten** that somebody will stay dry, how many people will get wet?*
   d. How many will stay dry?*

2. **swagger**—When you **swagger,** you walk and strut in a show-off way.
   • What's another way of saying **He strutted into the room?***

3. **accomplish**—When you **accomplish** something, you succeed in doing that thing.
   • What's another way of saying **They succeeded in the job?***

4. **gnarled**—Something that is **gnarled** is twisted and misformed.
   • What do we call something that is twisted and misformed?*

5. **decayed**—Another word for **rotted** is **decayed.**
   • What's another way of saying **The wood had rotted?***

6. **broth**—Clear soup is called **broth.**
   • What do we call clear soup?*

7. **masterpieces**—The finest works of art are called **masterpieces.**
   • What's another way of saying **She painted a fine work?***

PART C   Vocabulary Review

1	2
occupation	veer
dainty	immense
outrage	

1. Something that is very fine and delicate is _____.
2. Something that is a great insult is an _____.

PART D   Relevant Information

Here are two facts:

- Fact A: *Frank got on the bus.*
- Fact B: *Frank took out his keys.*

Some items below are relevant to fact A. Some items are relevant to fact B. Some items are irrelevant to both facts.

1. He was going to work.
   Is that relevant to fact A, relevant to fact B, or irrelevant? Ⓐ
2. He was wearing a round hat.
   Is that relevant to fact A, relevant to fact B, or irrelevant? Ⓑ
3. He did not own a car.
   Is that relevant to fact A, relevant to fact B, or irrelevant? Ⓒ
4. He wanted to get into his house. Is that relevant to fact A, relevant to fact B, or irrelevant? Ⓓ
- Write **relevant to fact A, relevant to fact B,** or **irrelevant** for items 1 through 4. Ⓔ

PART E   Story Items

1. **a.** In which part of New York City did the young women in this story live?
   b. What were the names of the two young women?
   c. They lived in an _____ colony.
2. **a.** What disease stalked the people in the colony that winter?
   b. Which young woman remained healthy?
   c. Which young woman was struck by the disease?
   d. The doctor reported that the sick woman had only one chance in _____ of surviving.
   e. The doctor said that she would have a chance of surviving if she had a reason for _____.
   f. How did this news make Sue feel?

3. **a.** Where did Sue take her drawing board after the doctor left?
   b. How did Sue try to act?
   c. What was Joan counting?
   d. When did Joan think she would die?
4. **a.** What did Sue want to buy if she sold her picture?
   b. Why did Joan suggest that Sue didn't have to buy any?
   c. How many leaves were left on the ivy branch at the end of the lesson?
   - 1   • 100   • 4   • 6
   d. Sue asked Joan to close her eyes until Sue had _____.
   e. Joan thought she was like an object. What object?

PART F   Main Idea

After the fun was over, Rupert went home with a hundred dollars, the citizens of Centerburg went home full of doughnuts, the lady and her chauffeur drove off with the diamond bracelet, and Homer went home with his mother when she stopped by with Aunt Aggy.

Write the main idea; then write three supporting details for the main idea. Use complete sentences to write the main idea and the supporting details. Write **1** in front of the main idea. Write **a, b, c** in front of the supporting details. Also, indent the supporting details.

PART G : Vocabulary Items

Use the words in the box to fill in the blanks or replace the underlined words.

dependable	tenants	mirage
predict	superb	dainty
occupation	outraged	twining
nourishment	meddle	

1. She ran toward something that looked like the store, but it turned out to be a _____ in the desert.
2. After waiting for three hours to get on the train, she was insulted to discover that there were no seats.
3. Their old black-and-white television was not always _____.

4. Milk and eggs contain a lot of _____.
5. Most of the apartments were empty, and there were only four _____ in the whole building.
6. He cooked a _____ meal.
7. She held a fine and delicate blue cup as she spoke to her guests.
8. Don't ever tamper with electrical wires.

PART H   Writing Assignment

Joan thought she was like a leaf. Some people think they are like an animal. If you had to be an animal, which one would you like to be, and why? Write a paragraph that explains your choice. Be sure the paragraph answers the following question:
● Why would you like to be that animal?

Make your paragraph at least **five** sentences long.

Lesson 28

PART A   Word Lists

1	2
Hades	**Vocabulary words**
Cerberus	scoff at
Demeter	canvas
prudent	palette
Persephone	easel
	contempt
	idiotic
	persistent

PART B   New Vocabulary

1. **scoff at**—When you mock or ridicule something, you **scoff at** that thing.
   ● What's another way of saying **She mocked the boy's behavior?***

2. **canvas**—**Canvas** is the cloth that artists paint on.

3. **palette**—A **palette** is used for mixing paint.

4. **easel**—The **easel** is a large frame that holds the canvas.

5. **contempt**—Another word for **hatred** is **contempt**.
   ● What's another way of saying **The queen showed hatred for the minstrel?***

6. **idiotic**—Something that is very stupid is **idiotic**.
   ● What's another way of saying **Their plan was very stupid?***

7. **persistent**—Something that won't give up is very **persistent**. A person who won't give up is a **persistent** person.
   ● What do we call a need that won't give up?

PART C   Vocabulary Review

1	2	3
stalks	decayed	swagger
broth	accomplish	squat
gnarled		

1. When you succeed in doing something, you _____ that thing.
2. When an animal tracks something and gets ready to attack, it _____ that thing.
3. Something that is twisted and misformed is _____.
4. Another word for **rotted** is _____.

PART D   Story Items

1. **a.** What was the name of the person who lived on the ground floor below the young women?
   - Mr. Franzin
   - Mr. Behrman
   - Mrs. Gottlieb
   b. What did that person do for a living?
   c. Describe **three** things about that person.
   d. How successful had that person been as an artist?
   e. After Sue and Mr. Behrman left his apartment, they went to see _____.

2. **a.** That next morning, what did Joan want to look at?
   b. How many leaves did Joan see on the wall?
   c. What was the weather like that night?
   d. How many leaves were there the next morning?
   e. On that day, Joan decided that she wanted to _____.

3. After the doctor came to see Joan, he had to see another person in the building.
   a. Who was that?
   b. What was wrong with that person?
   c. What happened to Mr. Behrman in the hospital?
4. Sue reported on how Mr. Behrman became sick. The janitor discovered him in his apartment several days before.
   a. Name at least **two** mysterious things that the janitor discovered.
   b. What was Mr. Behrman's masterpiece?
   c. When had Mr. Behrman painted it?
5. **a.** Here's something that Mr. Behrman said: "Vy do you allow dot?"
   Write that question in English.
   b. Here's another thing that Mr. Behrman said: "Dot poor leetle Miss Joan."
   Write that sentence in English.

PART E   Relevant Information

Read the facts and the items. If an item is relevant to fact A, write **relevant to fact A.** If an item is relevant to fact B, write **relevant to fact B.** If an item is irrelevant to both facts, write **irrelevant.**

- Fact A: *Janet opened her window.*
- Fact B: *Janet touched her toes.*

1. She was doing stretching exercises.
2. She was in the sixth grade.
3. Her room was quite hot.
4. She wanted some fresh air.

PART F Main Idea

Mr. Behrman climbed up the ladder.
When he got to the top, he took out his
brush and paints and began to work.
First he dipped the brush in the paint.
Then he carefully drew a brushstroke on
the brick wall. He paused to look at the
first stroke, then he continued. After
several hours, he had completed the leaf.
He climbed back down the ladder.

Write the main idea; then write three
supporting details for the main idea. Use
complete sentences to write the main idea
and the supporting details. Write **1** in
front of the main idea. Write **a, b, c** in
front of the supporting details. Also,
indent the supporting details.

PART G Review Items

Write which character could have made
each statement. Choose from **Joan, Sue,**
or **Mr. Behrman.**
1. "I am like a leaf."
2. "I must get help for my roommate."
3. "I have painted a masterpiece."
4. "I no longer feel like dying."
5. "I know how to save that young girl's
   life."

PART H Vocabulary Items

Use the words in the box to fill in the
blanks or replace the underlined words.

fine and delicate	veered
nourishment	plank
super	outraged
swells	dingy
tampered	seaworthy

1. Cows get their _____ from
   grass.
2. The intruders had evidently <u>meddled</u>
   with the safe, but they didn't succeed
   in opening it.
3. The little dolls on the shelf were
   dressed in <u>dainty</u> lace outfits.
4. The entertainment was <u>superb</u>.
5. After waiting in line for three hours
   to get tickets, he was <u>insulted</u> when it
   was announced that no tickets were
   left.
6. The eagle headed straight toward the
   cliff and suddenly <u>turned</u> to one side.
7. He climbed in the window of the
   castle and stood silently in the <u>dark</u>
   passageway.

PART I Writing Assignment

The story doesn't tell exactly what Mr.
Behrman did on the night that he painted
the leaf. Write a short story that describes
what he did. Be sure the story answers
the following questions:
- How did Mr. Behrman feel?
- What was he thinking?
- What was the weather like?

Make your story at least **ten** sentences
long.

Lesson 29

PART A Word Lists

1
sea nymphs
Hecate
Cerberus
dominions
triumphant
Hades

2
Persephone
necklace
demon
Demeter
nostrils

3
Vocabulary words
prudent
wilt
cavern
triumphant
sullen
excessive
massive
splendor

PART B New Vocabulary

1. **prudent**—Someone who is very wise and careful is **prudent.**
   - What's another way of saying **Mrs. Dunn always tried to be wise and careful?***

2. **wilt**—When plants **wilt,** they dry up and droop.
   - What's another way of saying **The leaves drooped and dried up?***

3. **cavern**—A large cave is a **cavern.**

4. **triumphant**—Another word for **victorious** is **triumphant.**
   - What's another way of saying **The Greek army was victorious at Troy?***

5. **sullen**—Someone who is **sullen** is somber and has no humor.

6. **excessive**—**Excessive** means too much. **Excessive** noise is too much noise.
   - What's another way of saying **The food at the banquet was too much?***

7. **massive**—Something that is very strong and large is **massive.**
   - What's another way of saying **The tree was large?***

8. **splendor**—Another word for **beauty** is **splendor.**
   - What's another way of saying **They stared at the beauty of the castle?***

PART C Vocabulary Review

1	2	3
gnarled	contempt	stalks
persistent	scoff at	decayed
canvas	idiotic	

1. When you mock or ridicule something, you _____ that thing.
2. Another word for **hatred** is _____.
3. Something that is very stupid is _____.
4. Something that won't give up is very _____.
5. Something that is twisted and misformed is _____.

PART D Story Items

1. **a.** What did Demeter rule over?
   b. What was the name of her daughter?
   c. How old was Demeter's daughter?
2. **a.** Who did Persephone want to visit while Demeter went to the fields?
   b. Demeter warned Persephone that the other gods might play _____.
   c. What did the sea nymphs make for Persephone?
   d. What did Persephone want to make for the sea nymphs?
   e. Did the sea nymphs want to go with Persephone into the fields?
   f. Why?
3. **a.** Why didn't Persephone like the first flowers that she saw?
   b. Just as Persephone was ready to return to the sea nymphs, she saw a large shrub, covered with incredible _____.
   c. What did she try to do to the shrub?
   d. After she pulled out the shrub, what happened to the hole that the shrub left in the ground?

4. A chariot appeared.
   a. Where did the chariot come from?
   b. What was pulling the chariot?
   c. Who was in the chariot?
   d. What did that character ask Persephone to do?
5. **a.** Who did Persephone call to for help?
   b. Why didn't that character answer?
   c. What did Hades do as soon as Persephone called out for help?
   d. As they rode off, Persephone left a trail of _____.

PART E Writing Assignment

What do you think Demeter will do when she finds out what has happened to Persephone? Write a paragraph that explains your answer. Be sure the paragraph answers the following questions:
- What evidence will Demeter use to try to find Persephone?
- What powers might Demeter use?

Make your paragraph at least **five** sentences long.

Lesson 30

PART A   Word Lists

1	2	3
illuminated	Cerberus	**Vocabulary words**
delicacies	crystal	illuminated
Hecate	Hades	lofty
morsel	spaniel	summon
threshold	soothe	morsel
		delicacies
		motive
		threshold

PART B   New Vocabulary

1. **illuminated**—When something is **illuminated,** it is lit up.
   - What's another way of saying **The park was lit up?***

2. **lofty**—Something that is very high is **lofty.**
   - What's another way of saying **The eagle's nest was on a very high cliff?***

3. **summon**—When you call somebody to come, you **summon** that person.
   - What's another way of saying **They called Henry to court?***

4. **morsel**—A bit of food is called a **morsel** of food.
   - What's another way of saying **She didn't have a bit of food?***

5. **delicacies**—**Delicacies** are the finest and richest foods.
   - What's another way of saying **Nancy had never seen such rich foods?***

6. **motive**—A person's **motive** for doing something is a person's reason for doing it.
   - What's another way of saying **Nobody could understand her reason for helping the beggar?***

7. **threshold**—The entrance of a place is the **threshold** of that place.
   - What do we call the entrance of a place?

PART C   Vocabulary Review

1	2
triumphant	stalks
prudent	persistent
excessive	gnarled
splendor	sullen
contempt	massive

1. Someone who is somber and has no humor is _____.
2. Something that won't give up is very _____.
3. Another word for **beauty** is _____.
4. When an animal tracks something and gets ready to attack, it _____ that thing.
5. Another word for **too much** is _____.
6. Someone who is very wise and careful is _____.
7. Another word for **victorious** is _____.
8. Another word for **hatred** is _____.

PART D   Story Items

1. **a.** Where did Hades want to take Persephone?
   b. Which place did Hades say was more magnificent, the earth or his underworld palace?
   c. Describe **three** things about his underworld palace.
   d. Hades hoped that Persephone's _____ would cheer up the rooms of his palace.
2. **a.** Who did Persephone pass as she rode in the chariot?
   b. What was wrong with Persephone's voice?
   c. What did Persephone try to do as she rode past?
   d. When did Hades's face become more satisfied?
3. At the gates to the underground kingdom was Cerberus.
   a. What was Cerberus?
   b. How many heads did Cerberus have?
   c. What was his tail?
   d. Hades pointed out that Cerberus becomes mean if somebody tries to _____ his kindgom or tries to _____ his kingdom.
4. **a.** In the underground kingdom, the walls had veins of _____.
   b. What was Persephone holding as Hades led her through the palace?

5. **a.** What did Hades order his servants to do?
   b. What liquid did Hades tell his servants to put by Persephone's plate?
   c. Why did Hades want Persephone to drink that liquid?
   d. Hades wanted Persephone to eat something, because if anybody in Hades's palace tasted any food, that person _____.
   e. Was Persephone tempted by the food that the cook prepared, or did the food take away her appetite?
   f. Name a food that would have tempted Persephone.

PART E   Outlining

Complete the following outline for *The Last Leaf.* Copy each main idea; then write three supporting details for each main idea. Use complete sentences to write the supporting details.

1. Joan thought she was going to die.
2. Mr. Behrman lived downstairs.
3. Joan did not die.

PART F   Writing Assignment

The story said that Hades's palace had a "tiresome magnificence." Write a paragraph about Hades's palace. Be sure the paragraph answers the following questions:
- What was magnificent about Hades's palace?
- What was tiresome about the palace?
- How would you feel if you had to live in Hades's palace?

Make your paragraph at least **five** sentences long.

Lesson 31

1
melancholy
pomegranate
wretched
recollect

2
innocent
enchantment
assure
Hecate

3
Vocabulary words
apt to
entice
melancholy
wretched
shriveled
behold
compose

PART B   New Vocabulary

1. **apt to**—When you are likely to do something, you are **apt to** do it.
   - What's another way of saying **He is likely to take a nap in the afternoon?***

2. **entice**—When you **entice** somebody to do something, you tempt that person to do it.
   - What's another way of saying **The queen tempted him to go into the secret garden?***

3. **melancholy**—Another word for **very sad** is **melancholy**.
   - What's another way of saying **She was very sad?***

4. **wretched**—Something that is miserable is **wretched**.
   - What's another way of saying **The miserable little boy walked in the rain?***

5. **shriveled**—**Shriveled** is another word for **wrinkled** and **withered**.
   - What's another way of saying **The apple was wrinkled and withered?***

6. **behold**—When you **behold** something, you observe it.
   - What's another way of saying **She observed the great mountains?***

7. **compose**—When you **compose** something, you make up that thing.
   a. What's another way of saying **She made up a letter to her friend?***
   b. What's another way of saying **They made up a song?***

PART C   Vocabulary Review

1	2
morsel	motive
stalks	illuminated
lofty	triumphant
delicacies	excessive
summon	persistent

1. The finest and richest foods are
   _____.

2. A bit of food is called a _____
   of food.

3. When something is lit up, it is
   _____.

4. When you call somebody to come, you
   _____ that person.

5. A person's reason for doing something
   is a person's _____ for doing it.

6. Something that is very high is
   _____.

7. Another word for **victorious** is
   _____.

8. Another word for **too much** is
   _____.

PART D   Story Items

1. Whose scream did Demeter hear when
   Hades's chariot was nearly out of
   sight?
2. Demeter left the fields in which she
   was working.
   a. Did Demeter believe that the
      shrieking sound had come from
      Persephone?
   b. But just to be sure, what did
      Demeter do?
   c. After Demeter left the field, the
      grain looked _____.
      ● ripe   ● magnificent
      ● unhealthy
3. a. After Demeter left home, who did
      she go to see first?
   b. Who had noticed footprints of
      Persephone in the sand?
   c. What had a shepherd observed?

4. a. What time of day was it when
      Demeter decided not to return
      until she found Persephone?
   b. What objects did Demeter discover
      on the path?
   c. Demeter knew that the flower had
      been created
      ● by itself.   ● by enchantment.
      ● by herself.
5. During the first night, Demeter asked
   many people about Persephone.
   a. Had any of those people seen
      Persephone?
   b. What magical object did Demeter
      carry?
   c. What could put out that object?
6. a. On the tenth day, Demeter came to
      a dark _____.
   b. Name the character who was
      sitting inside.
   c. That character talked to other
      people as if they were as _____
      as she.
      ● sad   ● happy   ● old

PART E   Outlining

Complete the following outline for
Persephone. Copy each main idea; then
write three supporting details for each
main idea. Use complete sentences to
write the supporting details.

1. One character was named Demeter.
2. One character was named Persephone.
3. One character was named Hades.

PART F   Writing Assignment

Write a paragraph that compares
Demeter's wandering with Odysseus's
wandering. Be sure the paragraph answers
the following questions:
● How was Demeter's wandering the
  same as Odysseus's wandering?
● How was her wandering different from
  his?

Make your paragraph at least **six**
sentences long.

Lesson 32

PART A   Word Lists

1
frivolous
elegant
exquisite
pomegranate
contradiction
recollect

2
Vocabulary words
exquisite and elegant
frivolous
recollect
indignant
gratifying
contradiction

PART B   New Vocabulary

1. **exquisite**—Something that is very splendid and fine is **exquisite**. Silverware that is very splendid and fine is **exquisite** silverware.
   - What do we call very splendid and fine silverware?*

2. **frivolous**—Someone who is foolish and not serious is **frivolous**.
   - What's another way of saying **The king was foolish and not serious?***

3. **recollect**—Another word for **remember** is **recollect**.
   - What's another way of saying **He could not remember the stranger's name?***

4. **indignant**—When you are **indignant**, you are angry and insulted.
   - What's another way of saying **She was angry and insulted over his unjust claim?***

5. **gratifying**—Another word for **satisfying** is **gratifying**.
   - What's another way of saying **His kind manner satisfied her?***

6. **contradiction**—A statement that is the opposite of something we know is true is a **contradiction**.
   - What do we call a statement that is the opposite of something we know is true?*

PART C   Vocabulary Review

1	2	3
wretched	entice	melancholy
summon	shriveled	morsel
behold	compose	apt to
persistent	excessive	lofty
illuminated		

1. Another word for **very sad** is _____.

2. When something is lit up, that thing is _____.

3. When you observe something, you _____ it.

4. Something that is very high is _____.

5. Another word for **wrinkled and withered** is _____.

6. Something that is miserable is _____.

7. When you are likely to do something, you are _____ do it.

8. Another word for **too much** is _____.

9. When you tempt somebody to do something, you _____ that person to do it.

10. When you make up something, you _____ that thing.

PART D Contradictions

Here's a rule about contradictions: *If a statement is true, a contradiction of that statement is false.*

Here's a statement: *Jack was in Chicago at 5:00 a.m. on July 1, 1983.*

If that statement is true, these statements are false:
- Jack was in New Orleans at 5:00 a.m. on July 1, 1983.
- Jack was in St. Louis at 5:00 a.m. on July 1, 1983.
- Jack was in Milwaukee at 5:00 a.m. on July 1, 1983.

These statements contradict the statement about being in Chicago because Jack couldn't be in Chicago and in any of the other places at the same time.

Here's another statement: *Yesterday Darla was fifteen years old.* These statements contradict the true statement:
- Yesterday Darla was twelve years old.
- Yesterday Darla was twenty years old.
- Yesterday Darla was eighteen years old.

These statements contradict the true statement because Darla can't be fifteen years old and any other age at the same time.

Let's say that this statement is true: *Maria is shorter than everybody else in her family—her father, her mother, and her sister, Jane.*
- Make up three statements that contradict the true statement about how short Maria is. Ⓐ

Let's say that this statement is true: *Mr. Green had red hair and brown eyes.*
- Make up three statements that contradict the true statement about Mr. Green's hair and eyes. Ⓑ

1. Let's say that this statement is true: *Phillip could speak only English.*
- Write three statements that contradict the true statement. Ⓒ

PART E Story Items

1. **a.** Had Hecate seen Persephone?
   b. Did Hecate have any evidence of Persephone being in distress?
   c. What evidence did Hecate have?
   d. Did Hecate want Demeter to seek her daughter?
   e. Where did Hecate want Demeter to live?

2. Demeter knew of one character who would know about Persephone.
   a. Which character was that?
   b. When Demeter found that character, what was he doing?
   c. What kind of thoughts did that character usually have in his head?
   - Pleasant   • Unpleasant
   - Neutral
   d. Did that character know what had happened to Persephone?
   e. Did that character think that Persephone was in excellent hands or in evil hands?
   f. Had that character ever seen the underground palace of Hades?
   g. Could that character enter Hades's kingdom?
   h. What would that character bring with him that was forbidden in Hades's kingdom?
   i. Demeter told Apollo bitterly, "You have a _____ instead of a _____."

3. **a.** After leaving Apollo, did Demeter find the entrance to Hades's dominions?
   b. What happened to Demeter's face as she continued to search?
   c. At last, Demeter became so bitter that she prevented something from happening. What was that?

PART F   Main Idea

Persephone saw a man who was richly dressed and had a crown on his head. He looked noble, and rather handsome. He kept rubbing his eyes, and shading them with his hand, as if he was not fond of the sunshine.

Write the main idea; then write three supporting details for the main idea. Use complete sentences to write the main idea and the supporting details. Write **1** in front of the main idea. Write **a, b, c** in front of the supporting details. Also, indent the supporting details.

PART G   Writing Assignment

Demeter told Apollo, "You have a harp instead of a heart." Write a paragraph that explains what she meant by that. Be sure the paragraph answers the following questions:
● How did Demeter feel about Apollo?
● What made Demeter think that Apollo didn't have a heart?

Make your paragraph at least **six** sentences long.

Lesson 33

PART A   Word Lists

1
juicy
snake
snaky
pomegranate
juiciest

2
Vocabulary words
of your own accord
pomegranate
detain

PART B   New Vocabulary

1. **of your own accord**—When you do something **of your own accord,** you do it willingly. Here's another way of saying **They stayed in the cave willingly: They stayed in the cave of their own accord.**
   a. What's another way of saying **They stayed in the cave willingly?***
   b. What's another way of saying **Will you go with me willingly?***

2. **pomegranate**—A **pomegranate** is a fruit that is red and that contains many seeds.

3. **detain**—When you delay somebody, you **detain** that person.
   a. What's another way of saying **They were delayed by the rain?***
   b. What's another way of saying **I will not delay you any longer?***

PART C Vocabulary Review

1	2	3
scoff at	exquisite	recollect
entice	gnarled	splendor
frivolous	indignant	immense
	gratifying	

1. Something that is very splendid and fine is _____ .
2. When you are angry and insulted, you are _____ .
3. When you tempt somebody to do something, you _____ that person to do it.
4. Another word for **beauty** is _____ .
5. Another word for **remember** is _____ .
6. Someone who is foolish and not serious is _____ .
7. Another word for **satisfying** is _____ .

PART D Contradictions

Assume that this statement is true: *Tom could not drive a car.* Then this statement is a contradiction: *Tom was driving a station wagon down Fifth Street.* Here is why the statement is a contradiction: If Tom could not drive a car, then he could not drive a station wagon down Fifth Street.Ⓐ

Assume that this statement is true: *Abby swam all morning.* Then this statement is a contradiction: *Abby rode her bike at 10:00 a.m.* Here is why the statement is a contradiction: If Abby swam all morning, then she could not have ridden her bike at 10:00 a.m. Ⓑ

1. Assume that this statement is true: *Gina loved to eat all fruits.* Then this statement is a contradiction: *Gina hated to eat pears.*
   Fill in the blanks to tell why the statement is a contradiction. Start by saying the true statement. Then tell what couldn't also be true.
   If _____ , then _____ . Ⓒ

2. Assume that this statement is true: *Jason always sleeps from noon to 6:00 p.m.* Then this statement is a contradiction: *Jason was fishing today at 3:00 p.m.*
   • Fill in the blanks to tell why the statement is a contradiction.
   If _____ , then _____ .Ⓓ
   • Explain the contradictions in items 1 and 2.Ⓔ

PART E Story Items

1. a. When Persephone went into Hades's dominions, she vowed never to _____ .
   b. How long had she kept that vow?
2. Hades gave Persephone objects that he thought were the most beautiful in the world.
   a. What objects?
   b. What objects did Persephone think were far more beautiful?
   c. Persephone told Hades, "I _____ you a little."
3. a. Hades again tried to tempt Persephone to _____ .
   b. Persephone said that the only thing she cared to eat was something _____ made.
4. Hades sent one of his servants to get something.
   a. Where did the servant go?
   b. Name at least **two** things the servant was to collect.
   c. Why couldn't the servant find most of those objects?
   d. What was the only thing that the servant found?
   e. What condition was it in?
5. a. Which god was concerned about the condition of the earth?
   b. Who did that god send to Hades's dominions with a message?
   c. What was that message?
   d. As that messenger stood at the door of the palace, what was one of Hades's servants doing?

PART F   Vocabulary Items

Use the words in the box to fill in the blanks or replace the underlined words.

excessive	lofty	enticed
summoned	motive	beheld
very sad	neglect	dusky
illuminated	shriveled	morsel
delicacy	triumphant	

1. The spotlights flashed on, and suddenly the side of the barn was <u>lit up</u>.
2. When they asked about her <u>reason</u> for saving string, she explained that she didn't like to waste anything.
3. He was thrown out of the game for <u>too much</u> violence.
4. He could not believe that French people consider large helpings of snails a delicious _____.
5. The meaning of the story was so <u>high</u> that I didn't understand it.

6. In an instant, the plate was cleaned and not a single _____ of food remained.
7. The prisoner was <u>called</u> by the judge.
8. Players on the losing team had <u>melancholy</u> expressions.
9. The boy <u>observed</u> the gray clouds.
10. The children were <u>tempted</u> by the strange-sounding musical instrument.
11. The fox sniffed at the <u>withered and wrinkled</u> grapes and turned away to look for more appetizing food.

PART G   Writing Assignment

Pretend you are Persephone. Would you have given Hades your hand? Write a paragraph that explains your answer. Be sure the paragraph answers the following questions:
● What are your feelings about Hades?
● What might happen because of your actions?

Make your paragraph at least **six** sentences long.

Lesson 34

PART A   Word Lists

1	2	3
curlew	oyster	**Vocabulary words**
efface	fatal	emerges from
liberty	idle	lush
emerge	idly	liberty
wardrobe		

PART B   New Vocabulary

1. **emerges from**—When something **emerges from** a place, it comes out of that place. Here's another way of saying **The campers came out of their tents: The campers emerged from their tents.**
   - What's another way of saying **The campers came out of their tents?***

2. **lush**—Plants that are very rich and green are **lush.**
   - What's another way of saying **The garden had very rich plants in it?***

3. **liberty**—Another word for **freedom** is **liberty.**

PART C   Vocabulary Review

1	2
apt to	gratifying
frivolous	lofty
indignant	entice

1. When you tempt somebody to do something, you _____ that person to do it.
2. When you are likely to do something, you are _____ do it.
3. Another word for **satisfying** is _____.
4. When you are angry and insulted, you are _____.

PART D   Contradictions

1. Assume that this statement is true: *Libby loved all vehicles.* Then this statement is a contradiction: *Libby hated motor scooters.*
   - Fill in the blanks to tell why the statement is a contradiction.
     If _____, then _____.Ⓐ
2. Assume that this statement is true: *At 6:00 a.m. yesterday, I was in Paris, France.* Then this statement is a contradiction: *At 6:00 a.m. yesterday, I was in London, England.*
   - Tell why the statement is a contradiction.
     If _____, then _____.Ⓑ

PART E   Story Items

1. The servant came to Persephone with an object.
   a. What object?
   b. At first, what did Persephone tell the servant to do with the object?
   c. The servant told her something about that object. What was that?
   d. What did the servant do with the object before leaving the room?
2. a. How long had it been since Persephone had eaten?
   b. As Persephone looked at the object, her appetite became
   _____.
      • strong • weak • neutral
   c. Persephone feared that unless she ate the object immediately, it would become so _____ that it would be unfit to eat.
   d. As Persephone was trying to _____ the pomegranate, she suddenly started to _____ it.
3. a. Name the two characters who entered the room at that moment.
   b. Had either of those characters observed what Persephone had done?
   c. Hades said that he had already considered doing something with Persephone. What was that?
   d. Did Persephone have any regrets about leaving the dominions of Hades?
4. a. In the meantime, where was Demeter sitting?
   b. What suddenly happened to the object Demeter was holding?
   c. Demeter thought that the earth was disobeying her because it _____.
   d. Why did Persephone and Demeter cry?

5. Persephone told her mother what had happened.
   a. Had Persephone taken a bite of the pomegranate?
   b. What was left in Persephone's mouth?
   c. For each seed, what did Persephone have to do?
   d. So how many months was Persephone to spend with Hades?
   e. And how many months was Persephone to spend with Demeter?
   f. What new season occurred when Persephone went back to the underground kingdom?
   g. In which season did Persephone return to Demeter?

PART F   Outlining

Complete the following outline for *Persephone.* Copy each main idea; then write three supporting details for each main idea. Use complete sentences to write the supporting details.

1. The underworld was an unusual place.
2. Demeter wandered all over the earth.
3. Persephone had to visit Hades for part of each year.

PART G   Writing Assignment

You have read about two people who lost hope. One was Persephone; the other was Joan. Write a paragraph that compares those two characters. Be sure it answers the following questions:
• How are those characters the same?
• How are those characters different?

Make your paragraph at least **six** sentences long.

Lesson 35

PART A   Word List

Henry Wadsworth Longfellow
hastens
efface
curlew
neigh

PART B   Vocabulary Review

1	2
liberty	frivolous
of your own accord	lush
emerges from	apt to
excessive	detain
gratifying	

1. When you do something willingly, you do it _____.
2. When you delay somebody, you _____ that person.
3. When something comes out of a place, it _____ that place.
4. Plants that are very rich and green are _____.
5. Another word for **freedom** is _____.
6. Someone who is foolish and not serious is _____.

PART C   Contradictions

Here's how to find a contradiction in a passage:

- Assume that what the writer says first is true.
- Read until you find a contradiction.
- Make up an **if-then** statement that explains the contradiction.

Here's a passage:
Andrea went to a museum when she was in Egypt. The museum was quite large. It had several sculptures and many different kinds of pottery. Andrea has never left the United States.

We assume that the underlined statement is true. If that statement is true, then it can't be true that Andrea has never left the United States.

Here's how we explain the contradiction:
If Andrea went to a museum when she was in Egypt, then she must have left the United States. Ⓐ

- Assume that the underlined statement is true. Find the statement that contradicts the underlined statement.

We have a club called the "Girls Only Club." We have meetings twice a week. John is a member of the club, and he loves it. We are thinking of building a clubhouse.
1. Which statement is a contradiction?
2. Explain the contradiction using an **if-then** statement.

PART D   Main Idea

Persephone could not help coming close to the table and eagerly examining this poor, dried pomegranate. Suddenly she felt six months of appetite. This was the first fruit she had seen in the underworld, and she feared that it might be the last one she would see.

Write the main idea; then write three supporting details for the main idea. Use complete sentences to write the main idea and the supporting details. Write **1** in front of the main idea. Write **a, b, c** in front of the supporting details. Also, indent the supporting details.

PART E   Writing Assignment

The Tide Rises, the Tide Falls tells about the sea. Make up a poem that tells about the wind or the rain. Here are some things you might tell about: cold rain, warm rain, rain with big drops, misty rain, the sound of rain, the smells of rain, the things that happen before the rain, the way things look and smell after the rain.

Make your poem at least **six** lines long.

Lesson 36

PART A　Word Lists

1
Cape Canaveral
decorate
bedstead

2
Frances Hodgson Burnett
Miss Minchin
tolerate
climate
possession

3
Vocabulary words
obliged to do something
frail
plumes
wardrobe
adorn
skylight

PART B　New Vocabulary

1. **obliged to do something**—When you are **obliged to do something,** you are required to do it.
   a. What's another way of saying **She was required to visit Mrs. Jones?***
   b. What's another way of saying **Her father was required to send her to England?***

2. **frail**—Somebody who is weak and delicate is **frail.**
   a. What's another way of saying **She was a weak and delicate person?***
   b. What's another way of saying **The leaf was weak and delicate?***

3. **plumes**—**Plumes** are large, fluffy feathers. People used to wear **plumes** on hats.

4. **wardrobe**—All the clothes you have are called your **wardrobe.**

5. **adorn**—When you **adorn** something, you decorate it.
   ● What's another way of saying **Her hat was decorated with plumes?***

6. **skylight**—A window in the roof of a house is called a **skylight.**

PART C　Vocabulary Review

1	**2**
detain	liberty
gratifying	emerges from
lush	

1. Plants that are very rich and green are _____.
2. When something comes out of a place, it _____ that place.

PART D   Contradictions

Here's how to find a contradiction in a passage:

- Assume that what the writer says first is true.
- Read until you find a contradiction.
- Make up an **if-then** statement that explains the contradiction.

Here's a passage:

Cape Canaveral is in Florida. Rockets are launched from the Cape, and many people work there. Every year we go to Alabama to visit Cape Canaveral. We love to watch rocket launchings.

We assume that the underlined statement is true. If that statement is true, then it can't be true that Cape Canaveral is in Alabama.

Here's how we explain the contradiction:
If Cape Canaveral is in Florida, then it can't be in Alabama. Ⓐ

- Assume that the underlined statement is true. Find the statement that contradicts the underlined statement.

The Camberra family was preparing a Fourth of July picnic. Mr. Camberra was frying chicken. Mrs. Camberra was making sandwiches. The children were packing cookies. They all thought it was a great way to celebrate Thanksgiving.
1. Which statement is a contradiction?
2. Explain the contradiction using an **if-then** statement.

PART E   Story Items

1. **a.** In which city did Miss Minchin live?
   b. Which country is that city in?
      - England • Canada • Ireland
   c. Which country had Sara come from?
   d. What was the weather like in that country?
   e. What effect did that weather have on Sara?

2. **a.** What kind of school did Miss Minchin run?
   b. How is that kind of school different from a regular school?
   c. How old was Sara when she came to Miss Minchin's school?
3. Captain Crewe bought Sara some clothes.
   a. Write the two words that describe the clothes he bought.
      - beautiful   • plain
      - practical   • extraordinary
   b. Write the names of the materials that her dresses were made of.
      - silk   • wool
      - cashmere   • velvet
      - polyester   • gingham
      - cotton
   c. What toy did Captain Crewe buy for Sara?
4. Captain Crewe left Sara with Miss Minchin.
   a. What country did he go back to?
   b. What did Sara do for several days after her father left?
   c. Which country would Sara rather have been in?
   d. How did Sara feel about Miss Minchin?
   e. Which animal did Miss Minchin remind her of?
   f. In what way was Miss Minchin like that animal?
   g. What would happen to Sara's back when Miss Minchin touched her?
5. Write which character each statement describes. Choose from **Miss Minchin, Sara,** or **Captain Crewe**.
   a. This character was an officer in the army.
   b. This character was like a fish.
   c. This character's wife had died.
   d. This character had an extraordinary wardrobe.
   e. This character ran a school.

PART F   Review Items

You read a poem about the sea. Write whether each statement describes **a person** or **the sea.**
1. This character leaves footprints that last for a short time.
2. This character erases the footprints left by the other character.
3. This character does things again and again.
4. This character does things only once.
5. This character hurries toward the town.
6. This character rises and falls, rises and falls.

PART G   Writing Assignment

What kind of school would you rather go to, a boarding school or a regular school? Write a paragraph that explains your answer.

Make your paragraph at least **five** sentences long.

Lesson 37

PART A   Word Lists

1
Bastille
distinguished
inherit

2
Vocabulary words
decked out
mount stairs
distinguished
inherit
bedstead
twitch

PART B   New Vocabulary

1. **decked out**—When you are **decked out,** you are all dressed up.

2. **mount stairs**—When you **mount stairs,** you climb them.

3. **distinguished**—A **distinguished** person is a noble or important person.
   - What's another way of saying **They met an important gentleman?***

4. **inherit**—When you **inherit** things, you receive them from somebody who has died.
   - What's another way of saying **Her father died and she received his fortune?***

5. **bedstead**—The frame of a bed is called the **bedstead.**

6. **twitch**—A **twitch** is a quick nervous gesture.

PART C   Vocabulary Review

1	2	3
wardrobe	detain	obliged to
adorn	frail	skylight
liberty		

1. When you are required to do something, you are _____ do it.
2. Somebody who is weak and delicate is _____.
3. All the clothes you have are called your _____.
4. When you decorate something, you _____ it.

PART D   Story Items

1. a. During Sara's first year at the boarding school, she was a _____ pupil.
   - favorite   • neglected
   - troublesome
   b. What did Miss Minchin think that Sara would inherit someday?
   c. Miss Minchin treated Sara well because she wanted some of Sara's _____.
2. Sara received a letter with bad news about her father.
   a. How old was Sara when that news arrived?
   b. How old had she been when she entered Miss Minchin's boarding school?
   c. What had Captain Crewe's friend done with the money?
   d. What did the jungle fever do to her father?
3. Sara went to see Miss Minchin.
   a. Why was Sara wearing a black dress?
   b. Whose eyes were cold and fishy?
   c. Whose eyes had dark rings around them?
   d. Who was the only friend that Sara still had?
   e. What would Miss Minchin no longer receive from Sara's father?
   f. Who would take care of Sara now?

4. Miss Minchin had a plan for Sara.
   a. What language would Sara help teach?
   b. Where did Miss Minchin threaten to send Sara if she didn't help her?
   c. Did Sara thank Miss Minchin for her kindness?
   d. How much money did Sara inherit?
5. a. Where was Sara's new room?
   b. What was the furniture like in that room?
   c. What would most children do if they felt like Sara did?
   d. Did Sara do that?

PART E   Relevant Information

Read the facts and the items. If an item is relevant to fact A, write **relevant to fact A**. If an item is relevant to fact B, write **relevant to fact B**. If an item is irrelevant to both facts, write **irrelevant**.

- Fact A: *Persephone spent six months with Hades.*
- Fact B: *Persephone spent six months with Demeter.*

1. The plants no longer grew.
2. Winter came upon the land.
3. She was sixteen years old.
4. The flowers started blooming.

PART F   Writing Assignment

What would you have done for Sara if you were Miss Minchin? Write a paragraph that explains your answer.

Make your paragraph at least **five** sentences long.

Lesson 38

PART A   Word Lists

1
accustomed
garret
vacant
Bastille

2
Cape Canaveral
craving
carving

3
Vocabulary words
accustomed to
outcast
garret
vacant
discard
craving

PART B   New Vocabulary

1. **accustomed to**—When you are used to something, you are **accustomed to** that thing.
   - What's another way of saying **They were used to fancy parties?***

2. **outcast**—An **outcast** is somebody who is thrown out of a group. Somebody who is thrown out of a country is an **outcast** of that country.

3. **garret**—Another word for an **attic** is a **garret**.

4. **vacant**—Another word for **empty** is **vacant**.
   - What's another way of saying **She stared at us with an empty expression?***

5. **discard**—When you **discard** something, you throw it away.
   - What's another way of saying **She wore clothes that had been thrown away?***

6. **craving**—When you have a **craving** for something, you have a great desire for that thing.
   a. What's another way of saying **He had a great desire for pickles?***
   b. What's another way of saying **She had a great desire for knowledge?***

PART C   Vocabulary Review

1	**2**	**3**
gratifying	frail	wardrobe
gnarled	adorn	lush

1. When you decorate something, you _____ it.
2. All the clothes you have are called your _____.
3. Something that is twisted and misformed is _____.

PART D   Story Items

1. The chapter described Sara's new life.
   a. What kinds of jobs did Sara do for Miss Minchin and the cook?
   b. Name at least **two** things about Sara that the other pupils didn't like.
   c. Sara thought that when people insult you, the best thing to do is to _____.
      - yell at them   • cry and argue
      - look at them and think
2. a. At first, who did Sara think understood her feelings?
   b. Did Sara like to admit the truth about that companion?
   c. Sara had a strong _____.
      - imagination • arm
3. a. Why did Sara have to go out in the cold on some days?
   b. On those days, it was _____ for Sara to pretend about Emily.
      - hard   • easy
4. One night, Sara was particularly cold and hungry.
   a. What did Emily say when Sara complained?
   b. Sara cried, "You are nothing but a _____."
   c. What did Sara do to Emily?
   d. Why didn't Emily say anything?
5. Sara pretended a lot. But sometimes it was hard for her to pretend. Tell whether it would be **hard** or **easy** for her to pretend at each of the following times.
   a. Sara is cold and miserable.
   b. Sara is reading a book.
   c. Sara is looking at the stars through her skylight.
   d. Sara is being made fun of.
   e. Sara is hungry.

PART E   Outlining

Complete the following outline for *Sara Crewe*. Copy each main idea; then write three supporting details for each main idea. Use complete sentences to write the supporting details.

1. One character was named Sara.
2. One character was named Miss Minchin.
3. One character was named Emily.

PART F   Review Items

You read a story about the underworld.
1. Who was the goddess of the earth?
2. Who was the god of the underworld?
3. Who had to spend half her time in the underworld?

PART G   Writing Assignment

Everybody pretends about certain things. Some people pretend to talk to dolls. Other people pretend what they will do when they grow up.

Write a paragraph that describes what you have pretended. Make your paragraph at least **five** sentences long.

Lesson 39

PART A   Word Lists

1
dramatic
awe
figurative

2
gypsies
fascinate
Bastille
revolution
gesture

3
Vocabulary words
has a gift
subscribe to
dramatic
forlorn
awe
crimson

PART B   New Vocabulary

1. **has a gift**—If somebody has a talent for something, that person **has a gift** for that thing.
   - What's another way of saying **She had a talent for making up poems?***

2. **subscribe to**—When you **subscribe to** a magazine, you pay money and receive each copy of the magazine that comes out.

3. **dramatic**—Speech or gestures that create emotion are **dramatic**. Here's another way of saying **Her gestures created emotion: Her gestures were dramatic.**
   - What's another way of saying **Her gestures created emotion?***

4. **forlorn**—Somebody who is **forlorn** is alone and lonely. A puppy that is alone and lonely is a **forlorn** puppy.
   - What would you call a child who is alone and lonely?*

5. **awe**—When you are amazed by something, you are **awed** by that thing.
   - What's another way of saying **She was amazed by her father's talent?***

6. **crimson**—Crimson is a deep red color.

PART C   Vocabulary Review

1	2
craving	inherit
accustomed to	distinguished
liberty	outcast
wardrobe	discard
frail	vacant

1. A noble or important person is a _____ person.
2. When you have a great desire for something, you have a _____ for that thing.
3. Another word for **empty** is _____.
4. Somebody who is thrown out of a group is an _____.
5. When you are used to something, you are _____ that thing.
6. When you throw something away, you _____ it.
7. When you receive things from somebody who has died, you _____ those things.

PART D   Figurative Language

Sometimes people use figurative language. When people use figurative language, they say things that are not really accurate. But the things they say give a good picture of what they mean. Ⓐ

Here are some examples of figurative language:
- *Her eyes were like emeralds.*
- *He ran like a rocket.*
- *The voice of Zeus sounded like thunder.*

Each statement tells how two things are the same.

1. The first statement says her eyes were like emeralds.
   a. How could her eyes and emeralds be the same? Ⓑ
   b. Name one way that her eyes and emeralds are not the same. Ⓒ
2. The second statement says he ran like a rocket.
   a. How could his running and a rocket be the same? Ⓓ
   b. Name one way that his running and a rocket are not the same. Ⓔ
3. The third statement says the voice of Zeus sounded like thunder.
   a. What two things are the same in that statement? Ⓕ
   b. How could those two things be the same? Ⓖ
   c. Name two ways those two things are different. Ⓗ

PART E   Story Items

1. a. How did most of Miss Minchin's pupils feel about reading?
   b. How did Sara feel about reading?
   c. What kinds of stories were in the magazines that Sara read?
      - Realistic
      - Romantic
      - Horror
      - Science fiction
2. a. Who sent Erma her books?
   b. How did Erma feel about reading?
   c. How would Erma's father find out if she had read the books?
   d. What did Erma decide to do with her books?
   e. What did Sara agree to do to help Erma?
3. Sara made her life easier by making everything sound like a _____.
   - story
   - lecture
   - poem
4. a. Name at least **two** things about Sara that Erma admired.
   b. How did Erma's friendship make Sara feel?
   c. Sara had one other friend besides Erma. Who was that?
5. a. Which prison did Sara compare the attic to?
   b. Which person did Sara compare Miss Minchin to?
   c. Which place did Erma decide to visit?
6. Write which character each statement describes. Choose from **Miss Minchin, Erma, Sara,** or **Captain Crewe.**
   a. This character had a strong imagination.
   b. This character needed help with her reading.
   c. This character was compared to a jailer.
   d. This character thought that everything was a story.
   e. This character got books in the mail.

PART F   Review Items

Pretend you are making a pot.
1. Which part do you use a flat piece of clay for?
2. You use coils of clay to make the _____ of the pot.
3. What do you use to smooth the clay?
4. What do you paint on the pot?
5. Why do you bake the pot?

PART G   Writing Assignment

Do you agree with Sara that everything is a story? Write a paragraph that explains your answer.

Make your paragraph at least **five** sentences long.

Lesson 40

PART A   Word List

fleecy
coral
sooty
quilt
corral

PART B   Vocabulary Review

1	2
subscribe to	forlorn
inherit	distinguished
dramatic	twitch
awed	

1. Somebody who is alone and lonely is
   _____.
2. When you are amazed by something,
   you are _____ by that thing.
3. When you pay money and receive each
   copy of a magazine that comes out,
   you _____ a magazine.
4. Speech or gestures that create emotion
   are _____.
5. A noble or important person is a
   _____ person.

PART C   Figurative Language

Sometimes people use figurative
language. When people use figurative
language, they say things that are not
really accurate, but the things they say
give a good picture of what they
mean.Ⓐ

Here are some examples of figurative
language:
- *Joan was like a leaf.*
- *Persephone was like a sunbeam.*
- *Miss Minchin was like a fish.*

Each statement tells how two things are
the same.
1. The first statement says Joan was like
   a leaf.
   a. How could Joan and a leaf be the
      same?Ⓑ
   b. Name some ways that Joan and a
      leaf are not the same.Ⓒ
2. The second statement says Persephone
   was like a sunbeam.
   a. How could Persephone and a
      sunbeam be the same?Ⓓ
   b. Name some ways that Persephone
      and a sunbeam are not the
      same.Ⓔ
3. The third statement says Miss
   Minchin was like a fish.
   a. What two things are the same in
      this statement?
   b. How could those two things be the
      same?
   c. Name two ways those two things
      are different.

PART D Story Items

1. **a.** Which room did Sara go to when she wanted to see the sunset?
   b. What did Sara stick her head through to see the sunsets?
   c. Name at least **two** things that Sara saw in the clouds.
2. Erma came to see Sara.
   a. How did Erma feel about the attic?
   b. Which animals did the two girls feed?
   c. What noise did Sara make to calm down the animals?
3. Sara described the attic to Erma.
   a. She said that it was so high up that it was like a _____ in a tree.
   b. Why couldn't Sara stand up at one end of the room?
   c. What could Sara look through when she was in bed?
   d. What did Sara try to count at night?
4. Sara described what the attic could be like.
   a. Erma saw what Sara described because Sara had a good _____.
   b. What could cover the cracks in the wall?
   c. What could be heating the stove?
5. **a.** After Erma left, what was the bed really like?
   b. What was the stove really like?
   c. Why do you think Sara let her head drop in her hands?

PART E Vocabulary Items

Use the words in the box to fill in the blanks or replace the underlined words.

used to	excessive
distinguished	triumphant
summon	inherit
outcast	hatred
vacant	lofty
tracked	

1. She shook hands with the <u>important</u> professor.
2. The lawyer was <u>accustomed to</u> reading the paper on the train in the morning.
3. The cowardly Indian was an _____ of his tribe.
4. Andrew did not <u>receive</u> any of his grandmother's money.
5. After the family removed the furniture, the apartment was totally <u>empty</u>.
6. She felt nothing but <u>contempt</u> for the horrible ruler of her <u>country</u>.
7. They <u>stalked</u> their prey for three days before catching up with it.
8. The smaller wolf was <u>victorious</u> in its fight with the older, stronger wolf.

PART F Writing Assignment

Write a paragraph that describes the room you are in now. Then write a paragraph that describes what it could be like.

Make each paragraph at least **three** sentences long.

Lesson 41

PART A　Word Lists

1
corral
coral
palace
place
rouse

2
Vocabulary words
inclined to
horrid
shuffle

PART B　New Vocabulary

1. **inclined to**—When you are **inclined to** do something, you have a tendency to do it. A person who has a tendency to talk loudly is **inclined to** talk loudly.

2. **horrid**—Something that is **horrid** is horrible or disgusting.

3. **shuffle**—When you **shuffle,** you walk slowly and drag your feet.

PART C　Vocabulary Review

1	2	3
awed	discard	frail
dramatic	forlorn	inherit
skeptical	wardrobe	outcast

1. Speech or gestures that create emotion are _____.
2. When you are very suspicious about something, you are _____ about that thing.
3. Somebody who is thrown out of a group is an _____.
4. When you are amazed by something, you are _____ by that thing.
5. Someone who is alone and lonely is _____.
6. When you throw away something, you _____ that thing.

PART D　Story Items

1. Sara heard a slight sound.
   a. What was making the sound?
   b. Why had the rat come out of his hole?
   c. Which other animal had Sara made friends with?
   d. Why did the rat have to come very close to Sara?
   e. What did Sara do when the rat came very close to her?
2. Erma heard Sara talking to somebody.
   a. Which animal was Sara talking to?
   b. What name had Sara given the rat?
   c. What kind of person did Erma think Sara was talking to?
   d. How did Erma feel when Sara told her about the rat?
   e. Where did Erma immediately jump?
3. Here are some things that people do. Write whether you think that Sara would or would not do each thing. Write **yes** if she would do it. Write **no** if she would not do it.
   a. Try to make friends with a dog.
   b. Set traps to catch mice.
   c. Get angry and hit somebody.
   d. Look at the bright side of things.
   e. Try to understand other people.

PART E   Main Idea

"You see," Sara went on, "the room really could be beautiful. There could be a thick Indian rug on the floor; and in that corner there could be a soft little sofa, with cushions; and just over it could be a shelf full of books; and there could be a fire, and pictures on the walls to cover up the cracks."

Write the main idea; then write three supporting details for the main idea. Use complete sentences to write the main idea and the supporting details. Write **1** in front of the main idea. Write **a, b, c** in front of the supporting details. Also, indent the supporting details.

PART F   Figurative Language

The statements in the next column use figurative language.

1. *The advertising man was like a sandwich.*
   a. Name two things that are the same in that statement.
   b. How could those two things be the same?
   c. Name two ways those two things are different.
2. *His feet felt like lead.*
   a. Name two things that are the same in that statement.
   b. How could those two things be the same?
   c. Name two ways those two things are different.

PART G   Writing Assignment

Do you think that animals understand people? Write a paragraph that explains your answer.

Make your paragraph at least **five** sentences long.

Lesson 42

PART A   Word Lists

1	2	3
impudent	unchildish	**Vocabulary words**
challenging	enraged	challenging
jostled	breathlessly	impudent
absurd	apologize	smarting
devour		absurd
simile		

PART B   New Vocabulary

1. **challenging**—Something that is **challenging** is very difficult to achieve. A race course that is very **challenging** is very hard to go over.

2. **impudent**—Somebody who is **impudent** is rude and bold.
   ● What's another way of saying **His remark was rude and bold?***

3. **smarting**—Something that is **smarting** is stinging or sore.
   ● What's another way of saying **Her cheek was stinging from the blow she received?***

4. **absurd**—Something that is ridiculous is **absurd.**

PART C   Story Items

1. **a.** Which piece of furniture was Erma on at the beginning of the chapter?
   b. Why had Erma jumped there?
   c. Why did Sara make a low whistling sound?
   d. How many different kinds of rat squeaks did Sara understand?
2. **a.** What did Sara think might happen to her if she didn't make up things?
   b. Name the animal Sara treated like a person.
   c. How much did Sara talk to Emily when she had other friends?
   d. Name three friends that took the place of Emily.
   e. Which place did Sara usually pretend the attic was?
   f. What happened to Erma the next day?
3. **a.** The next day, Sara began to pretend that she was a _____ .
   b. Which relative of hers was Sara imitating?
4. One day, Miss Minchin confronted Sara.
   a. What did Miss Minchin do to Sara?
   b. When Miss Minchin did that, Sara

   _____ .

   • laughed   • cried
5. Sara told Miss Minchin what she was thinking.
   a. What person was Sara pretending she was?
   b. Would Miss Minchin have slapped Sara if Sara was a real captain?
   c. Where did Miss Minchin order Sara to go?

PART D   Relevant Information

Read the facts and the items. If an item is relevant to fact A, write **relevant to fact A.** If an item is relevant to fact B, write **relevant to fact B.** If an item is irrelevant to both facts, write **irrelevant.**

- Fact A: *Sara pretended to be a captain.*
- Fact B: *Sara pretended that her doll was alive.*

1. She needed someone to talk to.
2. She needed to lift her spirits.
3. She had black hair.
4. She lived in London.

PART E   Figurative Language

The following statements use figurative language.

1. *Odysseus was like an eagle.*
   a. Name two things that are the same in that statement.
   b. How could those two things be the same?
   c. Name two ways those two things are different.
2. *The mesa is like a table.*
   a. Name two things that are the same in that statement.
   b. How could those two things be the same?
   c. Name two ways those two things are different.

PART F   Writing Assignment

Sara pretended to be a captain. What kind of person would you like to be? Write a paragraph that explains your answer.

Make your paragraph at least **five** sentences long.

Lesson 43

PART A Word Lists

1
tunic
tonic
simile
sized
seized
desparate

2
Vocabulary words
shock of hair
deprived of
draggled
jostled

PART B New Vocabulary

1. **shock of hair**—A **shock of hair** is a bunch of hair.

2. **deprived of**—When you are **deprived of** something, you are prevented from having that thing. Here's another way of saying **You are prevented from having your dinner: You are deprived of your dinner.**
   - What's another way of saying **You are prevented from having your dinner?***

3. **draggled**—Things that are **draggled** are muddy and limp.
   - What's another way of saying **The bird's feathers were muddy and limp?***

4. **jostled**—When you are pushed and jolted, you are **jostled.** If the crowd pushed and jolted the boy, the crowd **jostled** the boy.

PART C Vocabulary Review

1	2
awed	smarting
outcast	inclined to
distinguished	absurd
skeptical	impudent

1. A noble or important person is a _____ person.
2. Something that is ridiculous is _____.
3. Something that is stinging or sore is _____.
4. Somebody who is rude and bold is _____.
5. When you have a tendency to do something, you are _____ do that thing.

PART D   Similes

You have worked on these examples of figurative language:
- *Her eyes were like emeralds.*
- *His feet were like lead.*
- *The mesa is like a table.*

All those examples are called **similes.** Many similes contain the word *like.* Similes tell how two things are the same.Ⓐ

Here are some more similes. For each simile below, tell which two things the simile says are the same. Tell how those things could be the same. Then tell how the things are actually different.

1. *The schooner's sails were like a crane's wings.*
   a. What two things are the same in that simile?Ⓑ
   b. How could those things be the same?Ⓒ
   c. Name two ways those things are different.Ⓓ
2. *The lights of the ship were like two great eyes.*
   a. What two things are the same in that simile?
   b. How could those things be the same?
   c. Name two ways those things are different.

PART E   Story Items

1. a. When Sara went out on errands, what was the weather like?
   b. What happened to Sara's clothes?
   c. Why hadn't Miss Minchin given Sara any dinner?
   d. Why was it harder for Sara to pretend?
   e. Name the object Sara dreamed about finding.
   f. Name the object Sara actually found.
   g. What kind of shop did Sara see in front of her?
2. Sara headed for the bakery shop.
   a. Who did Sara see on the step of the shop?
   b. What did Sara think a captain would do for the girl?
3. Sara went into the shop.
   a. What did Sara ask to buy?
   b. How many of those could Sara afford?
   c. How did the woman show her kindness to Sara?
4. a. Who was still sitting on the step when Sara came out?
   b. How many buns did Sara give her?
      - 1   - 3   - 5
   c. Why didn't the girl give Sara any thanks?
   d. How many buns did Sara have left for herself?

PART F   Writing Assignment

Do you think that Sara did the right thing when she gave her food to the beggar girl? Write a paragraph that explains your answer.

Make your paragraph at least **five** sentences long.

Lesson 44

PART A Word Lists

1
luxurious
vague
luscious
pantry
exaggeration

2
Lascar
Odyssey
Odysseus

3
Vocabulary words
ponder
strollers
liver
tropical
luxurious
grate

PART B New Vocabulary

1. **ponder**—When you think about something or puzzle over it, you **ponder** it.
   - What's another way of saying **She thought about her future?***

2. **strollers**—**Strollers** are small carriages for very young children.

3. **liver**—The **liver** is an organ in your body. It is very important in helping you digest food.

4. **tropical**—**Tropical** parts of the world are very warm parts of the world. Things that come from tropical parts of the world are called **tropical.** Fruit from a warm part of the world is tropical fruit.

5. **luxurious**—Something that is very rich and elegant is **luxurious.**
   - What's another way of saying **His apartment was very rich and elegant?***

6. **grate**—The **grate** is part of a stove or fireplace. The **grate** is made up of bars that support the wood or material to be burned.

PART C Vocabulary Review

1	2
jostled	impudent
draggled	challenging
deprived of	shuffle
crimson	

1. When you are prevented from having something, you are _____ that thing.
2. When you are pushed and jolted, you are _____ .
3. Things that are muddy and limp are _drag_ .
4. Somebody who is rude and bold is _____ .

PART D   Story items

1. **a.** When the baker woman looked out her window, who did she see eating the buns?
   b. Why did the baker woman talk to the girl?
   c. The woman invited the girl to come into the _____.
   d. Why do you think the woman did that?
2. Sara named families that lived in the square.
   a. What did Sara name the family with many children?
   b. Did Sara find that family more interesting or less interesting than the Maiden Lady?
3. **a.** Who was the most interesting person in the square?
   b. Where was that person's house?
   c. Where had that person lived before?
   d. How was that person's health?
   e. Did that person have any relatives?
   f. Which animal lived with that person?
   g. Where did Sara think that animal wanted to be?
4. **a.** What did Sara call the servant?
   b. How did Sara surprise the servant one day?
   c. Sara knew the servant's language because she had lived in
   _____.
5. **a.** Sara heard rumors about the Indian Gentleman and his companions. Name **two** rumors that were true.
   b. What kind of expression did the Indian Gentleman always have?
   • Happy   • Greedy   • Lonely

6. Write which character each statement describes. Choose from **Sara, Miss Minchin, the Indian Gentleman,** or **the Lascar.**
   a. This character was surprised to hear his own language.
   b. This character had a problem with his liver.
   c. This character liked to imagine things about people.
   d. This character was very rich.
   e. This character served a gentleman.
   f. This character had been running errands.

PART E   Similes

1. *The miner's hands looked like a lump of coal.*
   a. What two things are the same in that simile?
   b. How could those things be the same?
   c. Name two ways those things are different.
2. *The sun was like a bloodstain.*
   a. What two things are the same in that simile?
   b. How could those things be the same?
   c. Name two ways those things are different.

PART F   Writing Assignment

Sara thought about three houses on the square: the Large Family's, the Maiden Lady's, and the Indian Gentleman's. Which house do you think Sara would like to live in? Write a paragraph that explains your answer.

Make your paragraph at least **five** sentences long.

Lesson 45

PART A Word Lists

1
directed
decided
exaggeration
respectable
concealed

2
Vocabulary words
vent your emotions
vague
luscious

PART B New Vocabulary

1. **vent your emotions**—When you **vent your emotions,** you let them show. When you **vent your anger,** you let your anger show.
   • Name something you might do to vent your frustration.

2. **vague**—If something is not clear it is **vague.** A comment that is not clear is a **vague** comment.
   a. What's another way of saying **a sight that is not clear?***
   b. What's another way of saying **an impression that is not clear?***

3. **luscious**—Something that is **luscious** is marvelous or delicious. Delicious fruit is **luscious** fruit.
   • What's another way of saying **a marvelous dress?***

PART C Vocabulary Review

1	**2**
tropical	ponder
jostled	strollers
luxurious	liver
grate	

1. When you think about something or puzzle over it, you _____ it.
2. Very warm parts of the world are _____ parts of the world.
3. Something that is very rich and elegant is _____.
4. When you are pushed and jolted, you are _____.

PART D Exaggeration

Exaggeration is another type of figurative language. When you exaggerate, you try to stretch the truth. You say that something is bigger or faster or longer than it really is.

1. Here's an example of exaggeration: *Frank worked for a year that afternoon.*
   a. How long does the statement say that Frank worked?Ⓐ
   b. Could Frank really have worked that long in the afternoon?Ⓑ
   c. What part of the statement stretches the truth?Ⓒ
   d. Use accurate language to tell what the exaggeration means.Ⓓ
2. Here's another example: *Camila ran one thousand miles an hour.*
   a. How fast does the statement say that Camila ran?
   b. Could Camila really have run that fast?
   c. What part of the statement stretches the truth?
   d. Use accurate language to tell what the exaggeration means.

PART E Story Items

1. a. When Sara came back to school, who met her in the hall?
   b. Why was that character angry?
   c. What did Sara receive for supper?
2. a. Why did it take Sara so long to climb the stairs to her room?
   b. It was difficult for Sara to pretend because she was so _____.
      • happy   • miserable   • rich
3. Sara opened the door.
   a. Describe what the stove was like.
   b. Describe what the bed was like.
   c. Describe what the floor was like.
4. Sara tried to figure out what she saw.
   a. At first, she thought it was part of her _____.
      • imagination   • reward
      • reality
   b. Sara thought these things had been given to her by _____.
      • a friend   • her father
      • Miss Minchin
   c. Why did that thought make Sara cry?
   d. How did Sara feel at the end of the chapter?

PART F Writing Assignment

Who do you think gave Sara all these things? Write a paragraph that explains your answer. Also tell how you think the person did it.

Make your paragraph at least **five** sentences long.

Lesson 46

PART A   Word Lists

1
incident
agitated
miscalculation
caress
Carmichael
metaphor

2
Vocabulary words
parcels
incident
scant

PART B   New Vocabulary

1. **parcels**—**Parcels** are packages.
   - What's another way of saying
   She received a package?*

2. **incident**—An **incident** is an event.
   An event that occurred last week is an
   incident that occurred last week.
   - What's another way of saying
   **There were five important events
   in her life?***

3. **scant**—If there is not enough of
   something, that thing is **scant.** If the
   food is **scant,** there is not enough
   food. If the greenery is **scant,** there is
   not enough greenery.
   - What's another way of saying
   There is not enough clothing?*

PART C   Vocabulary Review

1	**2**
jostled	luscious
ponder	vent your emotions
draggled	vague
tropical	

1. If something is not clear it is

   _____.

2. Something that is marvelous or
   delicious is _____.

3. When you let your emotions show, you

   _____.

4. Things that are muddy and limp are

   _____.

PART D Exaggeration

Exaggeration is another type of figurative language. When you exaggerate, you try to stretch the truth. You say that something is bigger or faster or longer than it really is.

1. Here's an example of exaggeration: *She aged five years in a week.*
   a. How much does the statement say she aged that week?Ⓐ
   b. Could she really have aged that much in a week?Ⓑ
   c. What part of the statement stretches the truth?Ⓒ
   d. Use accurate language to tell what the exaggeration means.Ⓓ
2. Here's another example: *The basketball player was about a hundred feet tall.*
   a. About how tall does that statement say he was?
   b. Could he really be that tall?
   c. What part of the statement stretches the truth?
   d. Use accurate language to tell what the exaggeration means.

PART E Story Items

1. Sara's room continued to change.
   a. Name at least **three** new things the room had.
   b. Before, Sara had made these things from her _____.
      • sewing box   • tool kit
      • imagination
   c. Now, she thought that she was *living* in a _____.
      • prison   • fairy story
      • basement
   d. Why was Sara able to bear Miss Minchin and the others now?
2. One day, some parcels arrived.
   a. Who were those parcels for?
   b. Did that character know who had sent them?
   c. What did those parcels contain?
   d. Who became irritated when Sara received the parcels?

e. What kind of person did Miss Minchin think Sara might have in the background?
f. Miss Minchin did not want that person to find out about the way Sara had been treated. Name **two** things Miss Minchin would not want that person to know.
g. How did Miss Minchin begin to treat Sara?

PART F Outlining

Complete the following outline for *Sara Crewe.* Copy each main idea; then write three supporting details for each main idea. Use complete sentences to write the supporting details.

1. Miss Minchin was mean to Sara.
2. Sara had a strong imagination.
3. Sara performed a good deed near a bakery shop.

PART G Similes

1. *He pounded on the door like a tiger.*
   a. What two things are the same in that simile?
   b. How could those things be the same?
   c. Name two ways those things are different.
2. *Hades's voice sounded like the rumbling of an earthquake.*
   a. What two things are the same in that simile?
   b. How could those things be the same?
   c. Name two ways those things are different.

PART H Writing Assignment

Sara's room looks very nice now. Write a paragraph that describes what you would like your own room to look like.

Make your paragraph at least **five** sentences long.

Lesson 47

PART A   Word Lists

1
elfish
scene
metaphor
desert
sense
dessert

2
Vocabulary words
caress
agitated
miscalculation
devoted

PART B   New Vocabulary

1. **caress**—When you **caress** someone, you hug that person.

2. **agitated**—Another word for **anxious** or **nervous** is **agitated**. A nervous gesture is an **agitated** gesture.
   - What's another way of saying **a nervous voice?***

3. **miscalculation**—A **miscalculation** is an error or a mistake.
   - What's another way of saying **He did not know about his mistake?***

4. **devoted**—Someone who is **devoted** is very loyal.
   - What's another way of saying **She had a loyal servant?***

PART C   Vocabulary Review

1	**2**
luscious	incident
impudent	tropical
scant	vague
absurd	parcels

1. Packages are _____.
2. An event is an _____.
3. If there is not enough of something, that thing is _____.
4. Somebody who is rude and bold is _____.
5. If something is not clear, it is _____.

PART D   Similes

Here's how to make up a simile. You start with an accurate statement such as: *Her eyes were blue.* Next, you name something that could be as blue as her eyes.**Ⓐ**

Here's a simile that tells what her eyes were like: *Her eyes were like a cloudless sky.***Ⓑ**

1. Make up a simile for this accurate statement: *The man ran fast.***Ⓒ**
   a. Name something that is fast.**Ⓒ**
   b. Make up a simile that tells how the man ran. Use the word **like** in your simile.**Ⓓ**
2. Make up a simile for this accurate statement: *The woman was very strong.*
   a. Name something that is strong.
   b. Make up a simile that tells how strong the woman was. Use the word **like** in your simile.

PART E   Story Items

1. **a.** Why did Sara write a note?
   b. Which animal did Sara find in her room a few nights later?
   c. What had that animal crawled through to get into Sara's room?
   d. Where did Sara take that animal?
2. **a.** The Indian Gentleman's face was
   _____.
   • pale   • red   • blue
   b. How did the Indian Gentleman seem to feel?
   • Content   • Ill   • Smug
3. The Indian Gentleman began to ask Sara some questions.
   a. Who had first taken her to the school?
   b. What had happened to her father's money?
   c. Then what happened to Sara's father?
   d. Who do you think the friend is who was responsible for her father's misfortune?
   e. What could the Indian Gentleman do for Sara?
4. At the end of the chapter the Indian Gentleman said, "Tell Carmichael that I have found the child."
   a. Which child was he referring to?
   b. What do you think the Indian Gentleman intends to do for that child?
5. Write which character each statement describes. Choose from the **Indian Gentleman, Captain Crewe, Sara,** or the **Lascar.**
   a. This character thought that all his money had been lost.
   b. This character had died in India.
   c. This character had hollow eyes.
   d. This character took care of a sick man.
   e. This character discovered who Sara really was.

PART F   Exaggeration

1. Here's an example of exaggeration: *The rain lasted forever.*
   a. How long does the statement say the rain lasted?
   b. Write an accurate statement that tells how long the rain lasted.
2. Here's another example: *Tatsu had a mountain of food on his plate.*
   a. How much food does the statement say that Tatsu had?
   b. Write an accurate statement that tells how much food Tatsu had.

PART G   Vocabulary Items

Use the words in the box to fill in the blanks or replace the underlined words.

rude and bold	rich and elegant
awed	smarted
delicious	vague
showed	obliged
subscribe to	deprived of
jostled	

1. Their hands <u>stung</u> from clapping so <u>hard.</u>
2. He was being punished, so he was _____ his bicycle for a week.
3. The cows <u>pushed and jolted</u> her as they <u>crowded</u> through the gate.
4. The little boy gave them <u>impudent</u> looks and then stuck out <u>his</u> tongue.
5. In the center of the room was a <u>luxurious</u> silk rug.
6. The cakes in the bakery looked <u>luscious.</u>
7. He <u>vented</u> his anger on the punching bag.
8. The teacher gave <u>unclear</u> answers to her questions.

PART H   Writing Assignment

Write a short story that explains why the Indian Gentleman hadn't found Sara before.

Make your story at least **five** sentences long.

Lesson 48

PART A   Word List

desert
dessert
dingy

PART B   Vocabulary Review

1	2
miscalculation	caress
incident	vague
devoted	scant
jostled	agitated

1. When you hug someone, you _____ that person.
2. An error or mistake is a _____.
3. Another word for **anxious** or **nervous** is _____.
4. Someone who is very loyal is _____.
5. If there is not enough of something, that thing is _____.

PART C   Similes

Here's how to make up a simile. You start with an accurate statement, such as: *His beard was rough*. Next, you name something that could be as rough as his beard.Ⓐ

Here's a simile that tells what his beard was like: *His beard was like sandpaper*.Ⓑ

1. Make up a simile for this accurate statement: *The city was crowded and busy*.
   a. Name something that is busy.Ⓒ
   b. Make up a simile that tells what the city was like. Use the word **like** in your simile.Ⓓ
2. Make up a simile for this accurate statement: *The monster's voice was very deep*.
   a. Name something that sounds deep.
   b. Make up a simile that tells how deep the monster's voice was. Use the word **like** in your simile.

PART D   Story Items

1. **a.** Who went to see Miss Minchin the next day?
   b. This character was the Indian Gentleman's _____.
   - doctor   - broker   - lawyer
   c. What was the Indian Gentleman's real name?
   d. Mr. Carmichael's _____ came over to explain everything to Sara.

2. Sara found out what had happened.
   a. Who had seemed to have lost her father's money?
   b. But after a while, the investment that he had made proved to be

   _____.
   - a disaster   - a success
   c. Who had Mr. Carrisford been wanting to find?
   d. Who had brought the gifts to Sara?
   e. How had that person entered Sara's room?
   f. Who else had entered Sara's room while she was gone?

3. **a.** Which family did Sara move in with?
   b. What name had Sara given that family before?
   c. When Sara was with that family, she felt as if she _____ somebody.
   - was punishing   - was hated by
   - belonged to
   d. Mrs. Carmichael thought that Sara had a _____ look in her eyes.
   - lonely   - bored   - arrogant

4. **a.** The one night at Miss Minchin's that Sara always remembered was the night that her _____ had changed.
   - doll   - room   - dress
   b. What good deed had Sara done on that same day?

PART E   Exaggeration

1. Here's an example of exaggeration: *Buckets of rain fell from the sky.*
   a. How much rain does the statement say fell?
   b. Write an accurate statement that tells how much rain fell.
2. Here's another example: *In the morning, the traveler had such an appetite that he ate about one hundred eggs for breakfast.*
   a. About how many eggs does the statement say the traveler ate?
   b. Write an accurate statement that tells how many eggs he ate.

PART F   Writing Assignment

If Sara had lived in another part of London, Mr. Carrisford might not have found her. Write a paragraph that describes at least five other things that might have kept Mr. Carrisford from finding Sara.

Make your paragraph at least **five** sentences long.

Lesson 49

Part A   Word Lists

1
desolate
quail
fiery
metaphor
grief

2
Vocabulary words
ex-
proposal
drab
suitable

Part B   New Vocabulary

1. **ex**—An **ex-** something is something that no longer exists. An **ex**-pupil is someone who is no longer a pupil. An **ex**-football player is someone who is no longer a football player.
   - What's an ex-musician?

2. **proposal**—A **proposal** is an offer or a plan to do something.
   a. What's another way of saying **She told her mother about her plan?***
   b. What's another way of saying **They did not like his plan for cutting down the trees?***

3. **drab**—Another word for **dreary** is **drab**.
   - What's another way of saying **She lived in a dreary room?***

4. **suitable**—Something that is appropriate is **suitable**.
   - What's another way of saying **His clothes were not appropriate?***

Part C   Metaphors

A **metaphor** is like a simile except that it doesn't contain the word *like*.Ⓐ

1. Here's an accurate statement: *The woman was very smart.* Here's a metaphor: *The woman was a walking encyclopedia.*
   a. What two things are the same in that metaphor?Ⓑ
   b. How could they be the same?Ⓒ
2. Here's another metaphor: *The man was a rattlesnake.*
   a. What two things are the same in that metaphor?Ⓓ
   b. How could they be the same?Ⓔ
3. Here's another metaphor: *Miss Minchin was a jailer.*
   a. What two things are the same in that metaphor?
   b. How could they be the same?

Part D   Story Items

1. a. Sara had nothing left to "suppose" because she had _____.
   b. Sara called Mr. Carrisford a

   _____.
   - magician • musician • mechanic

c. What was the family name of the children Sara played with?
   d. Name at least **two** things those children admired about Sara.
2. Miss Minchin tried to make up with Sara.
   a. What feelings did Miss Minchin pretend to have for Sara?
   b. Name at least **three** cruel things that Miss Minchin had done to Sara.
   c. Did Sara believe Miss Minchin when she said that she had always been fond of Sara?
3. Sara said, "You know why I would not stay with you."
   a. Who was Sara talking to?
   b. Did that person know why Sara wouldn't stay?
4. One night, Sara came up with a plan.
   a. Which child did she remember?
   b. What had she given to that child?
   c. Sara knew what it was like to be

   _____.
   - hungry • wicked • arrogant
   d. What did Sara want the baker woman to do?
   e. Who would pay for that?

5. a. Who was in the back room of the bakery?

b. Name **two** ways that person had changed.

c. What did Sara want that person to do?

PART E   Main Idea

Sara took off the damp clothes and put on the soft, warm robe before the glowing fire. She slipped her cold feet into the little wool-lined slippers she found near the chair. Then she made herself comfortable.

Write the main idea; then write three supporting details for the main idea. Use complete sentences to write the main idea and the supporting details. Write **1** in front of the main idea. Write **a, b, c** in front of the supporting details. Also, indent the supporting details.

PART F   Similes

Make up a simile for each accurate statement. Use the word *like* in your similes.

1. *Her dress was very light and airy.*
  a. Name something that is light.
  b. Make up a simile that tells what her dress was like.
2. *His heart had no feeling.*
  a. Name something that is unfeeling.
  b. Make up a simile that tells what his heart was like.

PART G   Review Items

Here are some things that people do. Write **yes** after each thing Sara might do. Write **no** after each thing that Sara would not do.

1. Give money to the poor.
2. Get bored with books.
3. Forget to thank somebody.
4. Speak to someone in a foreign language.
5. Like people just because they dress well.

PART H   Writing Assignment

What do you think Sara learned from her experiences? Write a paragraph that explains your answer.

Make your paragraph at least **five** sentences long.

PART I   Special Projects

1. (Individual Project) Memorize a poem or a part of a poem. Look in a book of poetry and find a poem that you like. Then memorize the poem and recite it to the class. The poem should be at least eight lines long.

2. (Group Project) The Greeks had dozens of gods and goddesses. Look in an encyclopedia and find out about at least ten new Greek gods and goddesses. Then draw a large chart that lists the gods and goddesses. Divide the chart into three parts. The top part should list the gods and goddesses who lived on Mount Olympus. The middle part should list the gods and goddesses who lived on the earth. The bottom part should list the gods and goddesses who lived in the underworld. If you like, draw pictures of each god or goddess on the chart.

3. (Group Project) Make up a play based on the last part of *Sara Crewe*. Start right after Sara's meeting with the beggar girl. Show Sara looking through the Indian Gentleman's window. Then show her discovering fairyland in her room. Finally, show how she finds out the truth about her father and his money. Figure out who will play each character; then figure out what each character will say. You can use words from the book or you can make up your own words.
Students who do not play characters can work on costumes or sets. When you are ready, perform the play for the class.

Lesson 50

PART A Word Lists

1
Guy de Maupassant
Matilda Loisel
humiliating
franc

2
Vocabulary words
pertains to
franc
humiliating
satin

PART B New Vocabulary

1. **pertains to**—Information that relates to something **pertains to** that thing.
   a. What's another way of saying **He discussed a plan that relates to the new school?***
   b. What's another way of saying **She gathered information that relates to her goals?***

2. **franc**—A **franc** is the basic unit of money in France.

3. **humiliating**—Something that is very disgraceful is **humiliating.**
   ● What's another way of saying **His proposal was disgraceful to her?***

4. **satin**—**Satin** is a fine fabric that is very shiny and smooth.

PART C Vocabulary Review

1	2
scant	suitable
agitated	ex-
devoted	drab
caress	proposal

1. Another word for **dreary** is _____.
2. Something that is appropriate is _____.
3. Something that no longer exists is an _____ something.
4. An offer or a plan to do something is a _____.
5. Someone who is very loyal is _____.

PART D Metaphors

A metaphor is like a simile except that it doesn't contain the word *like*.Ⓐ

1. Here's an accurate statement: *Gray clouds covered the sky.* Here's a metaphor: *The clouds were a gray ceiling.*
   a. What two things are the same in that metaphor?Ⓑ
   b. How could they be the same?Ⓒ
2. Here's another metaphor: *Sara's attic room was a nest in a tree.*
   a. What two things are the same in that metaphor?Ⓓ
   b. How could they be the same?Ⓔ
3. Here's another metaphor: *The boxer's arms were lightning bolts.*
   a. What two things are the same in that metaphor?
   b. How could they be the same?

PART E Story Items

1. **a.** What is the title of this story?
   b. Who is the author?
   c. What is the name of the main character in this story?
   d. What kind of job did her husband have?

2. **a.** Did the main character and her husband have the same tastes in things?
   b. Name **one** thing that he liked but that she didn't.
   c. Name **one** thing she liked but that he didn't.

3. One day Matilda's husband brought home an envelope.
   a. What was in that envelope?
   b. Why didn't Matilda want to go to the ball?
   c. How much did Matilda say a good dress would cost?
   d. Why did Matilda's husband grow a little pale when he heard about the amount?

4. **a.** After Matilda got a dress for the ball, what problem did she have?
   b. Her husband suggested that Matilda should go to a rich friend and do something. What?
   c. What did Mrs. Forester show Matilda?
   d. Describe what Matilda selected.

5. **a.** What time was it when the Loisels left the ball?
   b. What did they try to find on the street?
   c. What did Matilda discover at the end of part 1?

6. Matilda dreams about having certain things. Here are some items. Write **dream** for the items Matilda dreams about having. Write **reality** for the items Matilda actually has.
   a. Shining silverware
   b. Worn tablecloth
   c. Ugly curtains
   d. Eating trout for dinner
   e. Eating stew for dinner
   f. Golden plates

PART F Similes

Make up a simile for each accurate statement. Use the word **like** in your similes.

1. It was impossible to leave the palace.
   a. Name a place that is impossible to leave.
   b. Make up a simile that tells what the palace was like.

2. He had many exciting adventures in his life.
   a. Name something that is exciting.
   b. Make up a simile that tells what his life was like.

PART G Writing Assignment

Write a paragraph that compares Matilda with Sara Crewe. Tell what each character has. Tell what each character wants. Tell how the two characters are different, and how they are the same.

Make your paragraph at least **six** sentences long.

Lesson 51

PART A   Word Lists

1
anguish
unravel
rheumatism

2
route
headquarters
grocer
Ulysses

3
Vocabulary words
lobby
clasp
anguish
endure
rheumatism
unravel

PART B   New Vocabulary

1. **lobby**—The **lobby** of a hotel or apartment is an area just inside the door where people can sit and wait for others.

2. **clasp**—The **clasp** on a necklace or bracelet is the part that joins the two ends and holds them together.

3. **anguish**—Anguish is another word for **distress** or **torment**.
   - What's another way of saying **She felt great torment?***

4. **endure**—When you tolerate an experience that is painful, you **endure** that experience.
   - What's another way of saying **They could hardly tolerate the heat?***

5. **rheumatism**—Rheumatism is a disease of the bones and joints. People who have **rheumatism** have trouble walking or moving their joints.

6. **unravel**—When you pull on a single thread and take a garment apart, you **unravel** the material.

PART C   Vocabulary Review

1	2
franc	humiliating
pertains to	satin
parcels	drab

1. Information that relates to something _____ that thing.
2. Another word for **dreary** is _____.
3. Something that is very disgraceful is _____.

PART D   Metaphors

Some metaphors do not name the two things that are the same.

1. Here's an example: *The ship plowed the water*. That metaphor means that the ship was like something that plowed.
   a. What object could plow things?Ⓐ
   b. Use accurate language to tell what could be the same about the way a plow works and the way the ship moved through the water.Ⓑ

2. Here's another example: *Her voice twittered and chirped*.
   a. So, her voice was like something that _____.Ⓒ
   b. What could that something be?Ⓓ
   c. Use accurate language to tell how her voice and a _____'s voice could be the same.Ⓔ

PART E   Story Items

1. **a.** When was the last time that Matilda remembered feeling the necklace?
   b. Who went out and searched in different places for the necklace?
   c. Name at least **two** places that character went.
2. **a.** Matilda wrote a note to her friend and told her something about the necklace. What did she tell her friend?
   b. At the end of the week, Matilda and her husband decided to do something else. What was that?
3. The Loisels went to different jewelers.
   a. What did they finally find?
   b. How much did they pay for it?
   c. Mr. Loisel had some money. Where did they get the rest of it?
4. **a.** Why did the Loisels move?
   b. They moved into a _____.
      • palace   • shack   • garret
   c. What kind of job did Matilda get?
5. **a.** How long did it take for the Loisels to repay their loans?
   b. What did Matilda look like at the end of that time?
   c. What did Mrs. Forester look like?
   d. What did Mrs. Forester tell Matilda about the necklace?

PART F   Metaphors

1. *Her voice was silk.*
   a. What two things are the same in that metaphor?
   b. How could they be the same?
2. *Marlene was a wolf as she ate.*
   a. What two things are the same in that metaphor?
   b. How could they be the same?

PART G   Writing Assignment

The ending of *The Necklace* shows what the characters were really like. Write a paragraph that tells what the ending shows about Matilda and what she believed. Then tell what the ending shows about Mrs. Forester.

Make your paragraph at least **five** sentences long.

Lesson 52

PART A   Word Lists

1
busy
busied
Telemachus
lyre

2
Vocabulary words
appeal to
diversion
spurn
croon

PART B   New Vocabulary

1. **appeal to**—When you **appeal to** somebody's kindness, you make an earnest request for that person's kindness. If you **appeal to** somebody's sympathy, you make an earnest request for that person's sympathy.
   • What are you doing when you make an earnest request for somebody's sense of justice?

2. **diversion**—A **diversion** is something that pulls your attention away from something else. When you create a **diversion,** you pull people's attention from something they are interested in.
   • How could you create a diversion while your teacher is trying to teach the students about arithmetic?

3. **spurn**—When you **spurn** something, you vigorously reject it.
   a. What's another way of saying **Michael rejected their offer?***
   b. What's another way of saying **She rejected their sympathy?***

4. **croon**—When you **croon,** you sing or murmur.
   • What's another way of saying **She murmured the response?***

PART C   Vocabulary Review

1	2
endure	proposal
drab	humiliating
suitable	pertains to
anguish	

1. Something that is very disgraceful is _____.

2. Another word for **distress** or **torment** is _____.

3. When you tolerate an experience that is painful, you _____ that experience.

4. Information that relates to something _____ that thing.

PART D   Metaphors

Some metaphors do not name the two things that are the same.

1. Here's an example: *The images melted away.* That metaphor means that the images were like something that melts.
   a. What object could melt?Ⓐ
   b. Use accurate language to tell what could be the same about ice and the images.Ⓑ

2. Here's another example: *The river twisted and squirmed through the valley.*
   a. So, the river was like something that _____.Ⓒ
   b. What could that something be?Ⓓ
   c. Use accurate language to tell how the river and a _____ could be the same.Ⓔ

PART E Story Items

1. **a.** What was Homer doing when the sheriff drove up?
   b. Was the sheriff dressed in work clothes or in his Sunday clothes?
   c. What was the name of the character the sheriff was on his way to visit?
   d. Describe the well-known outfit that character wore.
   e. What does that character do to make her favorite outfit shorter?
   f. What does that character do with the material from that outfit?
2. Miss Terwilliger has two admirers.
   a. Who are they?
   b. Which character was called Telly?
   c. Which character was called Miss T?
3. **a.** What was Uncle Telly's hobby?
   b. About how far across was Uncle Telly's ball of string?
   c. Who had another ball of string that was about the same size?
4. Centerburg normally had an event at the fair, but there wasn't enough money for it this year.
   a. What event?
   b. What did the judge propose instead of that event?
5. **a.** If Uncle Telly wins, what will the sheriff have to do on Thursday afternoons?
   b. If the sheriff wins, what will Uncle Telly have to do on Sunday afternoons?
   c. After Telly and the sheriff agreed on the contest, they did something they hadn't done in years. What was that?

PART F Metaphors

1. *Geraldo's sorrow was a heavy weight.*
   a. What two things are the same in that metaphor?
   b. How could they be the same?
2. *Mrs. Forester's voice was ice.*
   a. What two things are the same in that metaphor?
   b. How could they be the same?

PART G Writing Assignment

Have you ever been to a county fair? If you have been to a county fair, write a paragraph that describes what it was like. If you haven't been to a county fair, write a paragraph that describes what it might be like.

Make your paragraph at least **five** sentences long.

Lesson 53

PART A   Word Lists

1
maneuver
plaid
diameter
unprecedented
mustache

2
edition
interruptions
frantically

3
Vocabulary words
maneuver
regard
diameter
contestant
unprecedented
plaid

PART B   New Vocabulary

1. **maneuver**—A skillful movement is a **maneuver.** Here's another way of saying **She skillfully moved her car through the traffic: She maneuvered her car through the traffic.**
   - What's another way of saying **They skillfully moved up the hill?***

2. **regard**—When you treat someone as an important person, you **regard** that person as an important person.
   a. What's another way of saying **They treat John as a winner?***
   b. What's another way of saying **Jane treated her mom as an important person?***

3. **diameter**—The **diameter** of a circle is the length of a line that goes through the widest part of the circle.
   - What do we call the length of a line that goes through the widest part of a circle?*

4. **contestant**—Somebody who is in a contest is called a **contestant.**

5. **unprecedented**—Something that is **unprecedented** is more exceptional than anything that occurred before. A meeting that is more exceptional than any other meeting is an **unprecedented** meeting.
   a. What's another way of saying **a meeting that is more exceptional than any other meeting?***
   b. What's another way of saying **a feat that is more exceptional than any other feat?***

6. **plaid**—**Plaid** is a design that is made up of rectangles of different sizes and colors.

PART C   Vocabulary Review

1	**2**
endure	spurn
devoted	appeal to
humiliating	proposal
diversion	

1. Something that is very disgraceful is _____ .

2. When you vigorously reject something, you _____ it.

3. Something that pulls your attention away from something else is a _____ .

4. When you make an earnest request for somebody's kindness, you _____ that person's kindness.

PART D   Story Items

1. **a.** Where would the contestants unroll their string?
   b. Who were the first two contestants?
   c. How many hours each day would the unwinding take place?
   d. The rules didn't mention a "gentleman's agreement." Which two characters had made that agreement?
   e. According to the "gentleman's agreement," what would the winner get to do?
2. **a.** The judge came to Uncle Telly's house and announced that there would be a new contestant. Who?
   b. Where did the new contestant get the pieces of yarn for her ball of string?
   c. How big was her ball of string?
   d. The movers had to use a _____ to transport her ball of string.
3. **a.** Uncle Telly admitted that her ball was the biggest, but he said, "It ain't _____ . You can poke your fist into it."
   b. Whose ball of string is the tightest?
   c. Whose ball of string is made of yarn?

PART E   Similes

1. *The party was like a dream.*
   a. What two things are the same in that simile?
   b. How could those things be the same?
   c. Name two ways those things are different.
2. *Her face was like a star.*
   a. What two things are the same in that simile?
   b. How could those things be the same?
   c. Name two ways those things are different.

PART F   Metaphors

1. *Felix was a real motor mouth.*
   a. What two things are the same in that metaphor?
   b. How could they be the same?
2. *In the pool, the athlete was a fish.*
   a. What two things are the same in that metaphor?
   b. How could they be the same?
3. *The express train flashed right through town.*
   a. So, the train was like something that _____ .
   b. What could that something be?
   c. Use accurate language to tell how the express train and that thing could be the same.

PART G   Writing Assignment

The judge uses a lot of big words when he talks. Pretend the judge is presenting an award to someone. Write a paragraph that tells what the judge might say.

Make your paragraph at least **five** sentences long.

Lesson 54

PART A Word Lists

1	2	3
reception	Iliad	**Vocabulary words**
parasol	Athena	best man
bough	Ithaca	parasol
deduction	Penelope	core
antelope		reception
egret		undisputed

PART B New Vocabulary

1. **best man**—The **best man** in a wedding is the man who is selected to accompany the man getting married during the marriage ceremony.

2. **parasol**—A **parasol** is an umbrella. Some **parasols** are used to protect people from hot sun, not from rain.

3. **core**—The **core** of thick objects is the part in the center. The **core** of an apple is the part in the center of an apple.

4. **reception**—A **reception** is a party that takes place after an important event. A party that takes place after a wedding is a wedding **reception.**
   - What do we call a party that takes place after a wedding?*

5. **undisputed**—If there is no doubt about something, that thing is **undisputed.** If there is no doubt that she won the race, she is the undisputed winner. If nobody doubts the fact that the world is round, that fact is undisputed.
   - What do we call a fact that we have no doubt about?

PART C Vocabulary Review

1	2
diversion	unprecedented
appeal to	anguish
regard	plaid
spurn	maneuver
endure	croon

1. When you treat a man as an important person, you _____ that man as an important person.

2. Something that is more exceptional than anything that occurred before is _____.

3. A skillful movement is a _____.

4. When you make an earnest request for somebody's kindness, you _____ that person's kindness.

5. When you vigorously reject something, you _____ it.

6. When you tolerate an experience that is painful, you _____ that experience.

7. Another word for **distress** or **torment** is _____.

PART D   Deductions

For each item, read the evidence and write the conclusion.
1. Here's the evidence:
   All living things need water.
   An antelope is a living thing.
   - What's the conclusion about an antelope? Ⓐ
2. Here's the evidence:
   Some birds cannot fly.
   An egret is a bird.
   - What's the conclusion about an egret? Ⓑ

PART E   Story Items

1. a. At the contest, the women were more interested in _____.
      - the clothes   • the string
      - the rules
   b. The men were more interested in
      _____.
      - the clothes   • the string
      - the rules
   c. After the first two times around the track, what problem did the sheriff and Uncle Telly have?
   d. So, what did some regular employees of the fair do?
   e. What did the contestants do?
2. Whose ball of string was the smallest at the beginning of the last day of the contest?
3. a. What color was Miss Terwilliger's outfit the first two days of the contest?
   b. What color was Miss Terwilliger's outfit on the last day?
   c. What did Miss Terwilliger hold her string in?
4. a. Name the object that was on the inside of the sheriff's ball of string.
   b. So, which contestant thought that he had won?
   c. Who really won the contest?
   d. Which contestant had started the last day with the smallest ball of string?
   e. What did Miss Terwilliger do with her blue dress as she walked around the track?
      - Patched it   • Ironed it
      - Unravelled it
5. a. Who did Miss Terwilliger marry?
   b. What did they invite the other suitor to do every Thursday evening?
   c. At the end of the story, what did the sheriff decide to start collecting?

PART F   Metaphors

Here's a metaphor: *The detective scratched and dug for clues.*
1. So, the detective was like something that _____.
2. What could that something be?
3. Use accurate language to tell how the detective and _____ could be the same.

PART G   Writing Assignment

In *Mystery Yarn,* the writer used the expression, "all's fair in love." What do you think that expression means? Write a paragraph that explains your answer. Use examples from the story to support your explanation.

Make your paragraph at least **five** sentences long.

Lesson 55

PART A Word Lists

1	2	3
heron	Circe	**Vocabulary words**
trio	Calypso	foster parent
Sylvia	Scylla	heron
wilderness		huckleberry
gallant		bough
pigeon		gallant
		trio
		game

PART B New Vocabulary

1. **foster parent**—A **foster parent** is somebody who brings up a child, but who is not the child's real parent.
   - What do we call somebody who brings up a child, but who is not the child's real parent?*

2. **A heron** is a large white bird. The picture shows a **heron.**

3. **huckleberry**—A **huckleberry** is a small purple berry that is very tasty.

4. **bough**—A **bough** of a tree is a branch of the tree.
   - What do we call a branch of a tree?*

5. **gallant**—Somebody who is very brave and noble is **gallant.**
   a. What's another way of saying **He was a noble warrior?***
   b. What's another way of saying **He was a noble prince?***

6. **trio**—A group of three is called a **trio.**
   - What's another way of saying **A group of three went to the river?***

7. **game**—Wild animals that are hunted are called wild **game.**
   - What do we call wild animals that are hunted?*

PART C Vocabulary Review

1	2
unprecedented	spurn
maneuver	endured
devoted	regard

1. A skillful movement is a _maneuver_.
2. When you treat a woman as an important person, you _regard_ that woman as an important person.
3. Something that is more exceptional than anything that occurred before is _unprecedented_.

PART D Deductions

For each item, read the evidence and write the conclusion.
1. Here's the evidence:
   No person can live forever.
   Lamar is a person.
   - What's the conclusion about Lamar?Ⓐ
2. Here's the evidence:
   Some Greek gods lived on Mount Olympus.
   Bacchus was a Greek god.
   - What's the conclusion about Bacchus?Ⓑ

PART E Story Items

1. **a.** At the beginning of *A White Heron,*
   Sylvia is driving a _____
   from the pasture, back to the
   house.
   b. What sound did Sylvia hear as she
   walked in the woods?
   c. What was the young man doing in
   the woods?
   d. What did the young man ask
   Sylvia?
   e. Was Sylvia quiet or loud?
   f. The town children had treated
   Sylvia _____ .
   - badly   - well
2. **a.** What was the name of Sylvia's
   foster mother?
   b. The stranger asked if he could
   have a night's _____ at
   Sylvia's house.
   c. Was the stranger's request
   granted?

PART F Metaphors

Here's a metaphor: *Odysseus swooped
down on the lazy suitors.*
1. So, Odysseus was like something that
   _____ .
2. What could that something be?
3. Use accurate language to tell how
   Odysseus and _____ could be
   the same.

PART G Exaggeration

The steak was tougher than a rubber tire.
1. How tough does the statement say the
   steak was?
2. Write an accurate statement that tells
   how tough the steak was.

PART H Writing Assignment

Sylvia lives on a farm that is far away
from other people. Would you like to live
in a place like that? Write a paragraph
that explains your answer.

Make your paragraph at least **five**
sentences long.

Lesson 56

PART A   Word Lists

1
endangered species
extinct
ecology

2
sympathetic
unsuspecting
Phacia
Demeter
pigeon
Bastille

3
Vocabulary words
New England
landmark
wilderness
crow
rare

PART B   New Vocabulary

1. **New England**—The **New England** area is the northeastern part of the United States. There are six New England states.

2. **landmark**—A **landmark** is an easily recognized feature of a landscape. A large hotel may be a **landmark** in a particular city. A cliff may be a landmark along a river.
   - What are some other **landmarks?**

3. **wilderness**—A wild place with no signs of people is a **wilderness.**
   - What do we call a wild place with no signs of people?*

4. **crow**
   - What is a **crow?**

5. **rare**—Something that is not common is **rare.** A book that is not common is a **rare** book.
   - What would we call a coin that is not common?*

PART C   Vocabulary Review

1	2
appeal to	gallant
diversion	undisputed
game	bough
heron	core
reception	pertains to
trio	

1. A party that takes place after an important event is a _____ .
2. Somebody who is very brave and noble is _____ .
3. A group of three is called a _____ .
4. If there is no doubt about something, that thing is _____ .
5. A branch of a tree is a _____ of the tree.

6. Something that pulls your attention away from something else is called a _____ .
7. When you make an earnest request for somebody's sympathy, you _____ that person's sympathy.
8. Information that relates to something _____ that thing.

PART D   Deductions

Complete each deduction.
1. Here's the evidence:
   Every bird has feathers.
   A heron is a bird.
   - What's the conclusion about a heron?Ⓐ
2. Here's the evidence:
   Some poems rhyme.
   Paradise Lost is a poem.
   - What's the conclusion about *Paradise Lost?*Ⓑ

PART E Inference

There are different types of questions about the passages you read. Some questions are answered by words in the passage. Some questions are not answered by words in the passage. You have to figure out the answer by making a **deduction.**Ⓐ

Read the passage below and answer each question.

Ecology

Over the past forty years, people have become increasingly interested in a subject called ecology. The study of ecology is the study of how the life of one living thing affects the lives of other living things. The more we study ecology, the more we discover that the life of a beetle in a faraway place may affect the lives of birds near us. And the lives of these birds may affect the lives of trees, or even the lives of people. We are finding that a change in any living thing affects many other living things.

1. **a.** What does a change in any living thing affect?Ⓑ
   b. Is that question answered by **Words** or by a **Deduction?**Ⓒ
2. **a.** If mice change, what might happen to cats?Ⓓ
   b. **Words** or **Deduction?**Ⓔ
3. **a.** Could a change in a cow's life affect the life of a rose?Ⓕ
   b. **Words** or **Deduction?**Ⓖ
4. **a.** What subject have people become interested in?Ⓗ
   b. **Words** or **Deduction?**Ⓘ

PART F Story items

1. Mrs. Tilley told the stranger about her life.
   a. What was the name of Mrs. Tilley's only real relative?
   b. Where was that relative?
   c. Who had Mrs. Tilley found in the town?

   d. Mrs. Tilley said that Sylvia was like Dan in some ways. Name **one** way.
   e. Name some creatures that Sylvia had tamed.
   f. Which creatures did Mrs. Tilley forbid Sylvia from bringing around the house?
2. **a.** What did the stranger collect?
   b. Does the stranger keep them penned up?
   c. Describe the condition of the things in the stranger's collection.
3. **a.** Name the kind of bird the stranger was following.
   b. Where had Sylvia seen that bird?
   c. How much did the stranger offer for information about the bird?
   d. Sylvia couldn't understand why the stranger _____ the birds he liked so much.
4. **a.** Half a mile from Sylvia's house was a landmark that could be seen from miles away. What was that landmark?
   b. What did Sylvia always dream of doing there?
   c. That landmark gave Sylvia an idea about how to locate the white heron. What did she plan to do?

PART G Writing Assignment

What would you rather look at, a stuffed bird or a live bird in the woods? Write a paragraph that explains your answer.

Make your paragraph at least **five** sentences long.

Lesson 57

PART A   Word Lists

1
Greenwich Village
Persephone
pigeon
extinct
Hades
Cerberus

2
Vocabulary words
pine pitch
birches and hemlocks
crest
slender
reveal

PART B   New Vocabulary

1. **pine pitch**—**Pine pitch** is a sticky material that comes from under the bark of pine trees.

2. **birches** and **hemlocks**—**Birches** and **hemlocks** are trees. **Birches** lose their leaves in the fall. **Hemlocks** are evergreens.

3. **crest**—A **crest** on a bird's head is a tuft of feathers on top of the bird's head.

4. **slender**—**Slender** is another word for **slim.**

5. **reveal**—When you **reveal** something, you take it out of hiding and show it or tell about it.
   • What's another way of saying **She told about her secret?***

PART C   Dialect

You will be reading a novel about a man named Pete. Pete is a pirate and the captain of a ship. He has trouble saying words like "wish." He says that word like this: weesh.

Frisco Kid is an orphan who has worked on ships for many years. He knows a great deal about sailing and the ocean.

The following scene takes place on Pete's ship, which is in the middle of a bay. When the scene begins, Pete has just discovered a dog on the ship, and he is very angry.Ⓐ

PETE: What eez thees? A dog? What eez a dog doing on thees sheep?

FRISCO KID: I bought him. I thought he'd keep me company at night.

PETE: Bought heem? Where deed you buy zees dog? Deed anyone see you?

FRISCO KID: A woman near the dock sold him to me. She doesn't know about what we do.

PETE: Let's hope not. Or else I weel be very angry. Tomorrow we are going to steal ze diamonds, and I don't want ze police after us. And as for ze dog, get reed of heem.

FRISCO KID: No, I won't. I want to keep him.

PART D   Inference

There are different types of questions about the passages you read. Some questions are answered by words in the passage. Some questions are not answered by words in the passage. You have to figure out the answer by making a **deduction.**Ⓐ

Read the passage on the next page and answer each question.

More about Ecology

A hundred years ago, people were not concerned with ecology. They believed that there was no end to the different types of wildlife. So, they killed wild animals by the hundreds of thousands. When we look back on those killings, we may feel shocked. But for the people who lived a hundred years ago, wild animals seemed to be as plentiful as weeds.

Those killings have caused more than a hundred types of animals to become extinct since the year 1800. A type of animal becomes extinct when there are no more animals of that type. One animal that has become extinct is the passenger pigeon. At one time, this bird was so plentiful that flocks of them used to blacken the sky. Now the passenger pigeon is gone forever. Think of that. Although the passenger pigeon lived for hundreds of thousands of years, you will never get to see it or any of the other animals that have become extinct. The only place you can see those animals is in a museum, where they are stuffed and mounted.

1. **a.** Are house cats extinct?**Ⓑ**
   b. Is that question answered by **Words** or by a **Deduction?Ⓒ**
2. **a.** Name one animal that has become extinct.**Ⓓ**
   b. **Words** or **Deduction?Ⓔ**
3. **a.** How many types of animals have become extinct since 1800?**Ⓕ**
   b. **Words** or **Deduction?Ⓖ**
4. **a.** The dodo bird is extinct. How many animals of that type are alive today?**Ⓗ**
   b. **Words** or **Deduction?Ⓘ**

PART E   Story Items

1. **a.** Sylvia went to the large tree _____ in the morning.
   • early   • late
   b. To climb the pine tree, Sylvia first climbed an _____ tree.

   c. Why did Sylvia climb the pine tree?
   d. What would be Sylvia's reward if she gave information to the stranger?
2. **a.** What time of day was it when Sylvia reached the top of the pine tree?
   • Sunset   • Sunrise   • Noon
   b. For the first time, Sylvia saw a body of water. What was that?
   c. What bird did Sylvia see in the hemlock tree?
   d. Where did the heron perch?
   e. Who did the heron call to?
   f. When the heron left, where did he go?
3. **a.** Who discovered that Sylvia was not in her room?
   b. The stranger suspected that Sylvia knew something. What was that?
   c. What condition were Sylvia's clothes in when she returned?
4. **a.** When Sylvia was questioned, what information did she give Mrs. Tilley and the stranger?
   b. Sylvia and the great bird had shared an experience. What had they watched together?
   c. So, which did Sylvia choose, the life of the heron or the hundred dollars and the friendship of the hunter?

PART F   Deductions

Complete each deduction.
1. Here's the evidence:
   Every element has an atomic weight.
   Argon is an element.
   • What's the conclusion about argon?
2. Here's the evidence:
   Horses eat grass.
   A palomino is a horse.
   • What's the conclusion about a palomino?

PART G Drawing Conclusions

Write a conclusion that tells what each person believed.

1. *Oliver believed that if he studied, he would pass the test. Oliver studied for the test.*
   - So, what did Oliver believe would happen?
2. *Nadia believed that if you ate an apple a day you would not get sick. Nadia ate an apple every day.*
   - So, what did Nadia believe would happen?

PART H Figurative Language

Write whether each statement is a **simile,** a **metaphor,** or an **exaggeration.**

1. Her face was like a pale star.
2. The apartment was a prison.
3. The day was like a dream.

PART I Writing Assignment

Sylvia wondered if the heron was a better friend than the hunter might have been. What do you think? Write a paragraph that explains your answer.

Make your paragraph at least **five** sentences long.

Lesson 58

PART A   Word Lists

1
endangered species
anon
Hermes
Odysseus
awesome
plough
ploughboy

2
Vocabulary words
rebel
smirk
suppress

PART B   New Vocabulary

1. **rebel**—When you **rebel**, you resist doing something you're expected to do. When you refuse to do the dishes, you **rebel** over doing the dishes.

2. **smirk**—A **smirk** is a sneer.

3. **suppress**—When you try to hold back an impulse, you **suppress** that impulse.
   a. What are you doing when you try to hold back laughter?*
   b. What are you doing when you try to hold back tears?*

PART C   Dialect

Pete and Frisco Kid are still discussing the dog. Pete wants the Kid to get rid of the dog, and Frisco Kid wants the dog to stay.Ⓐ

FRISCO KID: I bought the dog, so I'm the one who has the say about him.

PETE: Thees eez my sheep, and what I say goes! And I say ze dog has to go! A dog cannot pull heez own weight.

FRISCO KID: Look, I'll feed him and everything.

PETE: Oh, zat is good. And what about at night? I don't want ze dog to start barking when we sneak into shore. We would all get keeled. But maybe you can show heem how to steer ze sheep, no? I tell you, ze dog has to go.

FRISCO KID: If he goes, I go. And I mean it, Pete.

PETE: All right. You ween. You know zat I need your help. Just take good care of zees dog, and we weel see what happens.

PART D   Vocabulary Review

1	2
slender	landmark
rare	crest
crow	reveal

1. A tuft of feathers on top of a bird's head is the _____ of the bird's head.
2. Another word for **slim** is _____.
3. When you take something out of hiding and show it or tell about it, you _____ that thing.

PART E   Deductions

Complete each deduction.
1. Here's the evidence:
   All planets orbit around a sun.
   Pluto is a planet.
● What's the conclusion about Pluto?Ⓐ
2. Here's the evidence:
   Some plants bloom at night.
   A crocus is a plant.
● What's the conclusion about a crocus?Ⓑ

PART F   Inference

Read the passage below and answer each question.

Endangered Species

Once a type of animal becomes extinct, it is gone forever. Another word for **type** *is* **species.** *Over one hundred species of animals have become extinct since the year 1800. In addition to these animals, there are about four hundred species that are called endangered. An endangered species is one that is nearly extinct.*

The grizzly bear has become an endangered species. Once, its range used to extend through most of the western United States. Now it survives in only a few mountain ranges. The Alaskan brown bear, the African elephant, the bald eagle, and the sea turtle are just a few other endangered species.

The list of endangered and extinct species will continue to grow until people decide that the world should be a place for all living things. Grizzly bears may not get along well with people, but if we kill them all off, we won't be able to get them back if we should change our minds. Once an animal is extinct, it is extinct forever.

1. **a.** What is another word for **type?**
   b. Is that question answered by **Words** or by a **Deduction?**
2. **a.** The grizzly bear is an endangered species. Could it become extinct?
   b. **Words** or **Deduction?**
3. **a.** Name **four** endangered species.
   b. **Words** or **Deduction?**
4. **a.** The dodo bird is extinct. Can you have a dodo bird for a pet?
   b. **Words** or **Deduction?**

PART G   Drawing Conclusions

Write a conclusion that tells what each person believed.
1. *Isabel believed that if she used peach shampoo, she would make new friends. Isabel used peach shampoo.*
   ● So, what did Isabel believe would happen?
2. *Vernon believed that people who shined their shoes would get a good job. Vernon always shined his shoes.*
   ● So, what did Vernon believe would happen?

PART H   Outlining

Complete the following outline for *The Necklace.* Copy each main idea; then write three supporting details for each main idea. Use complete sentences to write the supporting details.

1. Matilda was a big success at the ball.
2. The Loisels had a hard life for ten years.
3. Ten years later, Matilda talked with Mrs. Forester.

PART I   Figurative Language

Write whether each statement is a **simile,** a **metaphor,** or an **exaggeration.**
1. He was so thirsty that he drank twenty gallons of water.
2. The waves were like mountains.
3. Her stomach growled.

PART J   Writing Assignment

Write a poem that describes what spring looks like in your neighborhood.

Make your poem at least **six** lines long. Your lines do not have to rhyme.

Lesson 59

PART A   Word Lists

1	2	3
Le Maire	vessel	**Vocabulary words**
forecastle	cyclops	forecastle
hoist	Odyssey	skiff
Farallons	Dazzler	loot
photosynthesis		
sarcasm		
carnivores		
herbivores		

PART B   New Vocabulary

1. **forecastle**—The **forecastle** is the part of the ship in which sailors sleep.

2. **skiff**—A **skiff** is a small rowboat.

3. **loot**—**Loot** is material that is stolen.
   ● What do we call material that is stolen?*

PART C   Vocabulary Review

1	2
smirk	slender
crest	suppress
reveal	rebel

1. When you try to hold back an impulse, you _____ that impulse.
2. A sneer is a _____.
3. When you resist doing something you're expected to do, you _____.

PART D   Sarcasm

Sometimes people say the opposite of what they really mean. But they give evidence that they don't mean what they say. When people speak in that way, they are using **sarcasm.**

1. Here's an example of sarcasm:
   A boy says, "I just love going to school. I love to sit there all day long and do boring things. I love to work and study when I could be outside playing and swimming with nobody to tell me what to do."
   a. How does the boy *say* he feels about school? Ⓐ
   b. The boy gives evidence that contradicts what he says. Name something he says about school that contradicts the idea that he loves it. Ⓑ

2. Here's another example of sarcasm:
   A woman says, "My, wasn't that a good television show. There's nothing I like more than watching two people argue about unimportant things, like cleaning the house. The show was almost as exciting as waiting for a bus in the rain."
   a. The woman says something that she later contradicts. What is that? Ⓒ
   b. Name one piece of evidence that contradicts her statement. Ⓓ

PART E   Story Items

1. a. What did the crew of the *Dazzler* sit on as they ate?
   b. The table in the cabin swung up on _____.
   c. Why was Joe impressed with Frisco Kid?

2. a. Twelve hours earlier, Joe Diaz had been a _____.
   b. When Joe thought of his mother, his feelings _____.
      ● softened   ● hardened
   c. When Joe thought of his father, his feelings _____.
      ● softened   ● hardened
   d. Which relative did Joe feel did not understand him?

3. **a.** Which two characters came on board the *Dazzler* after the others were in their bunks?
   b. Bill said that Joe had to keep his tongue between his teeth. What did he mean by that?
4. Nick argued with the captain.
   a. How many shares did Nick say that there should be?
   b. Pete said that there were now _____ shares for _____ men.
   c. Who won out in the end?
   d. Frisco Kid told Joe to keep away from _____.
   e. The only person that Joe felt he could trust was _____.

PART F Drawing Conclusions

Write a conclusion that tells what the person believed.
1. *Neil believed that if you could speak French, you would gain power. Neil learned to speak French.*
- So, what did Neil believe would happen?

PART G   Inference

Read the passage below and answer each question.

Photosynthesis

Plants and animals need food to survive, but they get their food in different ways. Animals must hunt for their food. Animals that eat plants must hunt for those plants. Animals that eat meat must hunt for other animals. They kill the animals and eat their meat.

*Green plants are different. Green plants actually manufacture their own food. The leaves of the plant need three ingredients—sunlight, water, and carbon dioxide. Leaves convert these ingredients into food for the entire plant. Plants don't have to hunt for food. So long as a plant has sunshine, water, and carbon dioxide, the plant will manufacture its own food. This process is called **photosynthesis.***

1. **a.** Name the three ingredients used by leaves to manufacture food for the entire plant.
   b. Is that question answered by **Words** or by a **Deduction?**
2. **a.** The process by which a plant manufactures its own food is called _____.
   b. **Words** or **Deduction?**
3. Write whether each living thing **hunts** for its food or **manufactures** its food:
   a. A giraffe
   b. An elm tree
   c. A snake

PART H   Figurative Language

Write whether each statement is a **simile,** a **metaphor** or an **exaggeration.**
1. The day lasted forever.
2. The sound floated across the water.
3. Her cheeks were roses.

PART I   Writing Assignment

Joe had many reasons for running away. Write a paragraph that explains his reasons. Tell what problems he had. Tell what he hoped would happen. Tell what might happen instead.

Make your paragraph at least **five** sentences long.

Lesson 60

PART A   Word Lists

1
Frisco Kid
private
herbivores
Farallons
mainsail
carnivores
jutted

2
Vocabulary words
hoist
collide
churn

PART B   New Vocabulary

1. **hoist**—When you **hoist** something, you raise it high.
   - What's another way of saying **They raised the mainsail high?***

2. **collide**—When two things run into each other, they **collide.**

3. **churn**—When liquid **churns,** it swirls and foams.

PART C   Sarcasm

Sometimes people say the opposite of what they really mean. But they give evidence that they don't mean what they say. When people speak in that way, they are using **sarcasm.**

1. Here's an example of sarcasm:
   A father told his son, "Thanks for all your help, Cleon. I really appreciated the way you looked on as I made your bed and picked up all your dirty clothes. I hope you're not all tired out."
   a. How does the father *say* he feels about Cleon's help?Ⓐ
   b. The father gives evidence that contradicts what he says. Name something he says about Cleon's help that contradicts the idea that he appreciates it.Ⓑ

2. Here's another example of sarcasm:
   Odelia says, "Oh, I feel just great. My right leg is broken in two places and I have a burn on my left hand. I'd like to have another accident as soon as possible."
   a. Odelia says something that she later contradicts. What is that?Ⓒ
   b. Name one piece of evidence that contradicts her statement.Ⓓ

PART D   Story Items

1. a. What time was it when the sloop began to sail?
   b. Did the men on board speak loudly or in quiet tones?
   c. What two boats was the *Dazzler* pulling?
   d. Who rowed the lifeboat to shore?
2. The men went to a place near a factory. What did they take from that place?
3. When Joe was on land, somebody appeared.
   a. What did that person flash at Joe?
   b. What noise did that person make?
   c. What did Joe do when that person appeared?
4. a. Which person got into the wrong boat?
   b. What almost happened to that boat?
   c. What did Joe do as the other two rowed toward the *Dazzler*?
   d. What happened to the lifeboat just as it approached the *Dazzler*?
5. a. At last, Joe realized that Pete and the others were _____.
   b. Joe had enough information about these men to send them to

   _____.

   c. At the end of the chapter, Joe decided that he would try to _____ at the first chance he had.

PART E   Inference

Read the passage below and answer each question.

Herbivores and Carnivores

Different kinds of animals eat different things. Animals that eat other animals are called **carnivores.** *Animals that eat plants are called* **herbivores.** *We can see that herbivores could not survive without plants. If there were no plants, herbivores would have nothing to eat and they would soon become extinct.*

But carnivores need plants as much as herbivores do. If there were no plants, herbivores would soon be extinct. Carnivores would then have to eat other carnivores. Before long there would be no more animals for carnivores to eat, and they would become extinct.

Herbivores feed **directly** *on green plants. Carnivores feed* **indirectly** *on green plants because they feed on animals that feed on plants.*

1. **a.** What are carnivores?
    b. Is that question answered by **Words** or by a **Deduction?**
2. **a.** What are herbivores?
    b. **Words** or **Deduction?**
3. Write whether each animal is a **carnivore** or a **herbivore:**
    a. A jackal eats other animals.
    b. An ape eats only fruit.
    c. Eagles eat living things that hunt.
4. **a.** Does a jackal feed directly on green plants?
    b. **Words** or **Deduction?**

PART F   Review Items

You have read two poems. Write whether each line is from *The Tide Rises, the Tide Falls,* or *Written in March.*
1. "The green field sleeps in the sun."
2. "The little waves, with their soft white hands."
3. "The twilight darkens, the curlew calls."
4. "The rain is over and gone."

PART G   Figurative Language

Write whether each statment is a **simile,** a **metaphor** or an **exaggeration.**
1. She jumped like a cat.
2. The dog's barking shattered my eardrums.
3. The sunshine danced on the water.

PART H   Writing Assignment

Joe has a serious problem. If he tries to escape, some bad things might happen. If he doesn't try to escape, some other bad things might happen. What do you think he should do? Write a paragraph that explains your answer.

Make your paragraph at least **five** sentences long.

Lesson 61

PART A   Word Lists

1
naval
puny
quarantine
Alcatraz
sardines
defy
bungle
marred
Felicia

2
Vocabulary words
bungle
puny
outwit
harsh
tow
naval
surge
principal

PART B   New Vocabulary

1. **bungle**—When a person **bungles**, that person makes stupid mistakes.
   - What's another way of saying **They did not make stupid mistakes when they fixed up the house?***

2. **puny**—Something that is small and weak is **puny**.
   - What's another way of saying **She had a small and weak voice?***

3. **outwit**—Another word for **outsmart** is **outwit**.
   - What's another way of saying **The duke outsmarted the knight?***

4. **harsh**—Something that is very cruel or bitter is **harsh**.
   - What's another way of saying **He tried to get out of the bitter wind?***

5. **tow**—When you **tow** something, you pull it by a chain or a rope.

6. **naval**—**Naval** refers to the navy. A plane that belongs to the navy is a **naval** plane.
   - What's a training station that belongs to the navy?*

7. **surge**—When something rolls or rises like waves, that thing **surges**.
   - What's another way of saying **The boat rolled like a wave?***

8. **principal**—The most important things are the **principal** things.
   a. What would you call the most important places in a city?*
   b. What would you call the most important mountains in a range?*

PART C   Vocabulary Review

1	2	3
bough	collide	suppress
loot	gallant	landmark
hoist		

1. When you raise something high, you _____ that thing.
2. When two things run into each other, they _____.
3. Material that is stolen is _____.
4. When you try to hold back an impulse, you _____ that impulse.

PART D   Conversations

Here are some characters you have read about:

- JOE is a sailor who is new on board ship. He must do all the hard jobs.

- FRISCO KID is an experienced sailor. He has been working on ships for ten years and has a good understanding of the sea.

- PETE is the captain. He is a rude man who gives orders and seldom speaks in a kindly way.

Write which character could have made each statement.
1. "Raise the sail, you landlubbers and loafers!" Ⓐ
2. "When the captain comes around, don't say anything or he'll get mad at you." Ⓑ
3. "Where is the main cabin?" Ⓒ
4. "Raise that mainsail or I'll throw you overboard!"
5. "What's the difference between a mainsail and a jibsail?"

PART E   Story Items

1. Joe sensed that there was an orderly confusion on the *Dazzler*.
   a. What event created the confusion?
   b. Give at least **one** reason that Joe thought the confusion was orderly.
   c. Why did the boys lower the mainsail halfway?
2. a. Joe realized that Frisco Kid was a

   _____.
   b. But how did Joe feel about him?
3. Joe tried to do something that was very dangerous.
   a. What was that?
   b. What happened to the towrope?
   c. Was Frisco Kid angry over that mishap?
   d. Had Frisco Kid ever made mistakes like the one that Joe made?
   e. Did the boys find the lifeboat?
   f. Who operated the tiller?

4. a. As dawn approached, Frisco Kid said that Joe should get some

   _____.
   b. Where did Joe remain?
   c. Name the city whose lights stretched for miles.
   d. In which city did Joe live?
   e. What people did he think about when he looked at that city?

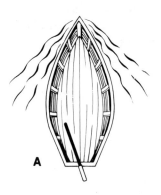

A

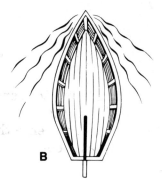

B

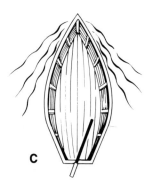

C

5. Look at the pictures. For each picture, write the direction the boat will turn. Write **left, right** or **straight ahead.**

PART F Relevant Information

Read the facts and the items. If an item is relevant to fact A, write **relevant to fact A.** If an item is relevant to fact B, write **relevant to fact B.** If an item is irrelevant to both facts, write **irrelevant.**

- Fact A: *Sylvia was an orphan.*
- Fact B: *Sylvia wanted to save the heron's life.*

1. She made friends with the heron.
2. She brought the cow home.
3. She did not tell anybody what she had discovered.
4. She lived with her foster mother.

PART G Sarcasm

Felicia was at a fast-food restaurant. She said, "The food in this place is simply marvelous. The hamburger buns taste like cardboard and the patties are as big as postage stamps. This place really goes all out to please its customers."

1. Felicia says something that she later contradicts. What is that?
2. Name two pieces of evidence that contradict her statement.

PART H Review Items

Write the title of the story in which each event occurred. Choose from *Mrs. Dunn's Lovely, Lovely Farm; The Last Leaf; Sara Crewe; The Voyage of the Northern Light;* or *The Spider, the Cave, and the Pottery Bowl.*

1. An old man saved a young woman's life by painting something.
2. An Indian girl found a bag of clay.
3. A woman from Ireland outwitted her landlord.
4. A nurse from Boston almost drowned.

PART I Writing Assignment

Joe has contradictory feelings about Frisco Kid. Write a paragraph about Joe's feelings. Tell what Joe likes about Frisco Kid, then tell what Joe dislikes about him. Tell which feelings are more powerful, and why.

Make your paragraph at least **five** sentences long.

Lesson 62

PART A   Word Lists

1
condensed
bicycle
bicyclists
Alcatraz
bungle
bugle

2
Vocabulary words
quarantine station
stirred
marred
keg
bait

PART B   New Vocabulary

1. **quarantine station**—A **quarantine station** is a place that is isolated because there may be sick people in that place. To prevent the disease from spreading, nobody can leave the **quarantine station** and nobody can enter.

2. **stirred**—When you are moved by the sight of something, you are **stirred** by the sight of that thing.
   - What's another way of saying **She was moved by his speech?***

3. **marred**—Things that are **marred** are spoiled or ruined in some way. Here's another way of saying **His pleasure was spoiled by hunger: His pleasure was marred by hunger.**
   - What's another way of saying **The evening was spoiled by Maria's accident?***

4. **keg**—A **keg** is a small barrel.
   - What do we call a small barrel?*

5. **bait**
   - What is **bait?**

PART C   Vocabulary Review

1	2
surges	outwit
loot	harsh
principal	rebel
hoist	bungles

1. The most important things are the _____ things.
2. When something rolls or rises like waves, that thing _____.
3. When a person makes stupid mistakes, that person _____.
4. Another word for **outsmart** is _____.
5. When you resist doing something you're expected to do, you _____.

PART D   Story Items

1. **a.** Frisco Kid gave Joe some chores when he woke up. Name **two** of them.
   b. Who cooked breakfast?

2. Joe had mixed feelings.
   a. The scene that he saw that morning made him feel
   _____.
   - happy   - shocked   - greedy
   b. His companions made him feel
   _____.
   - happy   - shocked   - greedy
   c. He resolved to be
   - clean and cunning.
   - strong and cunning.
   - clean and strong.

3. **a.** What was Pete doing as the boys ate breakfast?
   b. After breakfast, the boys went
   _____.
   - to sleep - swimming - home

4. Frisco Kid pointed out a quarantine station to Joe. People had to stay there because they had _____.

5. **a.** What did the boys decide to have for lunch?
   b. What did they use for bait?
   c. Whose fish tumbled on deck first?
   d. What did the boy who caught a fish last have to do?
   e. Who caught a fish last?
   f. What did the other boy do as the fish were cleaned?

6. After Joe had finished his chore, he carried out a plan.
   a. He planned to go to _____.
      - Oakland
      - Santa Cruz
      - the quarantine station
   b. How did he plan to get there?
   c. Why didn't he take his bundle of clothes with him?
7. As Joe approached the shore, somebody shouted at him.
   a. Who was that?
   b. What was that person pointing at Joe?

PART E   Conversations

Here are some characters you have read about:
- MISS MINCHIN runs a boarding school. She is very mean and has a cold heart.
- SARA used to be one of Miss Minchin's students. When Sara lost her money, Miss Minchin made Sara a servant.
- ANNE is a beggar girl. She has had nothing to eat for three days.

Write which character could have made each statement:
1. "Sweep the floors this instant, you miserable girl!"
2. "Please, sir, could you spare me a crust of bread?"
3. "You didn't treat me like this when I was rich."
4. "I hate it when she keeps ordering me around."
5. "Do what I tell you, or you'll regret it."

PART F   Sarcasm

Niko went to a baseball game with a friend. He said, "That Kirk McDermott is probably the finest player on the team. He has the speed of a snail, the power of a lamb, and the grace of an elephant. No wonder they traded half the team to get him."

1. Niko says something that he later contradicts. What is that?
2. Name **two** pieces of evidence that contradict his statement.

PART G   Deductions

Complete each deduction.
1. Here's the evidence:
   Some painters were impressionists.
   Monet was a painter.
   - What's the conclusion about Monet?
2. Here's the evidence:
   Vegetarians do not eat meat.
   Monika is a vegetarian.
   - What's the conclusion about Monika?

PART H   Similes

1. *The twigs scratched Sylvia like angry claws.*
   a. What two things are the same in that simile?
   b. How could those things be the same?
   c. Name two ways those things are different.
2. *The tree was like a great mast.*
   a. What two things are the same in that simile?
   b. How could those things be the same?
   c. Name two ways those things are different.

PART I   Writing Assignment

Today's chapter described all the sights that Joe saw from the *Dazzler*. Think of a place that you like. Write a paragraph that describes the sights you can see from that place.

Make your paragraph at least **five** sentences long.

Lesson 63

PART A   Word List

Vocabulary words
complicate
spurt
defy
wince
spunk
taunt

PART B   New Vocabulary

1. **complicate**—When you **complicate** something, you make it more involved or more difficult. Here's another way of saying **She made the arrangements more difficult: She complicated the arrangements.**
   - What's another way of saying **She made the arrangements more difficult?***

2. **spurt**—A **spurt** is a quick burst of energy.
   - What's a **spurt?***

3. **defy**—When you **defy** somebody, you challenge or oppose that person.
   a. What's another way of saying **He dared to challenge the captain?***
   b. What's another way of saying **She opposed the landlord's orders?***

4. **wince**—A **wince** is the kind of response you make when you are suddenly startled or hurt.
   - Show how you **wince**.

5. **spunk**—Someone who has a lot of spirit and determination has **spunk**.
   - What's another way of saying **She showed her determination when she talked to the neighbors?***

6. **taunt**—When you **taunt** people, you mock them and try to make them angry.
   - What's another way of saying **She mocked the prince?***

PART C   Vocabulary Review

1	2
outwit	marred
surges	principal
puny	bungles
stirred	bough

1. When you are moved by the sight of something, you are _____ by the sight of that thing.
2. Something that is small and weak is _____.
3. Things that are spoiled or ruined in some way are _____.
4. When something rolls or rises like waves, that thing _____.
5. When a person makes stupid mistakes, that person _____.

PART D   Story Items

1. As Joe approached the shore, he noticed some things happening on the *Dazzler*.
   a. Name at least **one** thing Joe observed.
   b. Would the soldier let Joe bring his boat to the island?
   c. Why?
   d. As Joe tried to row to another place on the island, which boat was chasing him?
   e. Who was watching the boats from the shore?
2. a. Name two things that Pete threatened to do to Joe.
   b. Who stuck up for Joe?
   c. Just as Pete was trying to catch Frisco Kid, the wind _____.
      - picked up   - stopped
      - stayed the same

d. What did Joe threaten to do to Pete if Pete didn't put him on shore?

e. Pete pointed out that Joe would go to that same place. Name **two** reasons Joe would go there.

3. a. What was Pete going to do to Joe when Frisco Kid interfered?

b. Who volunteered to cook lunch?

c. Could the boys trust Pete, even though he was being nice?

PART E   Map Skills

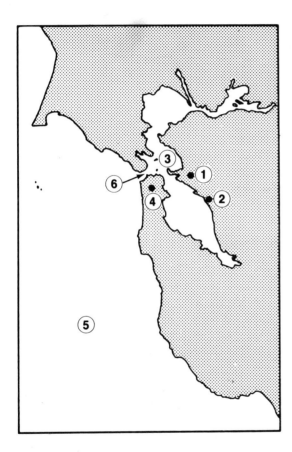

1. What city does circle 1 show?
2. Circle 2 shows where the pirates stole something. What was that?
3. Circle 3 shows an island where Joe tried to escape. That island had a _____ station.
4. What city does circle 4 show?
5. What ocean does circle 5 show?
6. What channel does circle 6 show?

PART F   Inference

Read the passage below and answer each question. Write **Words** if the question is answered by words in the passage. Write **Deduction** if the question is answered by a deduction.

The Herbivore's Eyes

Herbivores and carnivores eat different things. Herbivores eat plants, and carnivores eat other animals.

Herbivores and carnivores usually have different types of eyes. A carnivore's eyes point straight ahead. When a carnivore focuses on an object, both eyes see almost the same thing. But many herbivores are different. The left eye of a cow, for example, sees everything that is on the left side of the cow, while the right eye sees everything that is on the right side of the cow. When the cow's head is facing straight ahead, the cow is not really looking straight ahead; the cow is looking mostly to the right side and the left side. Both eyes can see only a little bit of what is straight ahead.

These eyes help the cow when it is eating grass. If the cow had the same kind of eyes that you have, it would be looking at the ground when it ate, and a carnivore could sneak up on it. But since the cow has eyes that see to the sides, it can watch out for carnivores as it eats.

1. a. What does the left eye of a cow see?

b. Is that question answered by **Words** or by a **Deduction**?

2. a. Would a cow be able to see a bear coming towards the cow's right side?

b. **Words** or **Deduction**?

3. a. When a carnivore focuses on an object, what do both eyes see?

b. **Words** or **Deduction**?

4. a. If you wanted to hide an object from a cow, would you put the object **in front** of the cow or **to the left** of the cow?

b. **Words** or **Deduction**?

PART G Drawing Conclusions

Write a conclusion that tells what the person believed.

1. *Edith believed that if you stopped watching television, you would get smarter. Edith stopped watching television.*
   - So what did Edith believe would happen?

PART H   Review Items

Write which character each statement describes. Choose from **Demeter, Sara Crewe, Matilda, Miss Terwilliger,** or **Sylvia.**

1. This character lost a fake necklace.
2. This character outwitted her suitors.
3. This character chose between a bird and a reward.
4. This character forced the plants to stop growing.
5. This character pretended to be a captain.

PART I   Writing Assignment

Joe said that he would send Pete to prison. Do you think that Frisco Kid should go to prison too? Write a paragraph that explains your answer.

Make your paragraph at least **five** sentences long.

Lesson 64

PART A   Word List

Vocabulary words
reform school
arouse
hail
skirt
untidy

PART B   New Vocabulary

1. **reform school**—Reform school is a place for young people who have broken the law. It is like a prison for people who are not yet adults.

2. **arouse**—When you wake up something or stir it, you **arouse** it.
   a. What's another way of saying **The sunset stirred his imagination?***
   b. What's another way of saying **They could not wake up the dog?***

3. **hail**—When you **hail** somebody, you wave and shout to that person.

4. **skirt**—When you **skirt** a place, you move around the outskirts of that place. Here's another way of saying **They moved around the outskirts of the city: They skirted the city.**
   ● What's another way of saying **They moved around the outskirts of the city?***

5. **untidy**—Something that is not neat or orderly is **untidy.**
   ● What's another way of saying **His room was not neat?***

PART C   Vocabulary Review

1	2
defy	taunt
marred	rebel
spunk	puny
complicate	forlorn
stirred	wince

1. Someone who has a lot of spirit and determination has _____.
2. The kind of response you make when you are suddenly startled or hurt is a _____.
3. When you mock people and try to make them angry, you _____ them.
4. When you make something more involved or more difficult, you _____ it.
5. When you challenge or oppose somebody, you _____ that person.
6. When you are moved by the sight of something, you are _____ by the sight of that thing.
7. Things that are spoiled or ruined in some way are _____.

PART D   Deductions

Complete each deduction.
1. Here's the evidence:
   Every newspaper has an editor.
   The Press-Herald is a newspaper.
   ● What's the conclusion about *The Press-Herald?*Ⓐ
2. Here's the evidence:
   Some substances are hard.
   Silicon is a substance.
   ● What's the conclusion about silicon?Ⓑ

PART E Story Items

1. Joe saw rows of people that he envied.
   a. Where were those people?
   b. Would Joe have rather been **with them** or **on the sloop**?
2. a. Frisco Kid pointed to the city and asked Joe if he had a _____ out there.
   b. When Joe asked Frisco Kid about his home, the Kid told him that he didn't _____.
   c. Who fixed lunch?
   d. How was the lunch?
3. a. What was the name of the sloop the *Dazzler* met?
   b. Which person went over to that sloop?
   c. At that time, were they **north** of San Francisco of **south** of San Francisco?
   d. Why do you think the *Reindeer* was built for speed?
4. Frisco Kid said that he liked life on the *Dazzler* but that he didn't like the _____.
5. The boys talked about running away together. Frisco Kid was concerned about what Joe's _____ would do.

PART F Conversations

Here are some characters you have read about:
- ODYSSEUS is the king of Ithaca. He has wandered all over the earth. He is very strong and cunning.

- PENELOPE is Odysseus's wife. She is suspicious of men who claim to be her husband. She refuses to marry any of her suitors.

- ANTINOUS is one of Penelope's suitors. He is a big bully, and he enjoys hurting other people. He also likes to brag.

Write which character could have made each statement:
1. "Get out of my way, you filthy beggar! I'm ten times as strong as you are."

2. "I have had many adventures, but this one is the most dangerous."
3. "What proof can you give me that shows who you really are?"
4. "I think I have figured out a way to get rid of the suitors."
5. "You, over there. Bring me more food, and do not waste any time!"

PART G Main Idea

Joe heard a creaking noise in the night and saw the men hoisting the huge mainsail above him. Then Bill and Nick untied the Dazzler from the dock. The Dazzler soon caught the breeze and headed out into the bay, pulling a lifeboat and the skiff. The waterfront lights of Oakland began to slip by.

Write the main idea; then write three supporting details for the main idea. Use complete sentences to write the main idea and the supporting details. Write **1** in front of the main idea. Write **a, b, c** in front of the supporting details. Also, indent the supporting details.

PART H Review Items

Joe and Frisco Kid are alike in some ways, and different in others. Tell whether each statement describes **Joe, Frisco Kid,** or **Both.**

1. _____ did not trust Pete.
2. _____ had a home in the city.
3. _____ knew all about sailing.
4. _____ did not like the stealing.
5. _____ was an orphan.
6. _____ was afraid of the city.

PART I Writing Assignment

Write a paragraph that explains why Frisco Kid was afraid of the land. Tell what might happen to him on the land.

Make your paragraph at least **five** sentences long.

Lesson 65

PART A   Word List

Vocabulary words
give somebody the slip
sic a dog

PART B   New Vocabulary

1. **give somebody the slip**—When you give **somebody the slip,** you escape from that person or hide from that person.

2. **sic a dog**
   - How would somebody **sic a dog** on another person?

PART C   Vocabulary Review

1	2
taunt	untidy
drab	wince
arouse	endure
collide	spurt

1. When you wake up something or stir it, you _____ that thing.
2. Something that is not neat or orderly is _____.
3. A quick burst of energy is a _____.
4. When you mock people or try to make them angry, you _____ them.
5. The kind of response you make when you are suddenly startled or hurt is a _____.

PART D   Story Items

1. Frisco Kid went below and got something to show Joe.
   a. What was it?
   b. The Kid asked Joe if his _____ looked like the one in the picture.
   c. How many brothers, sisters, and playmates did Frisco Kid have?
   d. Frisco Kid wanted to be like
      - Pete.
      - the people in the picture.
      - the captain of the *Reindeer*.
   e. When Frisco Kid thought of the pirates, the work, and the hard life, did the family seem **real** or **make-believe** to him?
   f. When Frisco Kid looked at the picture, did the family seem **real** or **make-believe** to him?
2. a. How many times had Frisco Kid run away from the pirates?
   b. When Frisco Kid learned how to do something, he found out that pirating was wrong. What did he learn to do?
      - Read   - Sail   - Steal
   c. Frisco Kid wanted Joe to tell him something about Joe's _____.
   d. How much information did Joe give?
   e. After the conversation, which people suddenly became very important to Joe?
3. a. Who called to the boys when they were in the cabin?
   b. Where was that person?
   c. What did that person want the boys to do?
4. Pete complained about the time that it took the boys to get the *Dazzler* moving.
   a. Somebody pointed out that the Kid was a good sailor. Who made that observation?
   b. Who first taught the Kid how to sail?

PART E Writing Assignment

Frisco Kid has strong feelings about a picture. Sara Crewe had strong feelings about a doll. Write a paragraph that compares their feelings. Tell how they are the same, then tell how they are different.

Make your paragraph at least **five** sentences long.

Lesson 66

PART A Word List

1
Vocabulary words
survey
strained
muffled

PART B New Vocabulary

1. **survey**—When you examine a scene closely, you **survey** that scene.
   - What's another way of saying **They closely examined the mountains?***

2. **strained**—Situations are **strained** if they make you feel anxious. Here's another way of saying **The night made us feel anxious: The night was strained.**
   - What's another way of saying **The night made us feel anxious?***

3. **muffled**—Sounds that are **muffled** are softened or deadened.
   - What's another way of saying **They spoke in voices that were softened?***

PART C   Vocabulary Review

1	2
principal	marred
hoist	defy
outwit	spunk
complicate	taunt

1. When you challenge or oppose people, you _____ them.
2. When you mock people and try to make them angry, you _____ them.
3. The most important things are the _____ things.
4. When you make something more involved or more difficult, you _____ it.
5. Things that are spoiled or ruined in some way are _____.

PART D   Substitute Words

In the following passage, some parts are underlined. Write the name of the person or thing that each underlined part refers to.

1. Martha was sick. <u>She</u> stayed in bed all day long.Ⓐ
2. Martha was watching a TV show, but she thought <u>it</u> was stupid.Ⓑ
3. She wished that she had gone to the library. She could have checked out several books <u>there</u>.Ⓒ
4. The books would be far better than the TV show, because <u>they</u> were not as stupid.Ⓓ

PART E   Story Items

1. a. Which boat was faster, the *Reindeer* or the *Dazzler*?
   b. After the *Dazzler* and the *Reindeer* dropped anchor, which two small boats went to shore?
   c. What kind of equipment did the men have with them?
   d. Who stayed on the *Dazzler*?
   e. The *Reindeer* was ready for a
      ● party. ● fast departure.
2. a. How did the boys plan to escape?
   b. Who called to them and warned them to stop?
   c. What did that person threaten to do if they tried to leave?
3. At one time, Frisco Kid had escaped from the pirates.
   a. What season was it when he escaped?
   b. Where did he try to find work?
   c. How much success did he have?
   d. Why?
   e. Frisco Kid was captured in a
      _____.
   f. Who captured him?
   g. What kind of place was Frisco Kid sent to after he was captured?
   h. How was Frisco Kid treated in that place?
   i. Where did he long to be?
   j. How did he get out of that place?
4. There were loud noises after the Kid had finished his story.
   a. What made those noises?
   b. What did the Kid and Joe do?
   c. What did the boy on the *Reindeer* do?
   d. Who did the noise wake up?
5. Write where Frisco Kid had each experience. Choose from the **country,** the **reform school,** or the **bay.**
   a. He did a lot of reading.
   b. He could not find any work.
   c. He became tired of stealing.
   d. People would sic their dogs on him.
   e. He would get into fights with other boys.

PART F   Conversations

Below is a conversation between Juan and Leroy. Write which person makes each statement.

"Look over there, Juan," Leroy said. "What is that thing?" ①

"Gee, I don't know. It sure is strange-looking." ② Juan looked more closely for a moment and then said, "Maybe it's a flying saucer." ③

The younger boy looked at Juan. "Do you really think it's a flying saucer?" he asked. ④

"Anything is possible," the elder boy said, with a stuffy tone in his voice. ⑤

"When you've lived as long as I have," he continued, "you'll know what I mean." ⑥

"If anything is possible, it's possible that you're wrong." ⑦

"All right, smart guy, let's go find out." ⑧

PART G   Inference

Read the passage below and answer each question. Write **Words** if the question is answered by words in the passage. Write **Deduction** if the question is answered by a deduction.

The Carnivore's Eyes

You learned that a herbivore has its eyes on the sides of its head. The herbivore's eyes see to the sides instead of straight ahead. This arrangement helps the herbivore when it is grazing, because the eyes can see if a carnivore is trying to sneak up.

Most farm animals are herbivores. Cows, goats, sheep and horses get all the nourishment they need by eating grass and other types of plants. All these animals have their eyes on the sides of their heads.

A carnivore is different. A carnivore must have a good image of the animal it is hunting. A carnivore needs to see as far forward as possible. Therefore, a carnivore's eyes look straight ahead. When a carnivore sees another animal in the distance, the carnivore focuses both eyes on that animal. And when the carnivore eats, its eyes show what its mouth is biting into.

1. **a.** A puma has eyes that look straight ahead. Is a puma a carnivore or a herbivore?
   b. Is that question answered by **Words** or by a **Deduction**?
2. **a.** A deer has eyes on the sides of its head. Is a deer a carnivore or a herbivore?
   b. **Words** or **Deduction**?
3. **a.** What do a carnivore's eyes show when the carnivore eats?
   b. **Words** or **Deduction**?
4. **a.** How do cows, goats and sheep get all the nourishment they need?
   b. **Words** or **Deduction**?

PART H   Writing Assignment

Frisco Kid explained how he returned to the pirates after he left reform school. Pretend that Frisco Kid is asking Pete for a job.

Make up a conversation between Pete and Frisco Kid. Have each character say at least **three** sentences.

Lesson 67

PART A   Word Lists

1
San Andreas
patron

2
Vocabulary words
loom up
gale
hurtle

PART B   New Vocabulary

1. **loom up**—When something **looms up,** it suddenly appears.
   - What's another way of saying **The wave suddenly appeared in front of them?***

2. **gale**—A **gale** is a terrible storm with great winds.

3. **hurtle**—When something **hurtles,** it moves with great speed.
   - What's another way of saying **The train moved with great speed down the mountain?**

PART C   Vocabulary Review

1	2
strained	untidy
defy	survey
bungle	spunk
muffled	surge

1. When you examine a scene closely, you _____ that scene.
2. Situations that make you feel anxious are _____.
3. Sounds that are softened or deadened are _____.
4. When you challenge or oppose people, you _____ them.
5. Someone who has a lot of spirit and determination has _____.

PART D   Story Items

1. The crews of the two sloops got ready to leave.
   a. What was wrong with Nelson when his skiff arrived?
   b. What had the men from the two sloops stolen?
   c. On which sloop did they put it?
   d. Which person said that the stolen object should be put on that sloop?
   e. Why didn't he want the stolen object on the other sloop?
2. Which country did Nelson plan to go to after they had escaped?
3. a. Joe thought about cutting down the sails, but he didn't do that because he was concerned about _____.
   b. The police boat tried to follow the *Dazzler,* but it crashed into something. What was that?
   c. What ocean was the *Dazzler* heading toward?
4. a. In the morning, the sky was gray and the wind almost had the force of a _____.
      - gate   • gale   • gape
   b. Frisco Kid didn't think that the police boat would have enough nerve to go through a certain place. Which place?
   c. Which craft had better sailors, the police boat or the *Dazzler*?
5. a. What did Joe see on the safe that surprised him?
   b. Who had owned that safe?
   c. What did the safe hold?

PART E   Map Skills

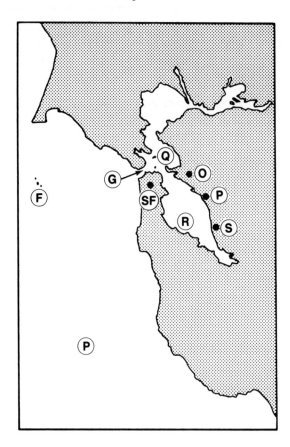

1. What city does circle **O** show?
2. What did the pirates steal at circle **P**?
3. The island at circle **Q** had a _____ station.
4. Which ship did the *Dazzler* meet at circle **R**?
5. What container did the pirates steal at circle **S**?
6. What channel does circle **G** show?
7. What ocean does circle **P** show?
8. What group of islands does circle **F** show?
9. What city does circle **SF** show?

PART F   Substitute Words

In the following passage, some parts are underlined. Write the name of the person or thing that each underlined part refers to.
1. Nathan lived in a dangerous building. <u>It</u> had many broken windows and the roof leaked.
2. Nathan's mother and father were poor, and <u>they</u> could not afford to leave the <u>building</u>.
3. Nathan said, "I can't stand it <u>here</u>."
4. His father answered, "<u>You</u> had better learn to stand it, because it will be a long time before we can move."

PART G   Metaphors

Here's a metaphor: *The sails began to snarl loudly.*
1. So, the sails were like something that _____.
2. What could that something be?
3. Use accurate language to tell how the sails and _____ could be the same.

PART H   Conversations

Below is a conversation between Harumi and Yoshio. Write which person makes each statement.

Harumi, a twelve year old girl, was glad to see her brother. "Yoshio," she said, "I can't believe that you are finally home."① She paused a moment, and smiled. "Is college really difficult?" she asked.②

"Oh, I think sixth grade was harder, because of Mrs. Ozu."③

"Yes, she is a very tough teacher. I am in her class now."④

"I know," Yoshio observed. "You told me in your letter."⑤ "Tell me," he asked, "does she still give a test every day?"⑥

"Not only that, but she won't give us any recess if we make too much noise."⑦

PART I Review Items

Sometimes, the sheriff would mix up his words. Here are some statements the sheriff might make. Rewrite each statement so that it is correct.

1. "That is the rest base I have ever seen."
2. "May I sorrow your bailboat?"
3. "That baseball player should have bought the call."
4. "The gad buys always wore hack blats."

PART J Writing Assignment

Joe has to figure out what to do with the safe. What do you think he should do? Write a paragraph that explains your answer.

Make your paragraph at least **six** sentences long.

Lesson 68

PART A   Word Lists

1
Farallon Islands
San Andreas
destination
quarantine

2
Vocabulary words
summit
poised

PART B   New Vocabulary

1. **summit**—The **summit** of something is the top or the peak of that thing.
   a. What's the peak of a mountain?*
   b. What's the top of a giant wave?*

2. **poised**—When something is **poised**, it is still and balanced.
   a. What's another way of saying **The ship was balanced on top of the wave?***
   b. What's another way of saying **The cat was balanced on the end of the branch?***

PART C   Vocabulary Review

1	2	3
arouse	gale	muffled
defy	strained	looms up
hurtles	survey	surges

1. When something suddenly appears, it _____.

2. A terrible storm with great winds is a _____.

3. When something rolls or rises like waves, that thing _____.

4. When something moves with great speed, it _____.

5. Sounds that are softened or deadened are _____.

6. When you wake up something or stir it, you _____ that thing.

7. Situations that make you feel anxious are _____.

PART D   Story Items

1. Joe now had a lot of responsibility.
   a. He felt responsible for the future of a friend. Who was that?
   b. He also had to protect somebody's property. Whose property?

2. When Joe and Frisco Kid went on deck, they saw something very frightening.

   a. What did they see?
   b. What did the police boat do as the *Dazzler* went through the Gate?
   c. Which boat arrived at the Farallon Islands first?
   d. In which direction did the sloops head from the Farallon Islands?
   e. As the sloops moved along, they stayed
      • in sight of the coast.
      • out of sight of the coast.

3. Frisco Kid had a plan.
   a. What did he plan to do with Pete?
   b. What did Joe think of that plan?
   c. Joe wanted to fix things so that Frisco Kid could get an _____, and be somebody other than a _____.

4. a. After lunch, what happened to the wind? *stronger*
   b. Which direction did it blow from?
      • Northwest   • Southeast
   c. Were the waves **taller** than the *Reindeer*'s sail or **not as tall?**
   d. To slow the *Dazzler,* Pete was going to launch a device. What was that?

5. Just as Pete was getting ready to launch that device, some things happened.
   a. Who fell into the water?
   b. What happened to the mast and the mainsail?
   c. What caused that problem?

PART E Map Skills

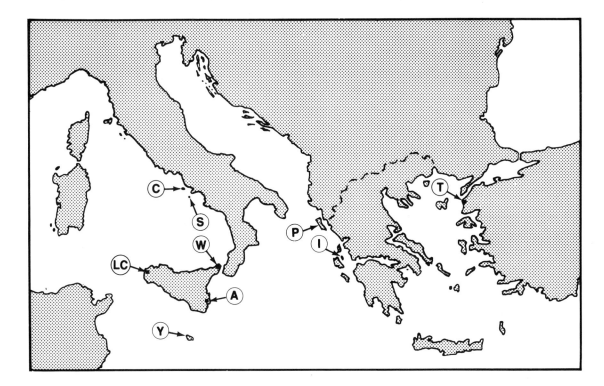

1. What is the letter of the place where Odysseus saw a whirlpool?
2. What is the name of island **I?**
3. What is the name of city **T?**
4. Which sorceress lived at place **C?**
5. At which letter did Odysseus hear an enchanting song?
6. What was the name of the creatures that sang the song?

PART F Inference

Read the passage below and answer each question. Write **Words** if the question is answered by words in the passage. Write **Deduction** if the question is answered by a deduction.

The Teeth of Carnivores and Herbivores

You have learned that carnivores and herbivores are different in two ways: they eat different things and they have different types of eyes. Carnivores eat meat, while herbivores eat plants; carnivores' eyes see straight ahead, while herbivores' eyes see to the sides of their heads.

Herbivores and carnivores also have different types of teeth. Herbivores have flat teeth. These flat teeth are designed to grind grass, leaves, and seeds.

Just as the teeth of herbivores are designed to grind food, the teeth of carnivores are designed to tear flesh. Carnivores' teeth are pointed and sharp, not flat. These teeth do not grind the food into small pieces. Instead, the teeth tear the food into chunks that are just small enough to be swallowed.

1. **a.** What kind of teeth do herbivores have?
   b. Is that question answered by **Words** or by a **Deduction?**
2. **a.** What kind of teeth do carnivores have?
   b. **Words** or **Deduction?**
3. **a.** A gazelle grinds its food. So is a gazelle a **herbivore** or a **carnivore?**
   b. **Words** or **Deduction?**
4. **a.** A ferret tears its food into chunks. Does a ferret eat **plants** or **meat?**
   b. **Words** or **Deduction?**

PART G   Writing Assignment

Pretend you are one of the sailors who watches the *Dazzler* go through the Golden Gate during the storm. Write a paragraph that describes what you see.

Make your paragraph at least **five** sentences long.

Lesson 69

PART A   Word List

Vocabulary words
forge ahead
vengeance

PART B   New Vocabulary

1. **forge ahead**—When you move forward with determination, you **forge ahead.**
   - What are you doing when you move forward with great determination?*

2. **vengeance**—Another word for **revenge** is **vengeance.**
   a. What's another word for **revenge?***
   b. What's another way of saying **They wanted revenge?***

PART C   Vocabulary Review

1	2	3
poised	spunky	untidy
taunt	arouse	muffled
strained	gale	summit

1. Sounds that are softened or deadened are _____.
2. The top or peak of something is the _____ of that thing.
3. When something is still and balanced, it is _____.
4. Situations that make you feel anxious are _____.
5. When you mock people and try to make them angry, you _____ them.
6. When you wake up something or stir it, you _____ that thing.

PART D Story Items

1. **a.** Was Pete hurt badly from the fall?
   b. How badly damaged was the *Dazzler*?
   c. What made it difficult for the *Reindeer* to come alongside the *Dazzler*?
   d. Who was the captain of the *Reindeer*?
   e. Joe admired the captain of the *Reindeer* for two things. Which two things?
   f. Joe hated the captain of the *Reindeer* for two things. Which two things?
2. **a.** Who jumped from the sinking *Dazzler* to the *Reindeer*?
   b. Who did not jump?
   c. What did the boys hope to rescue?
   d. What happened to the *Reindeer* as it came toward the *Dazzler* for the last time?
3. **a.** What did the boys do to try to keep the *Dazzler* from sinking?
   b. Did the *Dazzler* last through the storm?
   c. At first, why couldn't the boys sail the *Dazzler*?
4. **a.** The *Dazzler* was very close to
   ● the Farallon Islands.
   ● San Francisco.
   ● Santa Cruz.
   b. What did Frisco Kid use to make a sail?
   c. The *Dazzler* was heading
   ● toward the rocks.
   ● toward a river.
   ● toward a bridge.

PART E Outlining

Complete the following outline for *The Cruise of the Dazzler*. Copy each main idea; then write three supporting details for each main idea. Use complete sentences to write the supporting details.

1. Frisco Kid was afraid of the land.
2. Joe tried to escape near Angel Island.

PART F Exaggeration

His voice was so loud it shook leaves from the trees.
1. How loud does the statement say his voice was?
2. Write an accurate statement that tells how loud his voice was.

PART G Review Items

You have read two poems. Tell whether each line is from **The Tide Rises, the Tide Falls** or **Written in March**.
1. "There's joy in the mountains."
2. "The traveler hastens toward the town."
3. "But the sea, the sea in the darkness calls."
4. "The ploughboy is whooping—anon—anon."
5. "Darkness settles on roofs and walls."

PART H Writing Assignment

Pretend you are Nelson. Write a paragraph that tells what you think when you see the *Dazzler*'s accident. Tell the different feelings you have, then tell what you finally decide to do.

Make your paragraph at least **five** sentences long.

Lesson 70

PART A   Word Lists

1
wreathed
spheroid
pallor
patron

2
Vocabulary words
show promise
reception

PART B   New Vocabulary

1. **show promise**—When people **show promise,** they show that they have the talent to learn something.
   - What's another way of saying **She was a musician who showed talent to learn?***

2. **reception**—You know one meaning of a **reception.**
   a. What's that?
   b. Another meaning of a **reception** is a greeting.
   c. What's another way of saying **He didn't know what kind of greeting he would receive?***

PART C   Vocabulary Review

1	2
hurtles	poised
suppress	forge ahead
vengeance	loot
gale	hoist

1. A terrible storm with great winds is a _____.
2. When something moves with great speed, it _____.
3. When you move forward with determination, you _____.
4. Another word for **revenge** is _____.
5. When something is still and balanced, it is _____.

PART D   Story Items

1. a. Where did the boys go for breakfast?
   b. Where did Joe plan to go?
   c. How did Joe plan to get to that place?
   d. While Joe was gone, Frisco Kid was supposed to guard _____.

2. An article in the newspaper caught Joe's eye.
   a. What did the article describe?
   b. What did authorities think had happened to the two sloops?
   c. Who offered a reward for the return of the safe?
   d. How much was the reward?
3. a. Who did Joe go to see?
   b. Joe's father greeted him as if Joe had just come back from a _____.

4. Joe spoke to his father of the lessons he had learned.
   a. Joe learned that his family was _____ to him.
   b. He also learned that people are not all good or all bad. Which boy had taught Joe that lesson?
   c. What was good about Frisco Kid?
   d. What was bad about Frisco Kid?
5. a. Who was entitled to the reward?
   b. How much was each person to receive?
6. Joe and Frisco Kid agreed that one person was captain on land and one was captain on sea.
   a. Who was captain on land?
   b. Who was captain on sea?
   c. What did Joe's father agree to do with Frisco Kid's money?

d. Where were Joe and his father preparing to go at the end of the story?

PART E   Map Skills

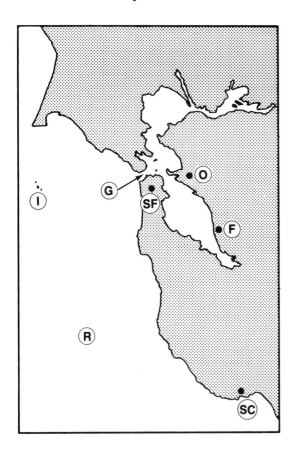

1. What city does circle **O** show?
2. What city does circle **SF** show?
3. What city does circle **SC** show?
4. The pirates stole a container from a factory at circle **F.** What was that?
5. Which circle shows the Golden Gate?
6. Which circle shows the place where the *Reindeer* sank?
7. Which circle shows the Farallon Islands?

PART F   Similes

Make up a simile for each accurate statement. Use the word **like** in your similes.
1. *The sloop bobbed up and down.*
    a. Name something that could bob up and down.
    b. Make up a simile that tells how the sloop bobbed up and down.
2. *He went straight back to his home.*
    a. Name something that could go straight.
    b. Make up a simile that tells how he went home.

PART G   Writing Assignment

At the end of the story, Joe was going home. Continue the story. Tell what might happen during the next few days.

Make your story at least **ten** sentences long.

Lesson 71

PART A   Word Lists

1
Ernest Thayer
despise
pallor
spheroid
vengeance
defiance
writhe

2
multitude
pudd'n
deathlike
rebound
patron
wreathed

3
Vocabulary words
despise
unheeded
remote

PART B   New Vocabulary

1. **despise**—When you **despise** something, you really hate it.
   a. What's another way of saying **She really hated snakes?***
   b. What's another way of saying **They really hate homework?***

2. **unheeded**—When you **heed** something, you pay attention to it or notice it.
   a. So, what is something that is **unheeded?**

   b. What's another way of saying **The little boy was unnoticed?***
   c. What's another way of saying **She attended to her father's advice?***

3. **remote**—Something that is far away is **remote.**
   • What's another way of saying **They observed a star that was very far away?***

PART C   Story Items

1. Some people left because they didn't feel that the star player would ever have a chance to bat.
   a. Why did they feel that way?
   b. Who was the star?
2. When Blake and Flynn got on base, who was the next batter?
3. Write whether each statement describes **Casey,** the **other players,** or the **audience.**
   a. A pallor wreathed their features.
   b. Two of them died at second.
   c. They sent up a joyous yell.
   d. There was pride in his bearing.
   e. There was ease in his manner.

PART D   Map Skills

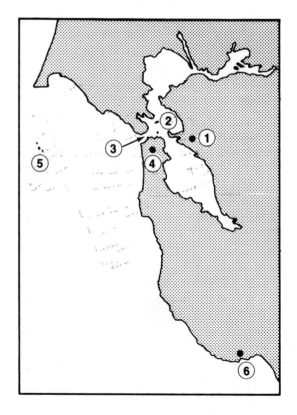

1. Which circle shows San Francisco?
2. Which circle shows the Farallon Islands?
3. Which circle shows Oakland?
4. Which circle shows Santa Cruz?
5. Which circle shows The Golden Gate?
6. Which circle shows Angel Island?

PART E   Inference

Read the passage below and answer each question. Write **Words** if the question is answered by words in the passage. Write **Deduction** if the question is answered by a deduction.

The Skulls of Herbivores and Carnivores

From what you have learned about herbivores and carnivores, you should be able to draw conclusions about the skulls of some animals.

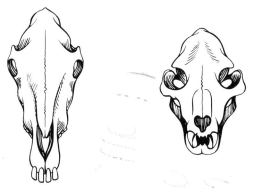

PICTURE 1   PICTURE 2

Picture 1 shows the skull of a herbivore. The eye sockets are pointed to the side, and the teeth are flat. The skull is light and thin, which means that the animal does not have much strength in its head.

Picture 2 shows the skull of a carnivore. The eye sockets are pointed straight ahead, and the teeth are strong and sharp. The skull of this animal is thick and strong. This animal has a lot of strength in its head. It can probably use its head as a weapon against other animals.

The skull of the animal in picture 1 belongs to a horse. The skull of the animal in picture 2 belongs to a lion.

PICTURE 3

Look at the skull in picture 3 and answer the following questions.
1. a. Is the skull in picture 3 that of a **herbivore** or a **carnivore?**
   b. Is that question answered by **Words** or by a **Deduction?**
2. a. Are the eye sockets of skull 3 like those of a **herbivore** or a **carnivore?**
   b. **Words** or **Deduction?**
3. a. Are the teeth of skull 3 like those of a **herbivore** or a **carnivore?**
   b. **Words** or **Deduction?**
4. a. Does skull 3 have the strength of a **herbivore** or a **carnivore?**
   b. **Words** or **Deduction?**
5. a. Which animal do you think skull 3 belongs to?
   b. **Words** or **Deduction?**

PART F   Sarcasm

Louise went to the City Movie Theater. She said, "Wow, this is really a great place. My feet are stuck to the floor because of the chewing gum. Somebody from the balcony threw popcorn in my hair. And the best part is that the people behind me talked all through the movie."

1. Louise says something that she later contradicts. What is that?
2. Name **two** pieces of evidence that contradict Louise's statement.

PART G   Writing Assignment

Casey at the Bat uses poetry to tell a story. Rewrite the first part of *Casey at the Bat* so that it is like a regular story. Tell what happened to the first two batters. Tell how the audience felt. Tell what happened to the next two batters. Tell what Casey was like.

Make your story at least **six** sentences long.

Lesson 72

PART A   Word Lists

1	2	3
haughty	defy	**Vocabulary words**
Christian	defiance	observatory
visage	pallor	astronomer
grandeur	fraud	scorn
tumult	writhe	overwhelm
observatory	spheroid	writhe
scholar		
astronomy		

PART B   New Vocabulary

1. **observatory**—A building that is designed to let people look at the stars is called an **observatory.**
   a. What do we call a building that is designed to let people look at the stars?*
   b. What kind of equipment would you find in an observatory?

2. **astronomer**—A person who studies the stars and planets is called an **astronomer.**
   • What do we call a person who studies the stars and planets?*

3. **scorn**—Another word for **hate** is **scorn.**
   a. What's another way of saying **They showed their hate?***
   b. If scorn means hate, what does scornful mean?

   c. What's another way of saying **His expression was full of hate?***

4. **overwhelm**—Something that **overwhelms** you, overpowers you.
   a. What's another way of saying **Winning the contest overpowered her?***
   b. What's another way of saying **There was so much information that it overpowered his mind?***

5. **writhe**—When something **writhes,** it squirms and wiggles vigorously.
   a. What's another way of saying **She squirmed with pain?***
   b. What's another way of saying **The can was full of wiggling worms?***

PART C Vocabulary Review

1	2	3
heed	reception	poised
despise	vengeance	summit
remote	muffled	unheeded

1. Something that is far away is
   _____.

2. When you really hate something, you
   _____ that thing.

3. When you pay attention to something
   or notice it, you _____ that
   thing.

4. Another word for **revenge** is
   _____.

5. A party that takes place after an
   important event is a _____.

6. When you don't pay attention to
   something or don't notice it, that
   thing is _____.

PART D Story items

1. a. How did the crowd react when the
      umpire called strike one?
   b. How did Casey respond to the
      umpire's call of strike one?

2. After there were two strikes on Casey,
   the pitcher threw another pitch. What
   happened when Casey swung at that
   pitch?

3. The last stanza of the poem says that
   there is joy in different places.
   a. In which place is there no joy?
   b. Why not?

PART E Similes

1. *From the benches, black with people,*
   there went up a muffled roar, like the
   beating of the storm waves on the stern
   and distant shore.
   a. What two things are the same in
      that simile?
   b. How could those things be the
      same?
   c. Name two ways those things are
      different.

2. *Like a monstrous bat, the ship passed*
   to the left of them in the gloom.
   a. What two things are the same in
      that simile?
   b. How could those things be the
      same?
   c. Name two ways those things are
      different.

PART F Review Items

Tell whether each statement describes
The Odyssey, The Voyage of the Northern
Light, or *The Cruise of the Dazzler.*
1. The ship in this story was powered by
   oars.
2. The ship in this story was a sloop.
3. The ship in this story was a schooner.
4. This story took place near Nova
   Scotia.
5. This story took place in the Pacific
   Ocean.
6. This story took place near Greece.

PART G Writing Assignment

Without looking at your textbook, try to
write the entire last stanza of *Casey at*
the Bat. If you can't remember all the
words, write the words that you do
remember.

After you finish, compare your version
with the original version.

If you made any mistakes, try to
memorize the stanza again.

Lesson 73

PART A   Word Lists

1
telescope
binoculars
scholar
winter
wintry

2
Vocabulary words
comet
grim
drawn
straggle

PART B   New Vocabulary

1. **comet**—A **comet** is an object that moves through space. It has a long tail that is made up of gas. The picture shows a comet.

2. **grim**—Something that is very terrible is **grim**.
   a. What's another way of saying **He moved ahead with very terrible determination?***
   b. What's another way of saying **She could think of nothing but very terrible possibilities?***

3. **drawn**—When a face is **drawn**, it has a strained expression.
   - What do we call a face that has a strained expression?*

4. **straggle**—People who **straggle** don't keep up with a group. They fall behind and move more slowly.
   - What are people doing when they fall behind and move more slowly?*

PART C   Vocabulary Review

1	2	3
writhes	astronomer	outwit
hurtled	overwhelms	unheeded
observatory	greeting	scorn

1. Something that overpowers you, _____ you.
2. Another word for **hate** is _____.
3. When something squirms and wiggles vigorously, it _____.
4. When you don't pay attention to something or don't notice it, that thing is _____.
5. A building that is designed to let people look at the stars is called an _____.
6. A person who studies the stars and planets is called an _____.

PART D   Story Items

1. a. What did the strange star finally collide with?
   b. What happened when the two planets collided?
   c. Which group of people recorded that event?
   d. The star became brighter and brighter because it was moving

   _____.
   - farther away   • closer
   - in the same spot

2. A schoolgirl figured out that something terrible might happen.
   a. Where was the star heading?
   b. The schoolgirl wondered what would happen if another object got in its way. Which object was that?
   c. What would happen?

3. a. Complete the rule about the rate of planet orbits: The closer a planet is to the sun, the _____ time it takes for that planet to orbit the sun.

b. Which planet takes the least amount of time to orbit the sun?

c. Which planet takes the longest amount of time to orbit the sun?

d. Which planet orbits the sun in less time, Mars or Saturn?

e. How long does it take the Earth to orbit the sun?

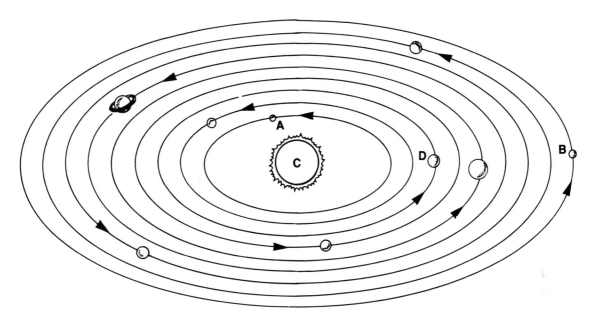

4. a. The map shows the _____ system.

b. What is the name of planet **D**?

c. What is the name of planet **A**?

d. What is the name of planet **B**?

e. What is the name of star **C**?

f. Which planet takes less time to orbit the sun, planet **B** or planet **D**?

g. Name the planet that was destroyed in the story.

PART E   Substitute Words

In the following sentences, some parts are underlined. Write the name of the person or thing that each underlined part refers to.

1. The people gathered their ropes. They were old and had been tied together where they had broken.

2. Sue was standing on a ladder and Linda was below her on the ground. She said, "Hand the paint brush up to me."

3. The rabbits quickly went into their holes. They huddled there and waited for the fox to leave.

4. They performed many dances at their celebrations. One of these was the pearl dance.

5. The people bought large pots. They were made of black metal.

PART F   Writing Assignment

Here is a part of today's story. "Beyond Pluto there is space, vacant space, without warmth or light or sound. There is nothing but blank space for twenty million times a million miles."

Imagine you are floating in that space. Write a paragraph that describes what you think it would be like. Tell how you would feel.

Make your paragraph at least **six** sentences long.

Lesson 74

PART A   Word Lists

1	2	3
ibex	halo	**Vocabulary words**
torque	politician	scholar
devastating	bathe	devastating
	tide	remnants
	tidal	
	bathed	

PART B   New Vocabulary

1. **scholar**—**Scholars** are people who have expert knowledge in some field. A scholar in arithmetic is an expert in arithmetic.
   - What would we call a person who is an expert in astronomy?*

2. **devastating**—Something that destroys another thing completely is **devastating.** An explosion that destroys something completely is a devastating explosion.
   a. What's an argument that is capable of destroying?
   b. What's a gale that destroys a small town?

3. **remnants**—The **remnants** of something are the pieces of that thing that remain after the thing no longer exists. The pieces of a house that remain after the house has been destroyed are the remnants of the house.
   - What do we call the pieces of her beliefs that remained after she changed her mind?

PART C   Vocabulary Review

1	2	3
drawn	comet	vengeance
straggle	heed	remote
despise	grim	reception

1. An object that moves through space and has a long tail that is made up of gas is a _____.
2. Something that is very terrible is _____.
3. When a face has a strained expression, it is _____.
4. People who don't keep up with a group _____.
5. When you really hate something, you _____ that thing.
6. When you pay attention to something or notice it, you _____ that thing.

PART D   Combined Sentences

Some sentences give information about the meaning of a new word. Here's a sentence that contains a new word. The new word is underlined. **The ibex lives in the mountains.**

Here's a second sentence that tells the meaning of the new word: **The ibex is a wild goat.**

To combine the sentences we start with the first sentence and leave a space after the new word: **The ibex _____ lives in the mountains.**

Then we put in the meaning of the new word. We put a comma at the beginning of the meaning and another comma at the end of the meaning. We also take out the word "is": **The ibex, a wild goat, lives in the mountains.**

- What is the new word that is presented in that sentence?Ⓐ
- What is an ibex?Ⓑ
- What does the sentence tell about the ibex?Ⓒ

Here is another pair of sentences. The first presents a new word. The second tells what that word means. **The torque was worn many years ago. The torque is a metal necklace.**

Here is the first sentence written with a space: **The torque _____ was worn many years ago.**

- What is the new word that is presented?Ⓓ
- What does that word mean?Ⓔ
- What does the first sentence tell about the new word?Ⓕ
1. Write the combined sentence. Remember to put a comma at the beginning of the meaning and another comma at the end of the meaning.Ⓖ

PART E   Story Items

1. a. Why did the astronomer tell her class that they had all lived in vain?
   b. What did her calculations show?
   c. Which planet did the astronomer think that the star would pass near?
   d. What would happen to the path of the new star as it came close to that planet?
   e. When the path changed, which planet would the star head toward?
2. a. Most people _____ their daily habits.
      - changed   • did not change
   b. At 7:15 London time, what was supposed to happen to the star?
   c. That evening, many people laughed when the star rose. Why?
   d. Why did they stop laughing?

PART F   Relevant Information

Read the facts and the items. If an item is relevant to fact A, write **relevant to fact A.** If an item is relevant to fact B, write **relevant to fact B.** If an item is irrelevant to both facts, write **irrelevant.**

- Fact A: *Casey was advancing to the bat.*
- Fact B: *Casey struck out.*

1. The game was on television.
2. The crowd sent up a joyous yell.
3. There is no joy in Mudville.
4. The air was shattered by the force of his blow.

PART G   Writing Assignment

What would you do if you knew that a star was going to destroy the world? Write a paragraph that explains what you would do, and why you would do it.

Make your paragraph at least **six** sentences long.

Lesson 75

PART A   Word Lists

1	2	3
toucan	China	**Vocabulary words**
chintz	Asia	blot out
torrent	tidal	invader
	Catherine	merge
	Moses	torrent

PART B   New Vocabulary

1. **blot out**—When something **blots out** something else, it covers up that thing. If a cloud covers up the sun, the cloud blots out the sun.
   a. What's another way of saying **The noise covered up her voice?***
   b. What's another way of saying **The smoke covered up the sun?***

2. **invader**
   • What's an **invader?**

3. **merge**—When things **merge,** they come together and form one thing.
   a. What's another way of saying **The three highways came together and formed one highway?***
   b. What's another way of saying **The two paths came together and formed a single path?***

4. **torrent**—A **torrent** is a wild flow. A wild flow of water is a torrent of water.
   a. What's a wild flow of words?*
   b. What's a wild flow of mud?*

PART C   Vocabulary Review

1	2
straggle	comet
remnants	drawn
grim	scholars
overwhelm	writhes
devastating	heed
scorn	

1. The pieces of something that remain after the thing no longer exists are the _____ of that thing.
2. An explosion that destroys something completely is a _____ explosion.
3. People who don't keep up with a group _____.
4. People who have expert knowledge in some field are _____.
5. Another word for **hate** is _____.
6. When something squirms and wiggles vigorously, it _____.
7. When a face has a strained expression, it is _____.
8. Something that is very terrible is _____.

PART D Combined Sentences

1. Below are two sentences. One introduces a new word; the other tells what the word means.

- *The toucan has bright feathers.*
- *The toucan is a tropical bird.*

   a. Combine the sentences so that the meaning comes right after the new word. Remember to put commas before and after the meaning. Also remember to take out the word "is."Ⓐ

   b. What is the new word in the combined sentence?Ⓑ

   c. What does the new word mean?Ⓒ

   d. What else does the sentence tell about the new word?Ⓓ

2. Below are two more sentences.

- *Chintz usually has bright colors.*
- *Chintz is a kind of cotton fabric.*

   a. Combine the sentences so that the meaning comes right after the new word. Remember to put commas before and after the meaning.

   b. What is the new word in the combined sentence?

   c. What does the new word mean?

   d. What else does the sentence tell about the new word?

PART E Story Items

1. a. What happened to the temperature of the Earth as the star approached?

   b. Name two other ways that the weather changed.

   c. Name **four** disasters that occurred as the planet approached.

2. Most of India was under water. Where had the people crowded?

3. A shadow suddenly crept across the star.

   a. What object made that shadow?

   b. The astronomer who had first calculated the path of the new star now realized that the star would _____ the Earth.
   - hit   - miss

   c. The astronomer realized that a certain object might save the Earth from total destruction. What was that object?

4. a. As the shadow passed across the Earth, what happened to the temperature?

   b. What would have happened if that shadow had not blocked the rays of the star?

   c. The next morning, the star rose _____ hours late.

   d. What was in front of the star?

5. a. At what time in Europe did the star collide with the sun?
   - 6:00 A.M. - Midnight - Noon

   b. After the sun and star collided, what happened to the size of the sun?

   c. The moon was _____.
   - closer to the Earth
   - closer to the sun

   d. What happened to the temperature of the Earth because of the change in the sun?

   e. What did that temperature change do to the ice near the poles?

PART F Writing Assignment

Imagine that your neighborhood was destroyed by the star. Write a paragraph that describes what it would look like.

Make your paragraph at least **six** sentences long.

PART G   Special Projects

1. (Individual Project) Draw a picture of the solar system on a large piece of paper. Draw the sun in the middle, then draw the planets orbiting the sun. Make each planet a different color. After you finish the picture, look up facts about each planet and write those facts on the picture.

2. (Group Project) Make a model of the solar system. Use balls of different sizes for the planets and the sun. Then figure out how to hang the balls in the air and how to make them orbit around the sun. You may want to paint the balls and put labels on each one.

3. (Group Project) A heron is a large bird. Look in an encyclopedia and find out about at least five other large birds. Draw or paste a picture of each bird on a large piece of paper. Then list facts about each bird under the pictures.

Lesson 76

PART A   Word Lists

1	2	3
quatrain	Maryland	**Vocabulary words**
noria	Pennsylvania	plantation
omnivore	tobacco	ruts
	runaway	

PART B   New Vocabulary

1. **plantation**—A **plantation** was a large farm with slaves. Plantations grew tons of cotton each year. There were large mansions for the slave owners and cabins for the slaves that worked on the plantation.

2. **ruts**—The dirt road was smooth for a few miles, but then it changed. It was now full of deep **ruts** that were caused by the vehicles that passed over it.
● What could the word **ruts** mean?

PART C Vocabulary Review

1	2	3
invader	remnants	writhes
torrent	grim	drawn
blots out	scholars	merge

1. When something covers up something else, it _____ that thing.
2. When things come together and form one thing, they _____.
3. Something that is very terrible is _____.
4. A wild flow is a _____.
5. Someone who goes to a place and tries to take over is called an _____.
6. When a face has a strained expression, it is _____.

PART D Combined Sentences

1. Below is a combined sentence that presents a new word and tells what the new word means. The new word is not underlined.
   - *This carved box was made in a hong, a Chinese factory.*
   a. What is the new word?Ⓐ
   b. What does the new word mean?Ⓑ
   c. What else does the sentence tell about the new word?Ⓒ
2. Here's another sentence:
   - *The noria, a kind of water wheel, is often seen in Spain.*
   a. What is the new word?
   b. What does the new word mean?
   c. What else does the sentence tell about the new word?

PART E Story Items

1. After a great war, slaves were freed in the United States.
   a. What was the name of that war?
   b. Name **two** states that had slaves before the war.
   c. Name **two** states that did not have slaves before the war.
2. a. What is the name of the narrator?
   b. In which state was he a slave?
   c. How old was he when he ran away?
   d. In what year did he run away?
   e. Just before he ran away, what job did he have on his master's plantation?
      - Hauling logs
      - Counting money
      - Feeding pigs
3. Jim Johnson heard about Moses.
   a. What was Moses's real name?
   b. The person who told about Moses was her _____.
   c. What was the signal that Moses was coming to the plantation?
   d. The day before Moses came, Jim was beaten for something that happened. What was that?
   e. If Jim ran away and got caught, what would happen?

PART F   Map Skills

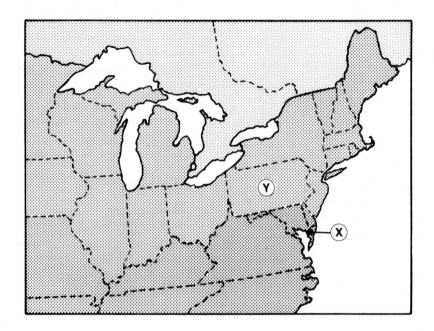

1. The **X** shows where Jim lived. In which state did he live?
2. Which state does the **Y** show?
3. Name one slave state on the map.
4. Name one free state on the map.
5. Which direction must Jim go to gain his freedom?

PART G   Combined Sentences

Below are two sentences. One introduces a new word; the other tells what the word means.

● *A quatrain always has four lines.*
● *A quatrain is a kind of poem.*

1. Combine the sentences so that the meaning comes right after the new word. Put commas before and after the meaning, and take out the word "is."
2. What is the new word in the combined sentence?
3. What does the new word mean?
4. What else does the sentence tell about the new word?

PART H   Inference

Read the passage below and answer each question. Write **Words** if the question is answered by words in the passage. Write **Deduction** if the question is answered by a deduction.

Omnivores

You have read about carnivores and herbivores, and how they are different. You know that herbivores eat plants, have eyes that look sideways, and have flat teeth. And you know that carnivores eat other animals, have eyes that look straight ahead, and have sharp, pointed teeth.

But what kind of animal is a person? A person has eyes that look straight ahead, so a person might be a carnivore. But a person's teeth are mostly flat, so a person might be a herbivore.

The answer is that a person is neither a carnivore nor a herbivore. A person eats both *plants and animals, and is called an* omnivore. *"Omni" is a word that means "all," so an "omnivore" is an animal that eats all kinds of things. Other omnivores include bears and pigs.*

1. **a.** What are herbivores like?
    b. Is that questions answered by **Words** or by a **Deduction?**
2. **a.** Rats eat both plants and other animals. So what kind of animals are rats?
    b. **Words** or **Deduction?**
3. **a.** What does the word "omni" mean?
    b. **Words** or **Deduction?**
4. **a.** What kind of teeth do carnivores have?
    b. **Words** or **Deduction?**
5. **a.** How are people like bears and pigs?
    b. **Words** or **Deduction?**

PART I   Review Items

You read a story about a strange star.
1. Which planet did the star destroy?
2. Which planet made the star change its course?
3. Which planet did the star narrowly miss?
4. What object did the strange star finally collide with?
5. What object saved the Earth?

PART J   Writing Assignment

Imagine that someone makes you a slave. Write a paragraph that describes how your life would be different. Tell what things you would no longer be able to do. Tell how you would feel.

Make your paragraph at least **six** sentences long.

Lesson 77

PART A Word Lists

1
ocelot
ocarina
limpkin

2
ricket
rickety
dull
dully

3
Vocabulary words
fit
licking
snicker

PART B New Vocabulary

1. **fit**—When somebody has a **fit,** that person loses consciousness and may writhe around.
   - What's a person having when that person loses consciousness and writhes around?*

2. **licking**—Tom was very angry with Joe. Tom said, "If you don't shut up, I'm going to stop talking and give you a **licking.**"
   - What could the words **give you a licking** mean?

3. **snicker**
   - Show me how you **snicker.**

PART C Vocabulary Review

1	2	3
ruts	invader	torrent
merge	grim	plantation

1. A wild flow is a _____.
2. Another word for **grooves** or **depressions** is _____.
3. Another word for a **large farm** is a _____.

PART D Story Items

1. The slaves ran away by going to different hiding places.
   a. What was the system of hiding places called?
   b. When would the slaves go from one hiding place to the next hiding place?
   c. What would the slaves do during the day?
   d. Guides led slaves from one hiding place to another. What were those guides called?

2. a. Where did Harriet and the slaves she was guiding spend their first night?
   b. What happened on the next night that frightened Jim?
   c. Jim pleaded with Harriet to let him do something. What did he want to do?
   d. How did Harriet respond to this plea?

3. The next night, Jim and the others came to a small town.
   a. Who did they expect to see in that town?
   b. Who did they see?
   c. The runaways ran quickly from that house because they knew that when the man woke up completely, he would realize something. What was that?
   d. After leaving town, Jim and the others came to a place that frightened Jim. What was that place?
   e. Suddenly, Harriet did something that was very unusual. What was that?

4. Henry explained that Harriet had received an injury.
   a. How old was she at the time?
   b. Who was she trying to protect?
   c. What happened to Harriet as she stood in the doorway?
   d. Did she ever fully recover from that injury?
   e. What would she sometimes do right in the middle of a conversation?
   f. Even with that injury was she a good worker?

5. When Harriet found out about a plan that her new master had, she decided to become a runaway slave.
   a. What plan was that?
   b. Who ran away with her?
   c. What did her brothers do after a while?

6. The system that helped runaway slaves was compared to a railroad.
   a. How was the system like a railroad?
   b. The system operated in secret, so it was called an _____ Railroad.

PART E   Combined Sentences

1. Below is a combined sentence that presents a new word and tells what that new word means. The new word is not underlined.
   - *Luigi played the ocarina, a small wind instrument.*
     a. What is the new word?
     b. What does the new word mean?
     c. What else does the sentence tell about the new word?

2. Below are two more sentences. One introduces a new word; the other tells what the word means.
   - *The coat of the ocelot is yellow with black spots.*
   - *The ocelot is a wild cat.*
     a. Combine the sentences so that the meaning comes right after the new word. Put commas before and after the meaning, and take out the word "is."

   b. What is the new word in the combined sentence?
   c. What does the new word mean?
   d. What else does the sentence tell about the new word?

PART F   Metaphors

Here's a metaphor: *The huge engine throbbed with power.*
1. So, the engine was like something that _____.
2. What could that something be?
3. Use accurate language to tell how the engine and a _____ could be the same.

PART G   Review Items

1. Name the war that broke out between the two parts of the United States.
2. In what year did that war begin?
   ● 1812   ● 1852   ● 1861   ● 1865
3. In what year did Jim Johnson run away?
   ● 1812   ● 1855   ● 1861   ● 1865

PART H   Writing Assignment

Do you think that Jim made the correct decision when he decided to escape? Write a paragraph that explains your answer.

Make your paragraph at least **six** sentences long.

Lesson 78

PART A Word List

wreathed
writhe
coral
corral

PART B Vocabulary Review

1	2	3
licking	grim	remnants
merge	vague	torrent

1. When things come together and form one thing, they _____.
2. Something that is very terrible is _____.
3. Another word for a **whipping** or **getting hit** is a _____.

PART C Story Items

1. When Harriet and the others got to Garret's shoe store, they learned that their trip would be longer than they had thought it would be.
   a. What was the name of the state they had first planned to go to?
   b. But a new law had been passed. Why did that law make it unsafe for the runaways in any state of the United States?
   c. Where did they have to go to be safe?

2. When the runaways got to Philadelphia, they met William Still.
   a. He told Jim and the others that Harriet had already delivered _____ people from the south.
   b. Still had a map that showed the journey they had to take to reach safety. How many miles did they have to go?
   c. How far had they gone already?
   d. What kind of transportation did they take from Philadelphia to Canada?

3. a. Who bought the tickets in the train station?
   b. When the man behind the counter _____, Jim knew that this man was a member of the Underground Railroad.
   c. How many times had Jim been in a train station before?

4. a. When the party was seated on the train, who noticed something that was alarming?
   b. What was it?
   c. Why didn't Harriet or Jim read what it said?
   d. According to the sign, how much was the reward?
   e. Whose capture was the reward for?

PART D   Map Skills

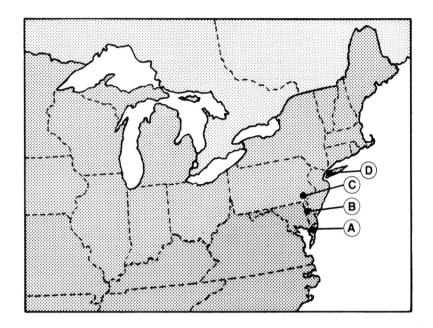

1. Dot **A** shows where Jim's home was. Which **state** was his home in?
2. Dot **B** shows where Jim spent the night above a shoe store. Which **state** was the shoe store in?
3. Dot **C** shows the city where Jim met William Still. Which **state** is that city in?
4. Dot **D** shows the city where Jim was going at the end of part 3. Which **state** is that city in?
5. Name one slave state on the map.
6. Name one free state on the map.

PART E   Combined Sentences

Below are two sentences. One introduces a new word; the other tells what the word means.

- *Plattsburgh has a population of about 25,000.*
- *Plattsburgh is a town in northeastern New York.*

1. Combine the sentences so that the meaning comes right after the new word. Put commas before and after the meaning, and take out the word "is."
2. What is the new word in the combined sentence?
3. What does the new word mean?
4. What else does the sentence tell about the new word?

PART F Similes

Make up a simile for each accurate statement. Use the word **like** in your similes.
1. *When he was on land, Frisco Kid did not know how to survive.*
   a. Name an animal that would have as much trouble surviving on the land as Frisco Kid.
   b. Make up a simile that tells what Frisco Kid was like on the land.
2. *The Earth became very hot as the blazing star approached.*
   a. Name something that could be as hot as the Earth.
   b. Make up a simile that tells what the Earth was like.

PART G Combined Sentences

The limpkin, a brown water bird, has a unique call.
1. What is the new word in this sentence?
2. What does the new word mean?
3. What else does the sentence tell about the new word?

PART H Review Items

Write which girl each statement describes. Choose from **Kate, Persephone, Sara Crewe,** or **Sylvia.**
1. This girl was taken to the underworld.
2. This girl saved the life of a bird.
3. This girl was the daughter of a goddess.
4. This girl found some clay.
5. This girl lived in an attic.

PART I Writing Assignment

Pretend you live in Maryland before the Civil War. You are grownup and you own a house. One day, someone asks to use your house for the Underground Railroad. What would you say? Write a paragraph that explains your answer.

Make your paragraph at least **six** sentences long.

Lesson 79

PART A Word List

visualize
Buffalo
visualizing
tumult

PART B Vocabulary Review

1	2
remnants	plantation
unheeded	ruts
torrent	scorn

1. Another word for **hate** is

   _____.

2. The pieces of something that remain after that thing no longer exists are the _____ of that thing.

3. When you don't pay attention to something and don't notice it, that thing is _____.

PART C Combined Sentences

Some sentences combine a main sentence and a part. The main sentence tells what is important. The part tells more about something in the main sentence. Here's an example: *The sun, red and pale, sank slowly in the west.*

Here's the main sentence: *The sun sank slowly in the west.*
Here's the part: *red and pale.*

- The part tells more about a word in the main sentence. What is that word?Ⓐ
- What does the part tell about the sun?Ⓑ

Here's how to combine a main sentence and a part that tells more about something in the main sentence. Start with the main sentence and leave a space for the part: **The sun _____ sank slowly in the west.** Then add the part that tells more about the sun: **The sun, red and pale, sank slowly in the west.**

Here's a main sentence and a part:
- *The sail was raised to the top of the mast.*
- *snarling in the wind*

- The part tells more about a word in the main sentence. What is that word?Ⓒ
- What does the part tell about the sail?Ⓓ
1. Write the combined sentence.Ⓔ

PART D   Story Items

1. At the beginning of part 4, two white men stopped near Jim and the others.
   a. What did the men read when they were in front of Jim and the others?
   b. What was Harriet pretending to do as the men paused in front of them?
   c. Why didn't the men recognize Harriet?
   d. Where did the train stop?
2. The next train that Jim and the others took left from New York City.
   a. In which country would it finally stop?
   b. On the way the train stopped at another city, where there was some trouble. What was the name of that city?
   c. Were most of the people in Jim's train car **black** or **white?**
   d. Just before the train was ready to leave the station, two people came through the train car. Who were they?
   e. Which person did not want to delay the train and search for runaways?
   f. Which person did the slave catcher identify as a runaway?
   g. Some of the white people at the other end of the train lied about Jim and the others in Harriet's party. What did they say?
3. a. What was the name of the falls that the train passed after leaving Buffalo?
   b. Jim was not interested in how beautiful the falls were. Why?
   c. What did Harriet say that cheered Jim greatly?
4. a. When the train crossed the middle of the bridge, Jim and the others were no longer in _____.
   b. They were now in _____.
   c. So, Jim was a _____ man.

PART E   Conversations

Here is a conversation between Connie and Jacob. Write which person makes each statement.

Connie answered the phone and said, "Hello."①

"Hello," said a shaking voice on the other end of the line. "Is this Connie? This is Jacob Drucker calling."②

"Oh," said the girl, with an icy tone in her voice. "And what do you want?"③ There was a long pause. "Well?" she asked.④

"Er, I was wondering, uh, if you, if you could go out tomorrow night."⑤

"You were, were you? Well, wonder no more. I'll go. See you then."⑥ And she hung up the receiver.

PART F   Review Items

Each of the following stories took place in or near a city. Name the city for each story. Choose from **London, Boston, New York City, San Francisco,** or **Mudville.**
1. *Mrs. Dunn's Lovely, Lovely Farm*
2. *The Cruise of the Dazzler*
3. *Casey at the Bat*
4. *Sara Crewe*
5. *The Last Leaf*

PART G   Writing Assignment

Write a paragraph that tells what might happen if Harriet stays in Canada, then tell what might happen if she leaves. Tell what you think she should do.

Make your paragraph at least **six** sentences long.

Lesson 80

PART A   Word List

bonnet
multitude
visage
grandeur

PART B   Vocabulary Review

1	2
overwhelms	scorn
straggle	heed
devastating	ruts

1. When you don't keep up with a group, you _____.
2. Something that destroys another thing completely is _____.
3. Something that overpowers you, _____ you.

PART C   Outlining

The passage below tells about two main things that happened. There is one main thing in each paragraph.Ⓐ

Just then, Joe was called to breakfast. Frisco Kid was as good a cook as he was a sailor. There were mush and condensed milk, beefsteak and fried potatoes, and all topped off with good French bread, butter, and coffee.

Pete did not join the boys, though Frisco Kid attempted to rouse him a couple of times. Pete mumbled and grunted, half opened his eyes, then started to snore again.

Make up an outline for the entire passage.
- Write the main idea for each paragraph.
- Under each main idea, write three supporting details.Ⓑ
- Use complete sentences to write the main idea and the supporting details.

PART D   Story Items

1. a. In which year does part 5 take place?
   b. What did Jim do for a living now?
   c. What country did he live in?
   d. Jim went to deliver a desk in _____, New York.
2. a. How much was the reward for Harriet at that time?
   b. Why did Harriet wait for warm weather to rescue her parents?
3. a. The lawyer who had ordered the desk wasn't in. Why was he at the sheriff's office?
   b. Jim saw Harriet Tubman as he was on his way back to the train station. Where was Harriet?
   c. At first, how much did Joe Nalle's master say he wanted for Joe's freedom?
   d. What did that master raise the price to?
4. a. When the sheriff ordered Harriet to clear the steps, what did she do?
   b. Who pushed Joe Nalle into the crowd?
   c. What did Harriet do to detain the sheriff?
   d. How did Harriet disguise Joe Nalle?
5. a. What kind of vehicle took Joe Nalle to the other side of the river?
   b. Jim and the others took a _____ to the other side.
   c. Which vehicle arrived at the other side first?
   d. Who grabbed Joe Nalle when he got out of the boat?
   e. When the ferry reached the other side, the mob went to the _____.
   f. Who drove Joe Nalle to a neighboring town?

PART E Combined Sentences

Here's a main sentence and a part:
- *The runner finally crossed the finish line.*
- *gasping for breath*
1. The part tells more about a word in the main sentence. What is that word?
2. Write the combined sentence.

PART F Writing Assignment

When the people freed Joseph Nalle, they broke the law. Do you think they were right to break the law? Write a paragraph that explains your answer. Try to think of other situations in which people might be right to break the law.

Make your paragraph at least **six** sentences long.

Lesson 81

PART A   Word Lists

1	2	3
Abraham Lincoln	face-first	**Vocabulary words**
Syracuse	crutches	regiment
Beaufort	realize	groggy
regiment	realization	agony
agony		reap
conscious		sensation
		raid
		surrender

PART B   New Vocabulary

1. **regiment**—A **regiment** is a large unit in the army.

2. **groggy**—When you are **groggy**, you are half-conscious or dopey.
   - What's another way of saying **He felt half-conscious after his fall?***

3. **agony**—**Agony** is **great pain**.
   - What's another way of saying **The wounded soldiers were in great pain?***

4. **reap**—When you cut down the ripe grain in a field, you **reap** the grain.
   - What do people do when they cut down the ripe grain in a field?***

5. **sensation**—Another word for a **feeling** is a **sensation**. A feeling of falling is a sensation of falling.
   - a. What is a feeling of fear?***
   - b. What is a strange feeling?***

6. **raid**—A **raid** is a sneak attack by a group.
   - What do we call a sneak attack by a regiment?***

7. **surrender**—When people **surrender**, they give up and stop fighting.
   - What's another way of saying **The army gave up?***

PART C   Story Items

1. a. What was the name of the woman that Jim married?
   b. What was the name of the war that broke out?
   c. In what year did that war begin?
      - 1812   • 1852   • 1861
      - 1865

2. Jim joined the army.
   a. Who persuaded him to do that?
   b. What state did Jim's regiment go to?
   c. When Jim arrived at that place, he heard many stories about
      _____.
   d. One story told how that person tricked the slaves into letting go of rowboats. How did she do that?

3. The next day, the regiment attacked Fort Wagner.
   a. What happened to Jim when he reached the beach?
   b. Who did Jim see again while he was in the hospital?
   c. How successful had Jim's regiment been in the attack on Fort Wagner?
   d. How many of the soldiers in Jim's regiment had been killed?
   e. At the end of the lesson, Jim experienced a deadly sick feeling as he looked to where Harriet was pointing. Why did he experience that feeling?

PART D   Combined Sentences

Here's a main sentence and a part:

- *The students began their summer vacation.*
- *jumping for joy*

1. The part tells more about a word in the main sentence. What is that word?
2. Write the combined sentence.

PART E   Outlining

Make up an outline for the following passage.
- Write a main idea for each stanza.
- Write three supporting details under each main idea.
- Use complete sentences.

There was ease in Casey's manner as
  he stepped into his place,
There was pride in Casey's bearing and a
  smile on Casey's face;
And when responding to the cheers he
  lightly doffed his hat,
No stranger in the crowd could doubt
  'twas Casey at the bat.

Ten thousand eyes were on him as he
  rubbed his hands with dirt,
Five thousand tongues applauded when
  he wiped them on his shirt;
Then when the writhing pitcher ground
  the ball into his hip,
Defiance glanced in Casey's eye, a sneer
  curled Casey's lip.

PART F   Vocabulary Items

Use the words in the box to fill in the blanks.

scholar	straggled
comet	devastating
overwhelm	grim

1. The wounded wolf _____ behind the rest of the pack.
2. Nobody laughed at her _____ joke.
3. The news that her cat had died was _____ to Sylvia.

PART G   Writing Assignment

Harriet Tubman used figurative language to describe the battle. She said that it was "like a storm over a field of corn." Then she explained her simile in detail.

Make up a simile that tells how you feel about war. Then write a paragraph that explains your simile.

Make your paragraph at least **four** sentences long.

Lesson 82

PART A   Word Lists

1
Confederate
deception
Auburn
debt
artificial
testify
sweetener

2
Vocabulary words
in debt
staggering numbers
artificial
deception
Confederate
hobble
testify

PART B   New Vocabulary

1. **in debt**—When somebody is **in debt**, that person owes money. If John owes money, John is in debt.
   - What if Mary owes money?

2. **staggering numbers**—**Staggering numbers** are numbers so great they make you stagger or they daze you. Here's another way of saying **an unbelievable number of cars on the freeway: a staggering number of cars on the freeway.**
   - What's another way of saying **That is an unbelievable number of wounded soldiers?***

3. **artificial**—Something that is not natural and that is made by people is **artificial.** A leg made by people is an **artificial** leg.
   a. What is a sweetener made by people?*
   b. What is a flower made by people?*

4. **deception**—When you deceive somebody, you are using **deception.**
   - What are you doing when you deceive somebody?

5. **Confederate**—The army of the South during the Civil War was called the **Confederate** Army.
   - What was the army of the South called?*

6. **hobble**—People who walk with a bad limp **hobble.**
   - What is a person doing when that person walks with a bad limp?*

7. **testify**—When you **testify,** you tell the truth about something you have observed. When you tell the truth about an accident you observed, you **testify** about the accident.
   - What do you do when you tell the truth about a robbery you observed?*

PART C   Vocabulary Review

1	2	3
agony	straggle	overwhelm
sensation	scorn	reap
drawn	unheeded	groggy

1. When you cut down the ripe grain in a field, you _____ the grain.
2. Great pain is _____.
3. When you are half-conscious or dopey, you are _____.
4. Another word for a **feeling** is a _____.
5. When a face has a strained expression, it is _____.
6. Another word for **hate** is _____.

PART D   Story Items

1. **a.** How much did Jim work during the first winter after he returned to New York?
   b. How frequently did Jim leave his house?
   c. What did Harriet drop off at Jim's place one evening?
   d. When Jim told Harriet that he couldn't work anymore, she said, "Cabinet makers work with their _____, not with their _____.
   e. Who were the shelves for?
   f. When Jim delivered the shelves, he discovered that Harriet had tricked him. What did he observe in Harriet's parents' house that made him realize he had been tricked?

2. **a.** Name at least **three** different jobs that Harriet held for the North during the Civil War.
   b. In what year did the war end?
      ● 1812   ● 1852   ● 1861   ● 1865
   c. On her last mission, Harriet worked as a _____.
   d. How much did the government pay Harriet for her services?
   e. How did Sarah Bradford raise money for Harriet?

3. In 1867, Harriet got married.
   a. How many years did that marriage last?
   b. Harriet received something from the government because she was Nelson's wife. What did she receive?

4. **a.** In what year did Harriet Tubman die?
   b. How old was Harriet when she died?
   c. Jim expressed his ideas about Harriet's life: Although she was born a _____, to him she lived like a _____ all her life.

PART E   Outlining

Make up an outline for the following passage.

● Write a main idea for each paragraph.
● Write three supporting details under each main idea.
● Use complete sentences to write the main idea and the supporting details.

It was the first day of the new year. On that day, an observatory announced that the motion of the planet Pluto had changed. Later that day, astronomers discovered a faint speck of light near Pluto. The speck of light was rapidly growing larger and brighter, and its motion was quite different from Pluto's.

The sun and its planets swim in a vacant space that almost overwhelms the imagination. Beyond Pluto there is space, vacant space, without warmth or light or sound. There is nothing but blank emptiness for twenty million times a million miles. Few people realize how remote our solar system is.

PART F   Writing Assignment

Write a paragraph that compares Jim and Harriet. Describe how they were alike, and how they were different.

Make your paragraph at least **six** sentences long.

Lesson 83

PART A   Word Lists

1
inflection
dumbfounded
majority
unanimously
initials

2
Vocabulary words
a rising inflection
at rise
beforehand
majority
unanimous
dumbfounded
initials

PART B   New Vocabulary

1. **rising inflection**—Say this sentence with a **rising inflection**:
   - Can you believe that?

2. **at rise**—**At rise** is an instruction in a play. It means: This is what you see when the curtain goes up.

3. **beforehand**—Something that happens **beforehand** happens before something else happens.

4. **majority**—The **majority** of a group is more than half the group. Let's say there are ten people in a group.
   a. What's the smallest number that would be standing up if a majority was standing up?*
   b. If six were standing, we would say: A majority is standing. What would we say?*

5. **unanimous**—If all members of a group vote the same way, the vote is **unanimous.**
   - What do we call the vote if all members vote the same way?

6. **dumbfounded**—When you are **dumbfounded**, you are stunned and you don't know what to say.
   - What's another way of saying **She was stunned by his rude remark?***

7. **initials**—Your **initials** are the first letters of your full name.

PART C   Vocabulary Review

1	2
Confederate	sensation
testify	deception
groggy	artificial
hobble	reap

1. When you deceive somebody, you are using _____.
2. People who walk with a bad limp _____.
3. When you tell the truth about something you observed, you _____.
4. Something that is not natural and that is made by people is _____.
5. The army of the South during the Civil War was called the _____ Army.

PART D   Story Items

1. At the beginning of the play, was Nancy already a member of the club?
2. How many kids were in the club?
3. How many votes did Nancy need to be elected into the club?
4. Why did Nancy say that Eddie could not become a member of the club?
5. Who came out of the clubhouse?
6. What news did that person give Nancy about the election?

PART E Map Skills

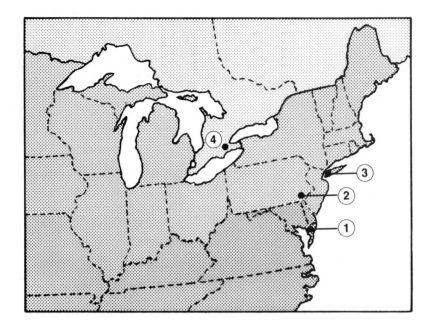

1. Which state is dot **1** in?
2. Which state is dot **2** in?
3. Which state is dot **3** in?
4. Which country is dot **4** in?

PART F Outlining

Make up an outline for the following passage.

- Write a main idea for each paragraph.
- Write three supporting details.
- Use complete sentences to write the main idea and the supporting details.

In a million towers and steeples, bells began to toll that night, summoning the people to gather in churches. And overhead, the oncoming star grew larger and brighter. The streets and houses were lit in all the cities, and the roads were lit and crowded all night long. And in all the seas, ships crowded with people were sailing north.

But not all of the world was in a terror because of the star. As a matter of fact, the old habits still ruled the world. In all the cities the stores opened and closed at their proper hours, the doctors and the lawyers worked as usual, and the workers gathered in the factories.

PART G   Combined Sentences

1. Below are two sentences. One introduces a new word; the other tells what the word means.

- *The fruit of the kapok produces a silky fiber.*
- *The kapok is a tree that grows in Malaysia.*

   a. Combine the sentences so that the meaning comes right after the new word. Put commas before and after the meaning, and take out the word "is."
   b. What is the new word in the combined sentence?
   c. What does the new word mean?
   d. What else does the sentence tell about the new word?

2. Below are two more sentences:

- *The man injured his patella.*
- *The patella is a bone in the knee.*

   a. Combine the sentences so that the meaning comes right after the new word. Put commas before and after the meaning, and take out the word "is."
   b. What is the new word in the combined sentence?
   c. What does the new word mean?
   d. What else does the sentence tell about the new word?

PART H   Writing Assignment

Before the play began, Nancy must have talked to Sidney about the club. Write a conversation between Nancy and Sidney.

Have each character say at least **three** sentences.

Lesson 84

PART A   Word Lists

1
astound
sulkily
treasurer
gavel
succinct

2
pronounce
hasty
hastily
pronouncing

3
Vocabulary words
one vote shy
make an exception
sulkily
dryly
astound
gavel

PART B   New Vocabulary

1. **one vote shy**—If a vote is **one vote shy**, it needs one more vote for the group to make a decision. Let's say that there are ten people in a group. The group will do something if a majority of the members vote for it.
   a. How many votes would be needed for a majority?
   b. How many would vote for it if the vote turns out to be one vote shy?*

2. **make an exception**—When you **make an exception**, you break the rules for a special case.
   ● What's another way of saying **The teacher broke the rules in Henry's case?***

3. **sulkily**—When you behave **sulkily**, you sulk or pout.
   ● Show me how you look when you're acting sulkily.

4. **dryly**—When you speak **dryly**, you speak without enthusiasm.
   ● What's another way of saying **She congratulated the winner without enthusiasm?***

5. **astound**—Another word for **amaze** is **astound**.
   a. What's another way of saying **Her performance amazed me?***
   b. What's another way of saying **The sunset was amazing?***

6. **gavel**—A **gavel** is a wooden hammer that the person in charge of important meetings pounds to quiet the group. The judge in a court uses a gavel.

PART C   Vocabulary Review

1	2
unanimous	reap
agony	majority
groggy	dumbfounded
rising inflection	sensation

1. More than half of a group is the _____ of the group.
2. A rising tone of voice is a _____ .
3. If all members of a group vote the same way, the vote is _____ .
4. When you are stunned and don't know what to say, you are _____ .
5. When you cut down the ripe grain in a field, you _____ the grain.

PART D   Story Items

1. Today's part of the play starts with the speech that Sidney made at the end of the last part.
   a. How many votes did Nancy receive?
   b. How many did Nancy need to be elected to the club?

PART D   Story Items

Below are some statements from stories you have read. Write which story each statement comes from.

1. "The sun and its planets swim in a vacant space that almost overwhelms the imagination."
2. "The rings of batter kept right on dropping into the hot fat, and an automatic gadget kept right on turning them over."
3. "The wave threatened to crush the tiny sloop like an eggshell."
4. "A white spot of the bird like a single floating feather came up from the dead hemlock and grew larger."
5. "But in summer I go back to the mesa where my grandmother lives."
6. "Any landlord who would offer me the use of his roof for a fine little garden must be a very likable man."
7. "Sometimes, when her husband was at the office, she sat down near the window, and thought of that gay evening of long ago."

PART E   Inference

Read the passage and answer each question. Write **Words** if the question is answered by words in the passage. Write **Deduction** if the question is answered by a deduction.

Organisms

Each living thing is called an organism. Some organisms, such as a giraffe or a rose bush, are very complicated. Other organisms are very small and simple. Some are so small that we cannot see them without using a microscope.

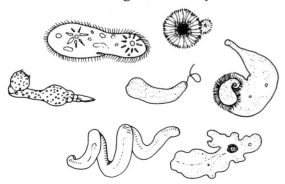

Millions of small organisms live in water. The picture shows what you might see if you looked at a drop of water through a microscope. You might see some organisms that have hairs and move like worms. Others might be shaped like spirals or flat, little circles.

These organisms are quite important to people, because many of them also live in our bodies. Some of them help us digest our food. But others can cause serious diseases, such as malaria and sleeping sickness.

1. **a.** How many small organisms live in water?
   b. Is that question answered by **Words** or by a **Deduction**?
2. **a.** Is an elephant a **complicated organism** or a **simple organism**?
   b. **Words** or **Deduction**?
3. **a.** What device do you use to see small organisms?
   b. **Words** or **Deduction**?
4. **a.** Do you need organisms to help you digest fruit?
   b. **Words** or **Deduction**?
5. **a.** Name two diseases that organisms can give you.
   b. **Words** or **Deduction**?

PART F   Writing Assignment

The poem *Miracles* describes things that the poet sees every day. Make up a poem that describes what you see every day. Tell how you feel about those things.

Make your poem at least **seven** lines long. Your lines do not have to rhyme.

Lesson 87

PART A   Word Lists

1
Tom Sawyer
Saint Petersburg
Huckleberry Finn
Saint Louis

2
Palermo
Albania
Sarajevo
Naples
syrup
Hannibal
Mississippi

3
Vocabulary words
corridor
landing
tradition

PART B   New Vocabulary

1. **corridor**—Another word for **hallway** is **corridor**.
   - What's another way of saying **She stood in the hallway?***
2. **landing**—A **landing** is a platform between two flights of stairs.

3. **tradition**—A **tradition** is a particular way of doing things that has been followed for a long time. The marriage ceremony is a tradition. The way people behave in church is a tradition. The way people behave in court is a tradition.

PART C   Vocabulary Review

1	2
majority	astound
unanimous	dryly
make an exception	sulkily

1. Another word for **amaze** is _____.
2. When you break the rules for a special case, you _____.
3. When you sulk or pout, you behave _____.

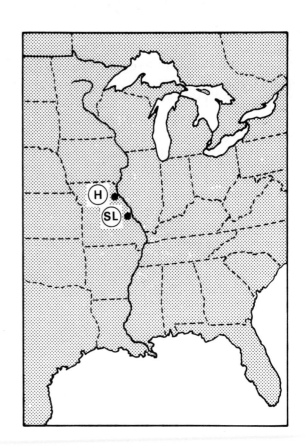

PART D   Story Items

1. **a.** What's the title of the next novel you will read?
   b. Who is the author of the novel?
   c. When does the novel take place?
2. The map shows where the novel takes place.
   a. What's the name of town H?
   b. What's the name of city SL?
   c. Which river does the map show?

For the remaining questions, pretend you live in Hannibal in the 1840's.

3. a. What type of power is not hooked up to your house?
   b. Because your house doesn't have this power, it is missing many things found in a modern home. Name at least five of these things.
   c. Why is your room cold in the morning?
   d. Why doesn't your house have a bathroom inside?
4. a. Which room is really the main room of the house?
   b. Which piece of furniture holds the plates and the silverware?
   c. Why doesn't anybody say anything during breakfast?
5. a. Explain how the water storage tank will work.
   b. Why do you have to walk to school?

PART E   Reference Skills

Which reference book would you use to find each of the following pieces of information?

1. Who won the 1937 World Series.
2. How many books Nathaniel Hawthorne wrote.
3. How many rivers are in the state of Maine.
4. How many definitions *for* has.
5. How to make pottery.

PART F   Review Items

Tell which story took place in each location. Choose from *All in Favor, The Cruise of the Dazzler, Sara Crewe, A White Heron, Harriet Tubman, Persephone, The Last Leaf, Casey at the Bat,* or *The Necklace.*

1. London, England
2. The underworld
3. San Francisco Bay
4. Mudville
5. Maryland
6. Greenwich Village

PART G   Writing Assignment

Write a paragraph that compares an 1840's breakfast with a modern breakfast. Tell what kinds of food people have for each type of breakfast. Also explain which type of breakfast you would rather eat and why.

Make your paragraph at least **six** sentences long.

Lesson 88

PART A Word Lists

1
irony
geography
unmistakable
Minneapolis
New Orleans
Memphis
Mississippi

2
Vocabulary words
rigid
ambush
legend

PART B New Vocabulary

1. **rigid**—Something that is **rigid** is **stiff.**
   - What's another way of saying **His arm was stiff?***
2. **ambush**—When you **ambush** people, you attack them from a hiding place. Here's another way of saying **The Confederate soldiers attacked the Union soldiers from a hiding place: The Confederate soldiers ambushed the Union soldiers.**
   - What's another way of saying **The cat attacked the dog from a hiding place?***
3. **legend**—A **legend** is a story that is passed from one generation to the next.
   - What do we call a story that is passed from one generation to the next?*

PART C Vocabulary Review

1	2
corridor	agony
tradition	reap
testify	landing

1. Another word for **hallway** is _____.
2. A platform between two flights of stairs is a _____.
3. A particular way of doing things that has been followed for a long time is a _____.

PART D Irony

Here's how irony works:
- A character believes something.
- The character does things that are based on the belief.
- Later, the character finds out that the belief was mistaken.

Here's an example of irony from *The Necklace:*
1. Matilda had a mistaken belief about the necklace. What was that?Ⓐ
2. Matilda did something that was based on that belief. What did she do?Ⓑ
3. What would she have done if she had known the truth about the necklace?Ⓒ

PART E   Story Items

1. a. What vehicles and animals used the streets of Hannibal?
   b. Describe the condition of the streets in Hannibal.
2. Why was the river so important to Hannibal?
3. a. How many rooms did the school have?
   b. How many teachers did the school have?
   c. How old were most students when they left school?
   d. What did the students sit on?
   e. Describe how the students were arranged.
   f. Why did the teacher keep a pile of birch rods?
4. The *McGuffey's Reader* contains a poem.
   a. Which country is the poem about?
   b. "Land of liberty" means land of _____.

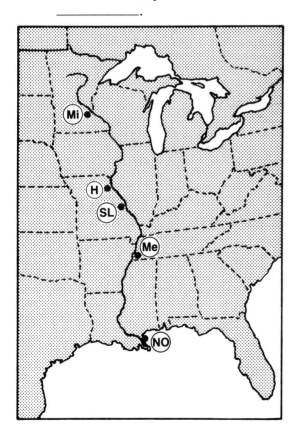

5. a. Which river does the map show?
   b. In which direction does the river flow?
   c. What is the name of the city at the northern end of the river?
   d. What is the name of the city at the southern end of the river?
   e. Name some of the goods that steamboats picked up along the river.
6. a. How were most things transported to and from Hannibal in the 1840's?
   b. What new form of transportation was being used in the eastern states in the 1840's?
   c. What was a big advantage of the newer form of transportation?

PART F   Exaggeration

The dog scooped out a vast crater in which to bury its bone.

1. How big does the statement say the hole was?
2. Write an accurate statement that tells how big the hole was.

PART G   Sarcasm

*"I really like this novel, **One Hundred Years of Boredom.** It is painfully long and dull. The characters in it are as lively as dead fish. The writing is ridiculous, and the plot is absurd. Because it is so big and heavy, the book makes a convenient paperweight."*

1. The writer says something that she later contradicts. What is that?
2. Name **two** pieces of evidence that contradict the writer's statement.

PART H   Writing Assignment

How were schools in the 1840's different from modern schools? Review what you have learned about schools in the 1840's, and then write a paragraph that describes at least five differences.

Make your paragraph at least **six** sentences long.

Lesson 89

PART A Word Lists

1
paddlewheel
biscuit
bushel

2
Vocabulary words
dwindle
stifles
bulky
plush
settlers

PART B New Vocabulary

1. **dwindle** — Something that **dwindles** becomes smaller and smaller.
   a. What's another way of saying **The image became smaller and smaller?***
   b. What's another way of saying **The noises became softer and softer?***
2. **stifles** — When something suppresses you, it **stifles** you. Here's another way of saying **Her embrace suppressed him: Her embrace stifled him.**
   - What's another way of saying **The foul air suppressed us?***
3. **bulky** — Something that is **bulky** is large and heavy.
   a. What is furniture that is large and heavy?*
   b. What is a package that is large and heavy?*
4. **plush** — Something that is very showy and expensive is **plush**.
   a. What's another way of saying **There was a showy, expensive carpet in the room?***
   b. What's another way of saying **He worked in a showy, expensive office?***
5. **settlers** — **Settlers** are people who come to live in a new area. The people who came to live in America were **settlers**.

PART C Vocabulary Review

1	2
corridor	rigid
tradition	legend
ambush	landing

1. Something that is stiff is _____.
2. When you attack someone from a hiding place, you _____ that person.
3. A story that is passed from one generation to the next is a _____.

PART D Irony

Here's how irony works.
- A character believes something.
- The character does things that are based on the belief.
- Later, the character finds out that the belief was mistaken.

Here's an example of irony from *Persephone:*
1. When she examined the pomegranate, Persephone had a mistaken belief about how long Hades was going to keep her. What was that?Ⓐ
2. Persephone did something that was based on the belief. What did she do?Ⓑ
3. What would Persephone have done if she had known the truth about how much longer Hades would keep her?Ⓒ

PART E Story Items

1. a. On a steamboat, what are the steam engines connected to?
   b. What does the steamboat do when the paddlewheels turn?
   c. Why are steamboat hulls better than sailboat hulls for river travel?
   d. What other advantage do steamboats have over sailboats for river travel?

2. Many types of passengers got off the steamboat.
   a. Which type was carrying tin boxes?
   b. Which type looked a little lost?
   c. Which types carried important papers?
   d. Which types had confident looks?
   e. Which type carried banjo and fiddle cases?
3. a. Name at least three acts from the circus.
   b. Do you think the mermaid act is real or fake? Why?
4. a. Name at least five types of goods that were unloaded from the steamboat.
   b. Name at least three types of goods that were loaded onto the steamboat.

PART F Map Skills

Look at the map below. Cities in *light type* have less than 100,000 people. Cities in medium type have between 100,000 and 500,000 people. Cities in **heavy type** have more than 500,000 people.

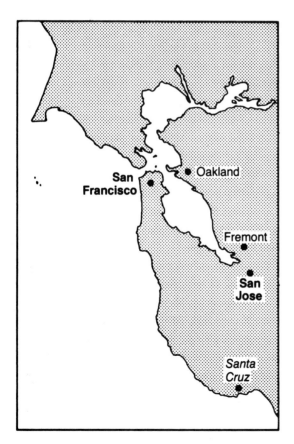

1. Which city is directly west of Oakland?
2. What is the shortest way to go from Santa Cruz to San Jose, by land or by water?
3. Is it possible to go from San Francisco to Oakland without crossing over any water?
4. Which city has more people, Fremont or San Jose?
5. The map shows where one of the stories you read took place. Which story?

PART G Reference Skills

Here's a fact: *Ocean water is bad for most crops.*
1. What kind of reference book would you use to support the fact?
● Read the passage below and find out why ocean water is bad for most crops.

Ocean water contains the kind of salt that is found in salt shakers. It also contains other types of salts. Ocean water cannot be used to water most crops because the salt in the water kills the crops. Corn, wheat, tomatoes, and other garden plants would die if they were watered with ocean water. Ocean water doesn't kill all crops, however. Certain kinds of barley will continue to grow if watered with ocean water.

2. Why is ocean water bad for most crops?

PART H Writing Assignment

You have read about many different kinds of boats: Odysseus's rowboat and raft; the schooner *The Northern Light;* the sloop *The Dazzler;* and the Mississippi River steamboat. Which boat would you most like to take a trip on? Write a paragraph that explains your answer.

Make your paragraph at least **six** sentences long.

Lesson 90

PART A   Word Lists

1	2
sensational	**Vocabulary words**
bilious	conquer
dropsy	supernatural
cholera	candlewick
malaria	systematically
	endure
	junction

PART B   New Vocabulary

1. **conquer**—When you **conquer** something, you are victorious over that thing. Here's another way of saying **She was victorious over her illness: She conquered her illness.**
   - What's another way of saying **The army was victorious over the fort?***
2. **supernatural**—An event is **supernatural** if that event seems magical and cannot be explained by science.
   - Name an event that would be **supernatural.**

3. **candlewick**—A **candlewick** is the string you light that runs through the middle of a candle.
4. **systematically**—Something that is done **systematically** is done in an organized way. If we clean a room in an organized way, we clean the room **systematically.**
   - What do you do when you examine a house in an organized way?
5. **endure**—Something that **endures** lives on or continues.
   a. What's another way of saying **The legend lived on?***
   b. What's another way of saying **Their ideas did not live on?***
6. **junction**—A **junction** is the place where two or more things join.
   a. What do we call a place where three roads join?*
   b. What do we call a place where two rivers join?*

PART C   Vocabulary Review

1	2
settlers	rigid
stifles	plush
dwindles	ambush
bulky	legend

1. Something that is very showy and expensive is _____ .
2. Something that gets smaller and smaller _____ .
3. When something suppresses you, it _____ you.
4. Something that is large and heavy is _____ .

PART D   Irony

Here's how irony works:
- A character believes something.
- The character does things that are based on the belief.
- Later, the character finds out that the belief was mistaken.

Here's an example of irony from *The Last Leaf:*
1. Joan had a mistaken belief about the painted leaf that she saw through her window. What was that?**Ⓐ**
2. Joan did something that was based on the belief. What did she do?**Ⓑ**
3. What would Joan have done if she had known the truth about the leaf?**Ⓒ**

PART E   Story Items

1. **a.** In the article, what was the family's main activity after dinner?
   b. What would a modern family's main after-dinner activity probably be?
2. **a.** Do you think it's a good idea to believe everything you read in the 1840's Hannibal newspaper? Why or why not?
   b. Do you think that *Old Sachem Bitters Wigwam Tonic* would make you as strong as an Indian chief? Why or why not?
3. **a.** Name three bad diseases that were common in the 1840's.
   b. Which disease was the worst?
   c. Why might doctors have been forced to rob graves in the 1840's?
4. **a.** How did some people believe they could guard themselves against malaria?
   b. What did some people think you could do with wood from a tree that had been struck by lightning?
5. Why were houses so quiet in the evening in the 1840's?

PART F   Map Skills

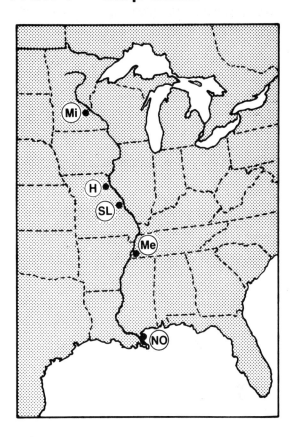

1. Which river does the map show?
2. What is the name of city **Mi?**
3. What is the name of city **SL?**
4. What is the name of city **Me?**
5. What is the name of city **NO?**
6. What is the name of town **H?**
7. What is that town called in the novel *Tom Sawyer?*
8. In which direction does the river flow?

PART G   Writing Assignment

Would you like to have lived in Hannibal in the 1840's? Write a paragraph that explains your answer. Use evidence from the article. Tell which parts of 1840's life you like, and which parts you don't like.

Make your paragraph at least **six** sentences long.

Lesson 91

PART A   Word Lists

1	**2**	**3**
conscience	newcomer	**Vocabulary words**
sidling	holiday	perplexed
vicious	Albania	conscience
	shabby	smug
	shabbier	smothered
	Palermo	traitor
	antelope	vicious
	smug	sidle
	smudge	

PART B   New Vocabulary

1. **perplexed**—When you are **perplexed**, you are puzzled.
   a. What's another way of saying **She had a puzzled expression?***
   b. What's another way of saying **The problem continued to puzzle him?***

2. **conscience**—Your **conscience** is the voice inside you that scolds you when you do something you shouldn't do.
   - What do we call the voice inside us that scolds us when we do something we shouldn't do?*

3. **smug**—When you feel **smug**, you feel very, very satisfied with yourself.
   a. What's another way of saying **She wore a very self-satisfied smile?***
   b. What's another way of saying **Nobody could stand Eric's self-satisfied attitude?***

4. **smothered**—When something is **smothered**, it is choked off or cut off from the air.
   a. What's another way of saying **The foam cut off the air from the fire?***
   b. What's another way of saying **His voice was choked off?***

5. **traitor**—A **traitor** is someone who is supposed to be on your side but who betrays you.
   - What do we call somebody who is supposed to be on your side but who betrays you?*

6. **vicious**—Something that is very cruel or evil is **vicious**.
   - What's another way of saying **The captain was cruel?***

7. **sidle**—When you **sidle** up to somebody, you approach that person by moving sideways.
   - What are you doing when you approach somebody by moving sideways?*

PART C   Vocabulary Review

1	2
systematically	stifles
supernatural	bulky
candlewick	conquer
junction	endures

1. When you are victorious over something, you _____ that thing.
2. Something that is done in an organized way is done _____.
3. Something that lives on or continues _____.
4. An event that seems magical and cannot be explained by science is _____.

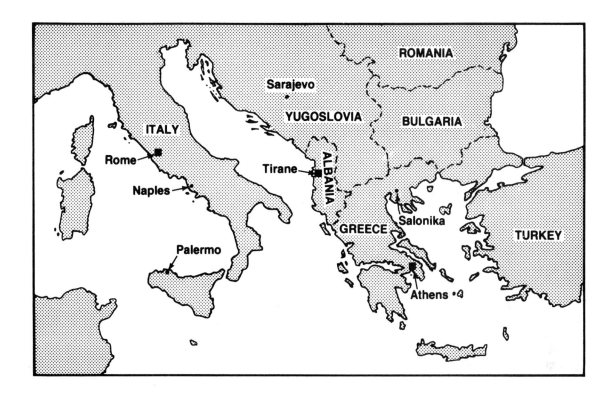

Look at the map above. The dots show large cities. The squares show towns that are capitals of countries.

Assume that the map is accurate. Examine the map carefully, and then read the statements below. Some of the statements contradict what is shown on the map.

1. Here's a statement: *Tirane is the capital of Albania.* Does that statement contradict what the map shows?Ⓐ

2. Here's a statement: *Athens is farther west than Rome.* Does that statement contradict what the map shows?

3. Here's a statement: *The shortest distance from Naples to Palermo is by land.* Does that statement contradict what the map shows?Ⓒ

● Write **yes** or **no** for items 1 through 3.

PART E   Story Items

1. a. What did Aunt Polly wear that was not very useful?
    b. What season was it in this chapter?
    c. Where was Tom hiding at the beginning of this chapter?
2. There were some clues about what Tom had been doing before Aunt Polly caught him.
    a. What were the clues?
    b. What had Tom been doing?
    c. How did Tom trick Aunt Polly and get through the open door?
3. a. Did Aunt Polly like to punish Tom?
    b. Did Aunt Polly's conscience bother her?
4. Tom met a stranger.
    a. What **two** things amazed Tom about the way that person was dressed?
    b. What kind of shoes did Tom wear?
    c. Tom lied to the stranger about something that he had. What was that?
    d. The other boy lied also. What did he claim to have?
    e. What did Tom and the stranger finally do?
5. a. When Tom went home, what time was it?
    b. How did Tom get into his bedroom?
    c. What ambush was waiting for Tom?
    d. What distressed Aunt Polly when she saw Tom?
    e. What condition were Tom's clothes in?
6. Aunt Polly resolved to make Tom do something the next day.
    a. What was that?
    b. What day of the week was the next day?

PART F   Irony

Below is an example of irony from *The Voyage of the Northern Light*.
1. The narrator had a mistaken belief about Jake's knife. What was that?
2. The narrator did something that was based on the belief. What did she do?
3. What would the narrator have done if she had known the truth about the knife?

PART G   Writing Assignment

Aunt Polly has complicated feelings about Tom. Pretend you are Aunt Polly. Write a paragraph that tells what you think when you ambush Tom crawling through the window.

Make your paragraph at least **six** sentences long.

Lesson 92

PART A Word Lists

1
philosopher
resume
contemplate
casual

2
whitewash
inspiration
melancholy
locust
alongside

3
Vocabulary words
brimming with
waver
tranquil
resume
suits
absorbed
fragment
philosopher

PART B New Vocabulary

1. **brimming with**—**brimming with** means **filled with**.
   - What's another way of saying **The pond was filled with fish?***

2. **waver**—When people **waver**, they begin to lose their determination.
   a. What's another way of saying **He wanted to climb the mountain, but now he began to lose his determination?***
   b. What's another way of saying **Jane's smug smile faded as she began to lose her determination?***

3. **tranquil**—Something that is **tranquil** is very calm.
   a. What's another way of saying **His mood was very calm?***
   b. What's another way of saying **The lake was very calm?***

4. **resume**—When you **resume** doing something, you start to do it again.
   a. What's another way of saying **He started working on his homework again.***
   b. What's another way of saying **Will you please start cleaning your room again?***

5. **suits**—If something **suits** you, you like it. Here's another way of saying **I like melons: Melons suit me.**

6. **absorbed**—When you are deeply involved in doing something, you are **absorbed** in that activity.
   a. What's another way of saying **She was deeply involved in her thoughts?***
   b. What's another way of saying **They were deeply involved in working the puzzle?***

7. **fragment**—A small piece is a **fragment**.
   a. What's another way of saying **a small piece of chalk?***
   b. What's another way of saying **a small piece of a plan?***

8. **philosopher**—A **philosopher** is someone who thinks about things and tries to explain them.
   - What do we call someone who thinks about things and tries to explain them?*

PART C   Vocabulary Review

1	2	3
traitor	smug	stifle
perplexed	smothered	legends
conscience	bulky	vicious

1. When you are puzzled, you are
   _____.
2. Someone who is supposed to be on
   your side but who betrays you is a
   _____.
3. When something is choked off or cut
   off from the air, it is _____.
4. When you feel very, very satisfied
   with yourself, you feel _____.
5. Something that is very cruel or evil is
   _____.
6. The voice inside you that scolds you
   when you do something you shouldn't
   do is your _____.

PART D   Graph Skills

To read a graph, you use the numbers
along the side of the graph and the
numbers along the bottom of the graph.

On the graph below, the numbers along
the side tell how many apples were
picked during a year.Ⓐ

The numbers along the bottom name the
years from 1975 through 1985.Ⓑ

1. Touch **R**.Ⓒ
   a. To find out the year, you go
      straight down from **R**. What year
      is on the same line as **R**?Ⓓ
   b. To find out how many apples were
      picked during that year, you go
      across from **R** to the apple
      numbers. What number is on the
      same line as **R**?Ⓔ
2. Touch **M**.Ⓕ
   a. Which year does **M** tell about?Ⓖ
   b. How many apples were picked in
      that year?Ⓗ
3. Touch **J**.Ⓘ
   a. Which year does **J** tell about?Ⓙ
   b. How many apples were picked in
      that year?Ⓚ

APPLE PRODUCTION AT THE EDEN APPLE ORCHARDS

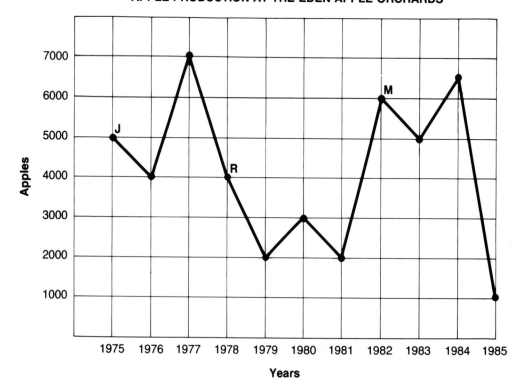

PART E   Story Items

1. a. What chore did Aunt Polly give to Tom?
   b. What day of the week was it?
   c. After Tom did a little work, he compared the amount that he had done with the amount he still had to do. Which amount was much greater?
   d. How did Tom feel when he realized that?
2. a. Who came out with a tin pail?
   b. What was the character going to do with the pail?
   c. Which chore did Tom prefer, working on the fence or the other chore?
   d. Why?
3. Tom offered to do two things for Sid.
   a. What object would he give Sid?
   b. What would he show to Sid?
4. a. Who ruined Tom's plan?
   b. After that person left, who got the water?
   c. Who worked on the fence?
5. Tom had an inspiration.
   a. Who was the first boy to come by after he had that inspiration?
   b. How did Tom actually feel about his chore?
   c. How did Tom pretend to feel about his chore?
   d. Name two things that Tom did when he pretended to feel that way.
   e. What did Ben finally offer Tom if Tom would let him do part of the chore?
6. a. How many coats of whitewash did the fence have by the middle of the afternoon?
   b. Who had an enjoyable time that day?
   c. Name **two** reasons why that person found the day enjoyable.
7. Tom learned a rule about human nature.
   a. According to that rule, how do you make somebody want something?
   b. What did Tom do to make the job of whitewashing difficult for the boys to get?

PART F   Irony

Below is an example of irony from *The Cruise of the Dazzler*.
1. At the beginning of the novel, Joe had a mistaken belief about what kind of person Pete was. What was that?
2. Joe did something that was based on the belief. What did he do?
3. What would Joe have done if he had known the truth about Pete?

PART G   Writing Assignment

After Tom tricked Ben Rogers into whitewashing, he tricked Billy Fisher into whitewashing. Reread the conversation between Tom and Ben Rogers. Then write a different conversation between Tom and Billy Fisher. Show how Tom tricked Billy, and what Billy offered Tom.

Make your conversation at least **six** sentences long.

Lesson 93

PART A   Word Lists

1
Staten Island
congregation
Harlem

2
crumpled
maidservant
drowsing
absurd

3
Vocabulary words
pride of
casual
worship
contemplate
drone

PART B   New Vocabulary

1. **pride of**—Something all the neighbors are proud of is the **pride of** the neighbors.
   - What would you call something the school is proud of?*

2. **casual**—When you act in a **casual** way, you act in a very relaxed way. You don't try to show off. If you dressed in a casual manner, you would dress in a relaxed manner.
   - How would you speak in a casual manner?

3. **worship**—When you **worship** something, you adore that thing and treat it as if it is more important than anything else.
   - What do you do to something when you adore that thing and treat it as if it is more important than anything else?

4. **contemplate**—When you think about something, you **contemplate** that thing.
   - a. What's another way of saying **She thought about the consequences?***
   - b. What's another way of saying **He thought about the stars?***

5. **drone**—When you speak in a very dull voice, you **drone** along.
   - Say something so that you drone along.

PART C   Vocabulary Review

1	2
fragment	absorbed
plush	dryly
tranquil	waver
corridor	resume

1. Something that is very calm is _____.
2. A small piece is a _____.
3. When you start doing something again, you _____ doing it.
4. When you are deeply involved in doing something, you are _____ in that activity.
5. When people begin to lose their determination, they _____.

PART D Graph Skills

To read a graph, you use the numbers along the side of the graph and the numbers along the bottom of the graph.

On the graph below, the numbers along the side tell how many centimeters of rain fell during a month.Ⓐ

The words along the bottom name the months.Ⓑ

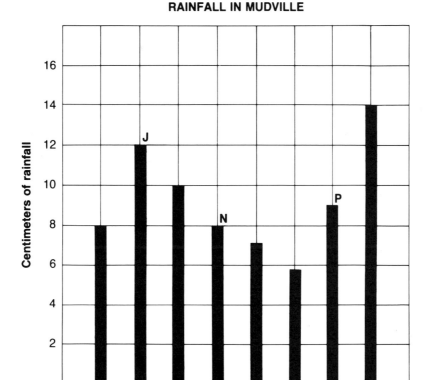

RAINFALL IN MUDVILLE

1. Touch **J.**Ⓒ
   a. To find out the month, you go straight down from **J.** What month is on the same line as **J?**Ⓓ
   b. To find out how much rain fell during that month, you go across from **J** to the rain numbers. What number is on the same line as **J?**Ⓔ

2. Touch **P.**Ⓕ
   a. Which month does **P** tell about?Ⓖ
   b. How much rain fell in that month?Ⓗ
3. Touch **N.**Ⓘ
   a. Which month does **N** tell about?Ⓙ
   b. How much rain fell in that month?Ⓚ

PART E   Story Items

1. **a.** What day was it in this chapter?
   b. What job had just been completed at the end of the last chapter?
   c. What was Aunt Polly doing when Tom entered the house?
   d. What did Tom announce to her?
   e. Did she believe that the job had been completed?
2. **a.** When Aunt Polly looked at the fence, how did she feel?
   b. How many coats of whitewash were on that fence?
   c. What did Aunt Polly tell Tom that he could do?
3. **a.** What activity did Tom join in with other boys at the public square?
   b. What rank did Tom have in that game?
   c. Which army won?
4. On his way home, Tom saw somebody.
   a. What did Tom feel when he saw that person?
   b. Tom tried to win that person's admiration. How did he do that?
   c. What object did that person throw over the fence?
   d. What did that person do after throwing the object?
5. **a.** Did Tom pick the object up right away?
   b. Why?
   c. How did Tom pick it up?
   d. What did Tom do with the flower when he was out of sight?
6. Tom stayed in front of the girl's house until nightfall.
   a. Name one thing he did during that time.
   b. After he left, he found something in the river. What was that?
   c. What place did he return to after leaving the river?
   d. Who was he hoping to see?
   e. What was thrown on Tom as he was in the girl's yard?

7. Later, Tom found out who the girl was.
   a. Who told him her name?
   b. What was her name?
8. This chapter had a funny example of irony.
   a. When Tom laid down under the window, who did he think would see him?
   b. Who actually appeared at the window?
   c. What did that character do to Tom?
   d. Why is that an example of irony?
     - Tom needed a bath.
     - Tom had a mistaken belief about who would appear in the window.
     - Tom knew who was at the window.

PART F   Writing Assignment

Pretend that you are the Adored Unknown Girl, Becky. Write a paragraph that explains how you feel about Tom and his antics.

Make your paragraph at least **six** sentences long.

Lesson 94

PART A Word Lists

1	2	3
gingerly	aisle	**Vocabulary words**
hymn	postmaster	justice of the peace
vulgar	mansion	lapse into
	fertile	minister
	furry	sermon
	fury	congregation
		pew
		gingerly

PART B New Vocabulary

1. **justice of the peace**—A **justice of the peace** is an official who deals with problems that are not as important as those a judge deals with.

2. **lapse into**—When you forget what you're doing and drift into thought, you **lapse into** thought.
   - What do you do when you forget what you're doing and drift into a dream?*

3. **minister**—A **minister** is the person who directs the services in some churches.

4. **sermon**—A speech that a minister delivers in church is a **sermon.**

5. **congregation**—A **congregation** is a group of people who attend a church service.

6. **pew**—A **pew** is a long bench that people sit on in church.

7. **gingerly**—When you do something **gingerly,** you do it cautiously.
   a. What's another way of saying **They entered the cave cautiously?***
   b. What's another way of saying **He petted the bear cautiously?***

PART C Vocabulary Review

1	2
contemplate	drone
conscience	casual
vicious	smug
absorbed	perplexed
traitor	bulky

1. When you act in a very relaxed way, you act in a _____ way.
2. When you think about something, you _____ that thing.
3. When you are puzzled, you are _____.
4. When you speak in a very dull voice, you _____ along.
5. When you feel very, very satisfied with yourself, you feel _____.
6. The voice inside you that scolds you when you do something you shouldn't do is your _____.

7. When you are deeply involved in doing something, you are _____ in that activity.

PART D Arguments

Some arguments are faulty because they break rules.

Here's a rule: *Just because two events happen around the same time doesn't mean one event causes the other event.*

The following argument breaks the rule.

"The last five times Joe tapped home plate, he hit a home run. He should always remember to tap home plate when he goes up to bat."
1. What two events happen around the same time?Ⓐ
2. What event does the writer think causes the home run?Ⓑ

PART E   Story Items

1. **a.** On which day of the week does this chapter take place?
   b. What sound announced that the church services were about to begin?
   c. Tom sat on the aisle because that seat was the farthest from the _____.
   d. What do you think Tom would have done if he had a chance?
2. **a.** Was the Widow Douglas **rich** or **poor?**
   b. What kind of place did she live in?
3. **a.** What did Tom observe during the minister's prayer?
   b. What did Tom do as the prayer ended?
   c. Who made him release his prisoner?
4. **a.** What did Tom count as the sermon went on?
   b. Many heads began to nod during the sermon. Why?
5. **a.** What prize did Tom bring from his pocket during the sermon?
   b. What was the first thing that animal did to Tom?
   c. Which animal began to play with the beetle?
   d. Finally, the dog _____ on the beetle.
      - sat down   • stepped
      - rolled
   e. Who did the dog finally go to?
   f. What did that person do with the dog?
   g. How did the congregation respond to the bug and the dog?
6. **a.** At the end of the chapter, Tom didn't mind the dog _____ with his pinch bug.
   b. But he did mind the dog _____.

PART F   Graph Skills

The graph below shows how much snow falls in the Red Hills. The numbers along the side tell how many centimeters of snow fell in a year. The numbers along the bottom tell how many meters high the hills are.

YEARLY SNOWFALL IN THE RED HILLS

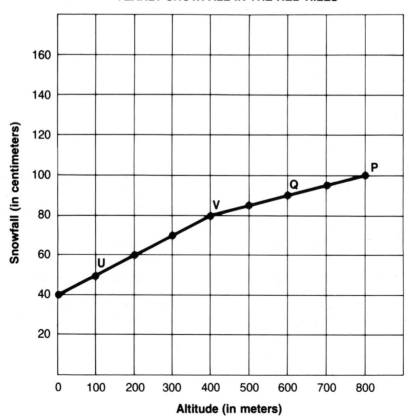

1. The letter **V** shows how many centimeters of snowfall occur at a certain altitude.
   a. Which altitude?
   b. How much snowfall?
2. Was there more snowfall at the **higher altitudes** or the **lower altitudes?**
3. Which point tells about a higher altitude, **U** or **P?**
4. How many centimeters of snow fell on hills that had an altitude of 800 meters?

PART G   Writing Assignment

Imagine what the minister said in his sermon. Then write part of his sermon. Try to make the sermon sound like the minister.

Make your sermon at least **six** sentences long.

Lesson 95

PART A   Word Lists

1	2	3
aggravated	infect	**Vocabulary words**
genuine	bedpost	ailment
mortified	hymn	considerable
juvenile	admirable	aggravate
		genuine
		mortified

PART B   New Vocabulary

1. **ailment**—An **ailment** is pain or a sickness.
   ● What's another word for **pain** or a **sickness?***

2. **considerable**—Another word for **fairly great** is **considerable.**
   a. What's another way of saying **He had fairly great talent?***
   b. What's another way of saying **She had fairly great wealth?***

3. **aggravate**—When you irritate something or make it worse, you **aggravate** that thing.
   a. What's another way of saying **Their discussion made the situation worse?***
   b. What's another way of saying **His behavior irritated Aunt Polly?***

4. **genuine**—Something that is **genuine** is real. It is not an imitation.
   a. What's another way of saying **The couch was made of real leather?***
   b. What's another way of saying **His tears were real?***

5. **mortified**—If a part of your body is dead, that part is **mortified.**

PART C Vocabulary Review

1	2	3
gingerly	smug	casual
absorbed	lapse into	perplexed
traitors	waver	plush
drone	stiff	conscience
tranquil		

1. When you forget what you're doing and drift into thought, you _____ thought.
2. When you do something cautiously, you do it _____.
3. The voice inside you that scolds you when you do something you shouldn't do is your _____.
4. When you feel very, very satisfied with yourself, you feel _____.
5. When you act in a very relaxed way, you act in a _____ way.
6. Something that is very showy and expensive is _____.
7. When you are deeply involved in doing something, you are _____ in that activity.
8. Something that is very calm is _____.
9. When you speak in a very dull voice, you _____ along.
10. When people begin to lose their determination, they _____.

PART D Arguments

Here's a rule: *Just because two events happen around the same time doesn't mean one event causes the other event.*

The following argument breaks the rule.

"When I went to Nova Scotia last year, it was snowing. When I went to Chicago later that year, it snowed. When I went to Buffalo this year, it was also snowing. I think I'll go to Philadelphia next year and make it snow there."

1. What two events happen around the same time? Ⓐ
2. What event does the writer think causes the snow? Ⓑ

PART E Story Items

1. a. On which day of the week does this chapter take place?
   b. How did Tom feel in the morning?
   c. What did he dread doing?
2. Tom examined himself as he lay in bed.
   a. What was he looking for?
   b. What was the first thing he discovered?
   c. What was the next ailment that he discovered?
   d. What did Tom do to act as if he was in pain?
3. a. Who was sleeping next to Tom?
   b. At first, what response did that person have to Tom's noises?
   c. What did that person want to do when he woke up and observed Tom's agony?
4. a. Sid ran downstairs. Why?
   b. Tom told Aunt Polly that his toe was _____.
      • injured   • mortified
      • bruised
5. a. What ailment did Aunt Polly cure?
   b. She sent Sid for some _____ and a chunk of _____.
   c. What did she do with one end of the silk thread?
   d. What did she do with the other end?
   e. What did she do with the hot coal?
   f. What did Tom do when she did that?
   g. What happened to the tooth?
   h. Why did the boys envy Tom as he went to school that morning?
6. In this chapter, Tom told some more lies. Write **truth** or **lie** for each statement.
   a. "Don't move around, Sid, you'll kill me."
   b. "Oh, please, auntie, don't pull it out."
   c. "*I* don't want to stay home from school."

PART F Graph Skills

The graph below compares tree width
and tree age. The numbers along the side
tell about the tree's width in inches. The
numbers along the bottom tell about the
tree's age in years.

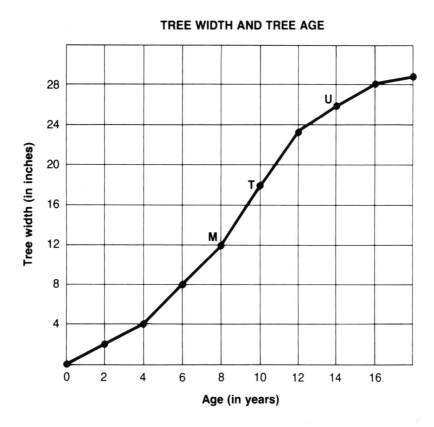

TREE WIDTH AND TREE AGE

1. Which point tells about trees that are eight years old?
2. Which point tells about trees that are 26 inches wide?
3. As trees get older, do they get **narrower** or **wider?**
4. Which point shows a wider tree, **M** or **T?**
5. How wide are trees that are six years old?

PART G   Map Skills

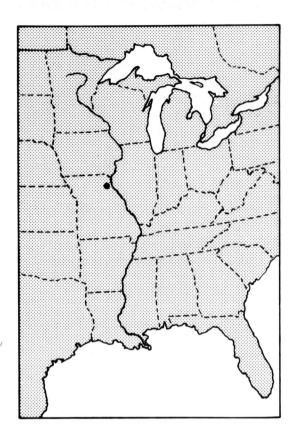

1. Which river does the map show?
2. The river flows from the _____ to the _____.
3. The dot shows where Tom Sawyer lived. What is the name of that place in the novel?
4. What is the name of that place in real life?

PART H   Writing Assignment

The boys Tom met on the way to school were interested in his missing tooth. Tom probably didn't tell those boys what had really happened. Write what you think he told them, and try to make your writing sound like Tom.

Write a paragraph that is at least **six** sentences long.

PART I   Special Projects

1. (Individual Project) Memorize a poem. Look in a book of poetry and find a poem that you like. Then memorize the poem and recite it to the class. The poem should be at least **twelve** lines long.

2. (Group Project) Draw a large map of the United States during the Civil War. Look in an encyclopedia or other reference book and find out which states were part of the South and which states were part of the North. Color the southern states gray and the northern states blue. Then make dots on the map to show where at least five important battles were. Label each dot and tell when the battle was fought.

3. (Group Project) Make up a play based on the whitewashing chapter of *Tom Sawyer*. Show Tom's conversation with Sid. Then show his conversation with Ben Rogers and the other boys. Figure out who will play each character, then figure out what each character will say. You can use words from the book, or you can make up your own words. Students who do not play characters can work on costumes or sets. When you are ready, perform the play for the class.

Lesson 96

PART A   Word Lists

1
lawless
idle
suspender
barely
barley

2
Vocabulary words
juvenile
vulgar
tick
wistful
dozing
lull

PART B   New Vocabulary

1. **juvenile**—A **juvenile** is a young person who is older than a child.
   - What's another way of saying **Tom was a young person who was older than a child?***

2. **vulgar**—Something that is very crude and disgusting is **vulgar**.
   a. What's another way of saying **His manners were crude and disgusting?***
   b. What's another way of saying **The sailors sang a crude and disgusting song?***

3. **tick**—A **tick** is an insect that digs into your skin and sucks out blood.

4. **wistful**—When you are full of desire and dreams, you are **wistful**.
   a. What's another way of saying **When she thought about her home, she became full of desire and dreams?***
   b. What's another way of saying **When they looked at the new car, they became full of desire and dreams?***

5. **dozing**—When you are **dozing**, you are sleeping.
   a. What's another way of saying **She slept for a few moments?***
   b. What's another way of saying **Stop sleeping in class?***

6. **lull**—Things that make you sleepy or drowsy **lull** you.
   a. What's another way of saying **The sound of the rain made her sleepy?***
   b. What's another way of saying **The constant humming sound made them drowsy?***

PART C   Vocabulary Review

1	2
aggravate	lapse into
casual	drone
considerable	contemplate
genuine	gingerly
ailment	

1. Another word for **fairly great** is _____.
2. Pain or a sickness is an _____.
3. Something that is real is _____.
4. When you irritate something or make it worse, you _____ that thing.
5. When you forget what you're doing and drift into thought, you _____ thought.
6. When you think about something, you _____ that thing.

PART D   Story Items

1. **a.** Who did Tom meet on his way to school?
   b. What did the mothers of the town think of that character?
   c. What did the children think of that character?
   d. Was Tom supposed to play with that character?
   e. So, how frequently did Tom play with him?
2. **a.** Name **three** things that Huckleberry Finn did not have to do.
   b. What prize did Huckleberry Finn have with him?
   c. What did Huck say that thing was good for?
   d. What did Tom think was better for getting rid of them?
   e. Both boys agreed there was another way to get rid of them. What was that way?
3. Huck Finn told Tom how to use a rat to get rid of warts.
   a. Where would you have to take the rat?
   b. Around what time would you go there?
   c. Then, when the devils were taking a corpse away, what would you do with the rat?
   d. When was Huck planning to use the rat?
4. Before the boys parted, Tom traded with Huck.
   a. What did Huck have?
   b. Where did Huck get it?
   c. What did Tom have?
   d. What did Tom do with the object he received from that trade?
5. Write whether each statement describes **Tom** or **Huck**.
   a. He didn't have to go to school.
   b. He was always the first boy to go barefoot in the spring.
   c. He knew how to get rid of warts with rats.
   d. He traded his tooth for a tick.

PART E   Similes

Make up a simile for each accurate statement. Use the word **like** in your similes.
1. *A thought went very quickly through his brain.*
   a. Name something that moves very quickly.
   b. Make up a simile that tells how the thought went.
2. *His face was hard.*
   a. Name something that could be as hard as his face.
   b. Make up a simile that tells what his face was like.

PART F   Arguments

Here's a rule: *Just because two events happen around the same time doesn't mean one event causes the other event.*

The following argument breaks the rule.

"Last Friday, I forgot to brush my teeth. Later that day, I got an A on a test. Last Monday, I didn't brush my teeth and I got an A on a test. The same thing happened to me on Tuesday. I have a test tomorrow, so I'd better not brush my teeth tomorrow."
1. What two events happen around the same time?
2. What event does the writer think causes the A's on his tests?

PART G   Graph Skills

RELATIONSHIP OF WEIGHT AND HEIGHT

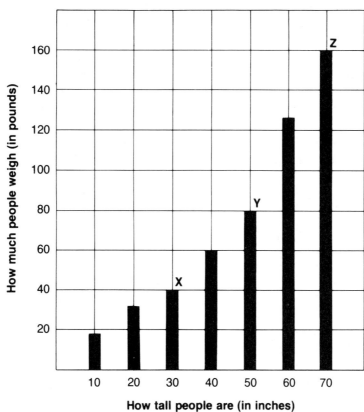

The graph above compares people's weight and height. The numbers along the side tell how many pounds people weigh. The numbers along the bottom tell how many inches tall people are.

1. How much does a person 50 inches tall weigh?
2. How tall is a person who weighs 160 pounds?
3. Which point tells about the smallest people: **X**, **Y**, or **Z**?
4. The taller people are, the _____ they weigh.

PART H   Irony

Below is an example of irony from *All in Favor.*
1. At the beginning of the play, Nancy had a mistaken belief about three people. What was that?
2. Nancy did something that was based on the belief. What did she do?
3. What would Nancy have done if she had known the truth about those three people?

PART I   Writing Assignment

Would you like to be Huckleberry Finn? Write a paragraph that explains your answer.

Make your paragraph at least **six** sentences long.

Lesson 97

1	2	3
critical	vacant	**Vocabulary words**
harass	tiptoe	critical of
engaged	redden	foolhardy
chemistry	tiptoeing	scrawl
	reddened	scuffle
		harass
		prod

PART B   New Vocabulary

1. **critical of**—When you are **critical of** something, you find fault with that thing. If you find fault with a meal, you are critical of that meal.
   a. What are you being if you find fault with a painting?*
   b. What are you being if you find fault with a person?*

2. **foolhardy**—Another word for **foolish** is **foolhardy**.
   ● What's another way of saying **They made a foolish decision?***

3. **scrawl**—When you write in a careless manner, you **scrawl**.
   ● What's another way of saying **She carelessly wrote her name on the sidewalk?***

4. **scuffle**—A **scuffle** is a small fight.
   ● What do we call a small fight?*

5. **harass**—When you **harass** somebody, you taunt and tease that person.
   a. What's another way of saying **They teased the new boy?***
   b. What's another way of saying **The dog taunted the stranger?***

6. **prod**—Another word for a **push** or a **shove** is a **prod**.
   ● What's another way of saying **Tom pushed the bug?***

PART C   Vocabulary Review

1	2
wistful	lull
unanimous	juvenile
gingerly	aggravate
dozing	perplexed
tranquil	vulgar
gavel	lapse into
considerable	

1. Something that is very crude and disgusting is _____.
2. Things that make you sleepy or drowsy _____ you.
3. When you are sleeping, you are _____.
4. When you are full of desire and dreams, you are _____.
5. A young person who is older than a child is a _____.
6. When you irritate something or make it worse, you _____ that thing.
7. When you do something cautiously, you do it _____.
8. Another word for **fairly great** is _____.
9. Something that is very calm is _____.
10. When you forget what you're doing and drift into thought, you _____ thought.

PART D Story Items

1. **a.** Was Tom on time when he reached school?
    b. Why?
2. Tom was going to lie to the schoolmaster.
    a. Then he noticed someone that made him change his mind. Who was that?
    b. Where was the only vacant seat in the schoolhouse?
    c. So, what excuse did Tom give for being late?
    d. How did the schoolmaster punish Tom?
3. **a.** What did Tom place on the desk of the Adored Unknown Girl?
    b. What picture did Tom draw on his slate?
    c. What did Tom say that he would teach the girl to do?
    d. When did he promise to do that?
    e. What was the girl's name?
4. Tom wrote something on the slate.
    a. What did he write?
    b. What part of Tom did the schoolmaster grab when he led Tom back to his seat?
    c. How did the other students respond?
5. **a.** What creature did Tom remove from his pocket when he was supposed to be studying?
    b. What was the name of the boy Tom started to play a game with?
    c. What did the boys use to guide the creature in their game?
      • Pens   • Pins   • Pans
    d. Who was more successful in playing with the creature?
    e. Who broke the rules of the game the boys were playing?
    f. Who put an end to the game the boys were playing?

6. Write which character each statement describes. Choose from **Tom, Becky Thatcher,** or **Joe Harper.**
    a. This character was impressed with a picture on a slate.
    b. This character had better luck with the tick.
    c. This character wrote the words "I love you."
    d. The schoolmaster ordered this character to sit on the other side of the room.
    e. This character finally accepted a peach.

PART E Drawing Conclusions

Write a conclusion that tells what the person believed.
1. *Huck believed that if you went to a graveyard at midnight, your warts would go away. Huck went to the graveyard at midnight.*
  • So, what did Huck believe would happen?
2. *Tom believed that if you acted sick, you could stay home from school. Tom acted sick.*
  • So, what did Tom believe would happen?

PART F Arguments

Here's a rule: *Just because two events happen around the same time doesn't mean one event causes the other event.*

The following argument breaks the rule.

"I went to a soccer game last week. I wore green socks, and my team won. I'm going to another game tomorrow. I'd better wear my green socks, or my team will lose."
1. What two events happen around the same time?
2. What event does the writer think causes the soccer team to win?

PART G Graph Skills

The graph below shows how many
bushels of corn were produced on the La
Grange Farm. The numbers along the
side tell how many bushels were
produced in a year. The numbers along
the bottom name the years.

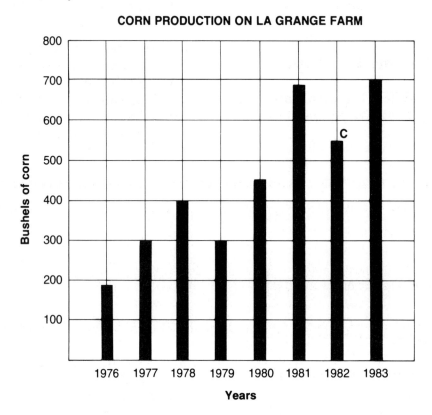

CORN PRODUCTION ON LA GRANGE FARM

1. In which year was corn production the lowest?
2. Did corn production increase from 1978 to 1979?
3. Corn production increased every year except for two. Which two years?
4. Which year does point **C** tell about?
5. How many bushels were produced in 1978?

PART H Writing Assignment

Do you think that Becky loves Tom?
Write a paragraph that explains your
answer. Use evidence from the story to
support your answer.

Make your paragraph at least **six**
sentences long.

Lesson 98

PART A   Word Lists

1
research
soothing
tiresome
scholars

2
Vocabulary words
engaged
blunder
coffin
pathetic

PART B   New Vocabulary

1. **engaged**—When two people are **engaged,** they have promised to marry each other.

2. **blunder**—A bad mistake is a **blunder.**
   - What's another way of saying **She made a bad mistake?***

3. **coffin**—A **coffin** is a large box that a dead person is placed in before the person is buried.

4. **pathetic**— Something that is very sad or sorrowful is **pathetic.**
   a. What's another way of saying **The wet dog looked sorrowful?***
   b. What's another way of saying **His expression was very sorrowful?***

PART C   Vocabulary Review

1	2	3
scrawl	prod	lull
critical of	wistful	scuffle
vulgar	harass	juvenile

1. When you find fault with something, you are _____ that thing.
2. When you write in a careless manner, you _____.
3. When you taunt and tease somebody, you _____ that person.
4. Another word for a **push** or a **shove** is a _____.
5. A small fight is a _____.
6. When you are full of desire and dreams, you are _____.

PART D   Arguments

Here's a rule: *Just because you know about a part doesn't mean you know about the whole thing.*

The following argument breaks the rule.

"You should buy this car. As you can see, the tires are in really good condition. Since the tires are in such good condition, you can be certain that the rest of the car is also in good condition."

1. Which thing in the argument is the part?Ⓐ
2. Which thing is the whole?Ⓑ
3. What does the writer conclude about the whole?Ⓒ

PART E   Story Items

1. a. Who did Tom arrange to meet at noon?
   b. What were the two going to do at that time?
   c. Tom told her to give her friends the slip and then meet him at _____.

2. a. What did Tom and Becky draw on the slate?
   b. What did Becky offer to share with Tom?
   c. Tom asked Becky if she had ever been _____ to be married.

3. Tom told her how to do that.
   a. First one person had to tell the other person, "I would never date _____."
   b. Then one person had to do something with the other person. What was that?
   c. What message had Tom written on Becky's slate earlier that day?

4. Tom made a blunder by starting to tell Becky something.
   a. What was that?
   b. How did Becky react?
   c. Tom tried to make up with her by giving her something. What?
   d. What did Becky do when he tried to give it to her?
   e. What did Tom do then?
5. That night, time seemed to pass very slowly for Tom.
   a. Where was he?
   b. Who was he going to meet?
   c. What were they going to do?
6. a. What signal was Tom waiting for?
   b. What did the neighbor do when the meowing started?
   c. Where were Tom and Huck at the end of this chapter?

PART F   Map Skills

Look at the map below. Dots like this ● show cities with less than 100,000 people. Squares like this ■ show cities with more than 100,000 people. Assume that the map is accurate. Examine the map carefully, and then read the statements below. Some of the statements contradict what is shown on the map.

Write **Contradictory** or **Not contradictory** for each statement.

1. Saint John is the largest city on the map.
2. You can go from Charlottetown to Saint John without crossing any water.
3. Halifax is smaller than Charlottetown.
4. When you sail from Saint John to Charlottetown, you pass by Halifax.
5. All of the cities on the map border on water.

PART G   Writing Assignment

Pretend you are Tom. What would you say or do to make up with Becky? Write a paragraph that tells what you would say or do.

Make your paragraph at least **six** sentences long.

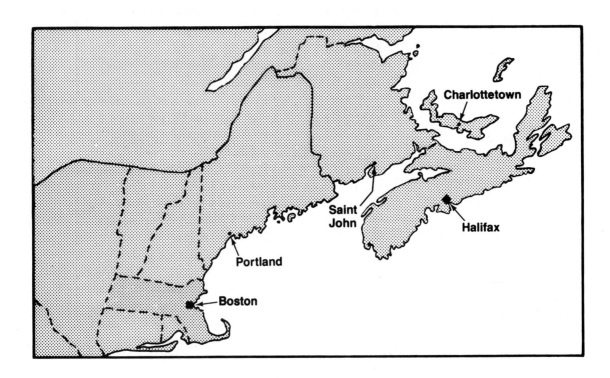

Lesson 99

PART A   Word Lists

1
cemetery
tannery

2
gone
goners
vague
blubbering

3
Vocabulary words
oath
swear
tannery

PART B   New Vocabulary

1. **oath**—An **oath** is a very solemn promise that must not be broken.
   - What do we call a very solemn promise that must not be broken?*

2. **swear**—When you take an oath, you **swear** to keep the oath. When you swear to keep the oath, you make a solemn promise to keep it.

3. **tannery**—A **tannery** is a place where people take hides of animals and make them into leather.
   - What do we call the place where people take hides of animals and make them into leather?*

PART C   Vocabulary Review

1	2
considerable	blunder
vulgar	juvenile
dozing	pathetic
lull	wistful
critical of	

1. A bad mistake is a _____.
2. When you find fault with something, you are _____ that thing.
3. Things that make you sleepy or drowsy _____ you.
4. Another word for **fairly great** is _____.
5. A young person who is older than a child is a _____.
6. Something that is very sad or sorrowful is _____.

PART D   Arguments

Here's a rule: *Just because you know about a part doesn't mean you know about the whole thing.*

The following argument breaks the rule.

"Mr. Williams works for the Ajax Company. Mr. Williams is very kind and careful. He also works very hard. Therefore, the Ajax Company must be a very kind and careful organization."

1. Which thing in the argument is the part?Ⓐ
2. Which thing is the whole?Ⓑ
3. What does the writer conclude about the whole?Ⓒ

PART E   Story Items

1. **a.** In which place does this chapter begin?
    b. The gravestones in that place were made out of _____.
     ● rock   ● metal   ● wood
    c. Why was the fence that surrounded the graveyard described as a crazy board fence?
2. **a.** When the party approached the graveyard, who did the boys first think it was?
    b. How many were in the party?
    c. What did two of the men do as the third sat by a tree?
3. **a.** What did one of the men then demand from the third man?
    b. Which man made that demand?
    c. Who had sent Outlaw Joe to jail?
    d. What did the doctor do when Joe threatened him?
4. **a.** When Outlaw Joe hit the doctor, what did the doctor's head strike?
    b. What did the two boys do at that time?
    c. What happened to the doctor after he fell?
5. **a.** Who made up a lie about what had happened?
    b. According to that person's story, _____ killed the doctor.
    c. Who really killed the doctor?

PART F   Arguments

Here's a rule: *Just because two events happen around the same time doesn't mean one event causes the other event.*

The following argument breaks the rule.

"My car can take either regular or premium gasoline. But the last time I put premium gasoline in my car, one of my tires went flat. I'll never use premium gasoline again."
1. What two events happen around the same time?
2. What event does the writer think causes the flat tire?

PART G   Review Items

Tell which poem each line is from. Choose from *Written in March, Casey at the Bat, Miracles,* or *The Tide Rises, the Tide Falls.*
1. "The rain is over and gone!"
2. "The exquisite delicate thin curve of the new moon in spring."
3. "Oh, somewhere in this favored land the sun is shining bright."
4. "The little waves, with their soft white hands."
5. "The ploughboy is whooping—anon—anon."

PART H   Writing Assignment

Pretend that Outlaw Joe sees Huck and catches him. Huck would plead with Outlaw Joe not to punish him. Write what Huck would say.

Write at least **six** sentences. Try to make your writing sound like Huck.

Lesson 100

PART A Word List

cemetery
initials
genuine
gingerly

PART B Vocabulary Review

1	2	3
prod	oath	droned
plush	vulgar	considerable
scrawl	wistful	genuine

1. A very solemn promise that must not be broken is an _____.
2. When you are full of desire and dreams, you are _____.
3. Another word for a **push** or a **shove** is _____.
4. Something that is very crude and disgusting is _____.
5. Another word for **fairly great** is _____.
6. Something that is real is _____.

PART C Graph Skills

Assume that the graph below is accurate. Examine the graph carefully, and then read the statements below. Some of the statements contradict what is shown on the graph. Write **Contradictory** or **Not contradictory** for each statement.

1. Seven thousand apples were produced in 1977.Ⓐ
2. Eight thousand apples were produced in 1982.Ⓑ
3. Apple production went up from 1977 to 1979.Ⓒ
4. More apples were produced in 1978 than in 1981.Ⓓ
5. The best year for apple production was 1982.Ⓔ

APPLE PRODUCTION AT THE EDEN APPLE ORCHARDS

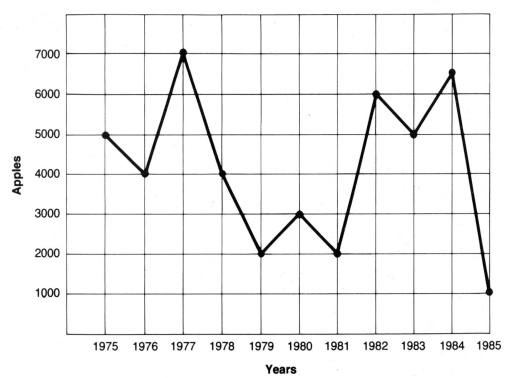

PART D   Story Items

1. **a.** What event had the boys witnessed that night?
   b. Where had that event taken place?
2. **a.** What place were the boys trying to reach at the beginning of this chapter?
   b. Who were the only people who could tell the truth about what had happened in the graveyard?
   c. Why couldn't Potter tell what had happened to the doctor?
   d. Who did Potter think had killed the doctor?
   e. Why did Potter think that?
3. The boys agreed to take an oath.
   a. What did they use to sign their names to the oath?
   b. Who wrote the oath?
   c. What did the boys use to prick their thumbs?
   d. What did they do with the blood?
   e. Which boy couldn't write?
   f. How did that boy know how to sign his initials?
   g. The oath said that if the boys ever told what happened, they would _____.
4. The boys were frightened by a dog's howling.
   a. Tom thought that if that dog faced him, he would be marked for _____.
   b. Was the dog a stray?
5. The boys had regrets about the way they had led their lives.
   a. Tom thought he should have been more like _____.
   b. Huck said that he wasn't even half as good as _____.
6. **a.** Was the stray dog facing the boys?
   b. What sounds did the boys hear from the other end of the building?
   c. What did they decide to do at the end of this chapter?

7. Tom and Huck are superstitious about some things. When you are superstitious, you believe that ordinary things can bring you good or bad luck. The statements below tell what Tom and Huck believed. Write whether each belief is **Superstitious** or **Not superstitious.**
   a. You can get rid of warts with a dead rat.
   b. Outlaw Joe is someone to be afraid of.
   c. You can wake somebody up by making noises.
   d. A howling dog means death.

PART E   Arguments

Here's a rule: *Just because you know about a part doesn't mean you know about the whole thing.*

The following argument breaks the rule.

"I went over to visit my friend Toshio the other day. We played in her garage. The place was a mess. There were bottles and newspapers everywhere, and a huge pile of dirty rags in one corner. The rest of Toshio's house must be a mess too."

1. Which thing in the argument is the part?
2. Which thing is the whole?
3. What conclusion does the writer draw about the whole?

PART F   Writing Assignment

Do you think the boys were right to keep quiet about what they saw? Write a paragraph that explains your answer. Tell what might happen if they continue to keep quiet, then tell what might happen if they tell what they saw.

Make your paragraph at least **six** sentences long.

Lesson 101

PART A   Word Lists

1
pathetic
ghastly
decomposer
jealousy
randomly

2
tannery
fascination
crest
crestfallen
antics

3
Vocabulary words
play hooky
electrified
ghastly

PART B   New Vocabulary

1. **play hooky**—When you **play hooky** from school, you don't go to school when you're supposed to.
   - What do people do when they don't go to school when they're supposed to?*

2. **electrified**—When something is **electrified,** it suddenly becomes very active and excited, as if electricity were surging through it. Here's another way of saying **The village suddenly became very excited: The village became electrified.**

   a. What's another way of saying **The village suddenly became very excited?***

   b. What's another way of saying **The swarm of bees suddenly became very active and excited?***

3. **ghastly**—Something that is very horrible or shocking is **ghastly.**
   - What's another way of saying **The drapes were a horrible color?***

PART C   Vocabulary Review

1	2	3
considerable	genuine	pathetic
casual	lull	prod
harass	blunder	conscience

1. Things that make you sleepy or drowsy _____ you.
2. Another word for **fairly great** is _____.
3. A bad mistake is a _____.
4. Something that is very sad or sorrowful is _____.
5. Something that is real is _____.
6. When you taunt and tease somebody, you _____ that person.

PART D Graph Skills

Assume that the graph below is accurate.
Examine the graph carefully, and then
read the statements below it. Some of the
statements contradict what is shown on
the graph. Write **Contradictory** or **Not
contradictory** for each statement.

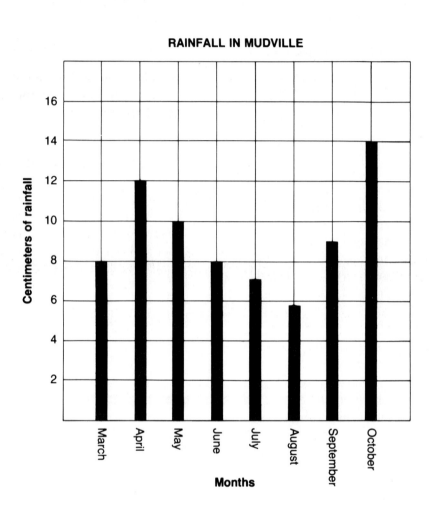

1. Fourteen centimeters of rain fell in
   April.Ⓐ
2. Eight inches of rain fell in June.Ⓑ
3. September was the rainiest month.Ⓒ
4. August was the driest month.
5. More rain fell in March than in July.

PART E Story Items

1. The boys identified the sleeping form in the tannery.
   a. Who was the sleeping form?
   b. Who was the stray dog facing when it howled?
   c. What did Tom think that meant?
2. a. When Tom returned home, how did he enter his bedroom?
   b. Who observed him?
   c. What was that person pretending to do?
3. a. What time was it when Tom awoke?
   b. Did Aunt Polly know that Tom had been out all night?
   c. How did she find out?
4. When Tom got to school he discovered a hard object on his desk.
   a. What was the hard object?
   b. Who had returned it to him?
   c. If she returned the object, it meant that she no longer _____.
5. a. What news electrified the village that morning?
   b. Where did many of the people from the village go that afternoon?
   c. Who did the sheriff lead to the graveyard?
6. a. Who told the story of what had happened?
   b. Tom and Huck thought that lightning would strike Joe because he was _____.
      • telling the truth
      • keeping quiet
      • lying
   c. Did the lightning come?
   d. Tom and Huck thought that Joe had sold himself to the

   _____.

PART F Arguments

Here's a rule: *Just because you know about a part doesn't mean you know about the whole thing.*

The following argument breaks the rule.

"That brown duck can swim under water. Therefore, all brown ducks can swim under water."

1. Which thing in this argument is the part?
2. Which thing is the whole?
3. What conclusion does the writer draw about the whole?

PART G Writing Assignment

The howling stray dog seemed to predict bad luck for Muff Potter. Does that make you believe that howling stray dogs mean death? Write a paragraph that explains your answer. Use evidence from the story.

Make your paragraph at least **five** sentences long.

Lesson 102

PART A Word Lists

1
independent
hero
heroic
indifferent
decomposer

2
Vocabulary words
antics
crestfallen
independent
random

PART B New Vocabulary

1. **antics**—Silly, show-off behavior is called **antics**.
   a. What's another way of saying **Tom tried to impress her with his show-off behavior?***
   b. What's another way of saying **I'm tired of her silly behavior?***

2. **crestfallen**—When someone is **crestfallen**, that person feels very sad, as if the whole world has fallen.
   a. What's another way of saying **Tara was very sad?***
   b. What's another way of saying **Victor walked away with a very sad expression?***

3. **independent**—When something doesn't depend on other things, it is **independent**. Here's another way of saying **The country didn't depend on other countries: The country was independent.**
   a. What's another way of saying **The country didn't depend on other countries?***
   b. What's another way of saying **Cindy felt that she didn't depend on others?***

4. **random**—Things that follow no pattern are **random** things. If her behavior followed no pattern, her behavior was **random**.
   a. What would we call events that followed no pattern?*
   b. What would we call numbers that followed no pattern?*

PART C Vocabulary Review

1	2	3
ghastly	electrified	blunder
pathetic	harass	oath

1. Something that is very horrible or shocking is _____.
2. A very solemn promise that must not be broken is an _____.
3. When something suddenly becomes very active and excited as if electricity is surging through it, that thing is _____.

PART D Arguments

Here's a rule: *Just because a person is an expert in one field doesn't mean that person is an expert in another field.*

The following argument breaks the rule.

"Professor Jones teaches chemistry at the university. He knows all about chemistry and has won many prizes for his research. So when Professor Jones tells us that we need a new airport, we should listen to what he says."

1. Who is the expert in the argument?Ⓐ
2. In which field is that person an expert?Ⓑ
3. That person makes a statement about another field. Which other field?Ⓒ
4. Does the argument show that the person is an expert in the other field?Ⓓ

PART E   Story Items

1. **a.** What evidence did Aunt Polly and Sid have that something was disturbing Tom?
   b. What did Tom do to prevent talking in his sleep at night?
   c. What did Tom bring to Muff Potter while he was in jail?
2. **a.** Tom became concerned with Becky because she had failed to come to

   _____.
   b. Tom kept looking down the road from the schoolyard. Who was he looking for?
   c. How did Tom feel when that person did not appear?
   d. Name some things Tom did when that person finally appeared.
   e. At last, that person expressed an opinion of Tom's feats. Was she impressed?

PART F   Arguments

Here's a rule: *Just because two events happen around the same time doesn't mean one event causes the other event.*

The following argument breaks the rule.

"Last week, I put on a red shirt, and I got a rock in my shoe. Just yesterday, I put on a red shirt, and I got another rock in my shoe. I don't think I'll be wearing any more red shirts."

1. What two events happen around the same time?
2. What event does the writer think causes the rocks in his shoes?

PART G   Inference

Read the passage below and answer each question. Write **Words** if the question is answered by words in the passage. Write **Deduction** if the question is answered by a deduction.

Decomposers

Some things will rot when they are left in the air. Another word for **rot** *is* **decompose.** *Things that decompose start out as one material and turn into another material. For example, leaves decompose and turn into a soggy mass that no longer looks like leaves. Dead animals also decompose. Their flesh becomes rotten, and their bodies shrivel up.*

Tiny organisms are responsible for much of the change that occurs when matter decomposes. These organisms are called **decomposers.** *Decomposers are very small plants. They get their food by eating the flesh or waste material of other organisms.*

The world would be vastly different if there were no decomposers. Leaves from thousands of years ago would be piled on the ground, along with the bodies of dead animals. It is unlikely that we could live in such a world.

1. **a.** How do decomposers get their food?
   b. Is that question answered by **Words** or by a **Deduction?**
2. **a.** Do dead birds decompose?
   b. **Words** or **Deduction?**
3. **a.** When leaves decompose, they turn into a _____.
   b. **Words** or **Deduction?**
4. **a.** What might happen to us if there were no decomposers?
   b. **Words** or **Deduction?**
5. **a.** What would be piled on the ground if there were no decomposers?
   b. **Words** or **Deduction?**

PART H Review Items

Name the Greek god, goddess or poet each statement describes. Choose from *Athena, Demeter, Hades, Hermes, Homer,* or *Zeus.*
1. This god was the chief god.
2. This goddess often disguised Odysseus.
3. This god was the messenger god.
4. This goddess was the goddess of the earth.
5. This poet was blind.
6. A character in the story *Mystery Yarn* was named after this poet.

PART I Irony

Here's an example of irony from *Casey at the Bat.*
1. Before Casey came to bat, the crowd had a mistaken belief about Casey. What was that?
2. The crowd did something that was based on the belief. What did they do?
3. What would they have done if they had known the truth about Casey?

PART J Writing Assignment

Tom has been having terrible dreams. Write a paragraph that describes what happens in one of his dreams.

Make your paragraph at least **six** sentences long.

Lesson 103

PART A Word Lists

1
cozy
cozily
folly
proceedings

2
Vocabulary words
indifferent
flirt
jealousy
spite

PART B New Vocabulary

1. **indifferent**—When you don't care about things, you are **indifferent** about those things.
   a. What's another way of saying **They didn't care about the weather?***
   b. What's another way of saying **They didn't care about school?***

2. **flirt**—People **flirt** when they are trying to court somebody. They flirt by joking around and acting in a way that they think will make the other person interested in them.

3. **jealousy**—Another word for **envy** is **jealousy.** When you are jealous, you feel great envy.

4. **spite**—When you do things out of **spite,** you do them to get even or to get revenge.
   ● What's another way of saying **He didn't go to her party out of vengeance?***

PART C   Vocabulary Review

1	2
independent	antics
oath	electrified
crestfallen	wistful
ghastly	random

1. Silly, show-off behavior is called _____.

2. When something doesn't depend on other things, it is _____.

3. When someone feels very sad, as if the whole world has fallen, that person feels _____.

4. Things that follow no pattern are _____ things.

5. Something that is very horrible or shocking is _____.

PART D   Story Items

1. a. How did Tom react to Becky when she appeared in the schoolyard in the morning?
   - Greeted her warmly
   - Ignored her   • Argued with her

   b. Becky became upset when she discovered that Tom was talking to _____.

   c. Why was Becky bothered by this?

   d. What news did Becky announce to Mary Austin and the other students?

   e. Which two students did not ask for an invitation to that affair?

2. Becky had another plan for getting back at Tom.

   a. What did she do?

   b. When Tom observed Becky at recess, he felt great _____.
   - eagerness   • jealousy
   - happiness

   c. Which girl did Tom want to get rid of when he observed Becky?

3. a. Did Tom stay around at noon to observe Becky and Alfred?

   b. So Becky began to feel that she had carried her plan _____.
   - too far   • out well
   - not far enough

c. At last, Becky told Alfred, "I _____ you!"

4. Tom had encountered Alfred before, just after Alfred moved to town. What had happened at that time?

5. To get even with Tom, Alfred did something to a possession of Tom's.

   a. Which possession?

   b. What did Alfred do to it?

   c. At first, Becky resolved to tell Tom about what Alfred did. Then she changed her mind. Why?

6. Write whether each statement describes **Tom, Becky,** or **Both.**

   a. _____ felt anger toward the other character.

   b. _____ looked at pictures with Alfred Temple.

   c. _____ had an imaginary fight with Alfred Temple.

   d. _____ saw Alfred Temple do something evil in the classroom.

   e. Deep down inside, _____ wanted to make up with the other person.

PART E   Arguments

Here's a rule: *Just because a person is an expert in one field doesn't mean that person is an expert in another field.*

The following argument breaks the rule.

"Nadia Griggs is one of the funniest comedians in the world. She can make you laugh just by looking at you, and after two or three of her jokes, your side is splitting. So if she recommends Marko Jeans, you know they have to be good. Take it from Nadia: If you want to feel good, listen to her jokes; if you want to look good, wear Marko Jeans."

1. Who is the expert in the argument?
2. In which field is that person an expert?
3. That person makes a statement about another field. Which other field?
4. Does the argument show that the person is an expert in this other field?

PART F   Arguments

Here's a rule: *Just because you know about a part doesn't mean you know about the whole thing.*

The following argument breaks the rule.

"Here's a good way to check a carton of eggs. Open the carton and take out one egg. Hold the egg up to the light and see if it has any cracks in it or if it has a strange color. If the egg looks good, the other eggs will also be good."

1. Which thing in the argument is the part?
2. Which thing is the whole?
3. What conclusion does the writer draw about the whole?

PART G   Writing Assignment

Make up a conversation between Tom and Amy Lawrence. Have Tom explain to Amy why he is interested in her again.

Have each character say at least **three** sentences.

Lesson 104

PART A   Word Lists

1	2	3
anatomy	impatient	**Vocabulary words**
isolated	sphere	anatomy
villain	atmosphere	flustered
lynch	topic	proceedings
diary	use	folly
	abuse	sensation
		diary
		villain

PART B   New Vocabulary

1. **anatomy**—**Anatomy** is the study of a body and its parts. Human **anatomy** is the study of the human body and its parts.

2. **flustered**—Another word for **embarrassed and bewildered** is **flustered.**
   a. What's another way of saying **He was so bewildered that he couldn't talk straight?***
   b. What's another way of saying **When she flirted with him, he became completely embarrassed?***

3. **proceedings**—The things that occur during an event are the **proceedings** of that event. The things that go on in a trial are the **proceedings** of a trial.

   ● What would we call the things that go on during an argument?*

4. **folly**—Something that is very foolish is **folly.**
   a. What's another way of saying **His idea was very foolish?***
   b. What's another way of saying **They were amazed by his foolishness?***

5. **sensation**—When something makes a **sensation**, it makes a very strong impression that people talk about.
   a. What's another way of saying **The circus made a strong impression that people talked about?***
   b. What's another way of saying **The trial made a strong impression that people talked about?***

6. **diary**—A **diary** is a book that you write in and tell about the things that happened to you.
   ● What do we call a book that you write in and tell about the things that happened to you?*

7. **villain**—A person who does evil things is a **villain.**
   ● What do we call a person who does evil things?*

PART C   Vocabulary Review

1	2
jealousy	independent
random	indifferent
oath	ghastly
spite	antics
pathetic	

1. When you don't care about things, you are _____ about those things.
2. Things that follow no pattern are _____ things.
3. Another word for **envy** is _____.
4. Something that is very horrible or shocking is _____.
5. When you do things to get even or to get revenge, you do them out of _____.
6. When something doesn't depend on other things, it is _____.

PART D   Story Items

1. a. When Tom came home for lunch, what kind of mood was he in?
   b. When he left for school again, what kind of mood was he in?
   c. Who did Tom meet?
2. a. Tom told that person that he was so _____ for what he had done.
   b. The other person said, "I will never _____."
3. a. What had the schoolmaster always wanted to be?
   b. What kind of book did he keep secretly in his desk?
   c. Who discovered that book?
   d. What picture was that person observing when Tom came into the classroom?
   e. What happened to the picture?
4. a. Who got punished for the ink spilled on Tom's spelling book?
   b. Who knew which person really spilled the ink?
   c. Did Becky tell what had happened?

5. The novel says that when Mr. Dobbins reached for his book, "there were two that watched his movements with intent eyes."
   a. Which two characters watched him with intent eyes?
   b. Tom had planned to do something before Mr. Dobbins opened the book. What was that?
6. Somebody sprang to his feet and said "I done it!"
   a. Who was that?
   b. Who was Mr. Dobbins questioning at the time?
   c. What was Tom's punishment?
   d. Tom knew that somebody would be waiting for him when his punishment had ended. Who?
   e. That night, Tom remembered Becky's last words: "Tom, how *could* you be so _____!"

PART E   Arguments

Here's a rule: *Just because you know about a part doesn't mean you know about the whole thing.*

The following argument breaks the rule.

"Warren is probably the greatest hockey player I have ever seen. He can skate circles around everybody else, and he can really control a hockey stick. The team he plays for, the Fairbanks Polar Bears, must be a great team."

1. Which thing in the argument is the part?
2. Which thing is the whole?
3. What conclusion does the writer draw about the whole?

PART F Combined Sentences

Below are two sentences. One introduces a new word; the other tells what the word means.

- *The scientist used a barometer.*
- *A barometer is a device that measures air pressure.*

1. Combine the sentences so that the meaning comes right after the new word. Put commas before the meaning, and take out the word "is."
2. What is the new word in the combined sentence?
3. What does the new word mean?
4. What else does the sentence tell about the new word?

PART G Arguments

Here's a rule: *Just because a person is an expert in one field doesn't mean that person is an expert in another field.*

The following argument breaks the rule.

"Gilbert Irving is a very active man. He jogs three times a week, and swims on the other four days. He also skis and plays tennis when he gets a chance. Shouldn't a person who is that active be the next president of the United States?"

1. Who is the expert in the argument?
2. In which field is that person an expert?
3. That person makes a statement about another field. Which other field?
4. Does the argument show that the person is an expert in this other field?

PART H Writing Assignment

In your own words, tell the story of Tom and Becky's romance, from the first time they met each other to when they made up.

Make your story at least **ten** sentences long.

Lesson 105

PART A Word Lists

1
ceremonies
secure
insecure
mortal
immortal

2
Vocabulary words
stand trial
atmosphere
topic
abuse
lynched
isolated

PART B New Vocabulary

1. **stand trial**—When somebody **stands trial,** that person is tried for a crime.

2. **atmosphere**—The **atmosphere** of a setting is the mood that surrounds that setting.
   a. What's another way of saying **The mood of the church was solemn?***
   b. What's another way of saying **The mood of the stadium was electric?***

3. **topic**—A **topic** is a subject that people discuss. If people discuss a trial, that trial is the **topic** of their discussion.
   a. What do you know about a trial if people discuss it?
   b. What do you know about a school if people discuss that school?

4. **abuse**—When you **abuse** something, you treat it badly.
   a. What's another way of saying **He treated his bike badly?***
   b. What's another way of saying **He treated his toy badly?***

5. **lynched**—When a person is **lynched,** that person is hanged without being tried by a court of law.

6. **isolated**—Things that are **isolated** are not close to other things. Here's another way of saying **The house was not close to other houses: The house was isolated.**
   ● What's another way of saying **Sara was not close to other people?***

PART C Vocabulary Review

1
villain
indifferent
sensation
antics
independent
scuffle

2
proceedings
random
ghastly
flustered
diary

1. Another word for **embarrassed and bewildered** is _____.
2. The things that occur during an event are the _____ of that event.
3. A book that you write in and tell about things that happened to you is called a _____.
4. When something makes a very strong impression that people talk about, it makes a _____.
5. A person who does evil things is a _____.
6. When something doesn't depend on other things, it is _____.
7. Things that follow no pattern are _____ things.
8. When you don't care about things, you are _____ about those things.

PART D Arguments

Here's a rule: *Just because the writer presents some choices doesn't mean that there are no other choices.*

The following argument breaks the rule.

"Whenever there are fairs, the ground gets littered. People drop cups, popcorn, candy wrappers, and all other types of litter onto the ground. We have to pay thousands of dollars to clean up this litter, and we can't afford it anymore. Either we go broke or we close down all the fairs."

1. Which two choices does the writer present?Ⓐ
2. Name another choice that could be possible.Ⓑ

PART E Story Items

1. At first, Tom's summer vacation was boring. But then something happened that stirred the whole village.
   a. What happened?
   b. Tom met secretly with somebody to talk about the crime. Who did he meet with?
   c. What secret knowledge did both of those people have?
   d. They had taken an _____ not to tell about it.
   e. Had both parties kept their word?
2. a. After the boys had talked, what place did they go to that evening?
   b. They hoped that something would happen to save _____.
   c. Did any miracles occur?

3. a. What did they give the person they visited?
   b. That person responded with
      • fear   • anger   • gratitude
   c. Who were the only two boys in the village that were kind to Potter?
   d. Name **two** things that Potter said he had done for the other boys in town.
   e. Tom and Huck were kind to Potter because they _____ him.
      • pitied   • hated
      • made fun of
   f. What would Tom and Huck have to do to free their consciences?
4. If Huck and Tom keep their oath, some things might happen. If Huck and Tom break their oath, other things might happen. Write **keep the oath** or **break the oath** for each thing that might happen.
   a. Muff Potter will be hanged if they _____
   b. Huck and Tom will be in serious danger if they _____.
   c. Outlaw Joe might be captured if they _____.
   d. Outlaw Joe will go free if they _____.
   e. Muff Potter will go free if they _____.

PART F Graph Skills

Assume that the graph on the next page is accurate. Examine the graph carefully, and then read the statements below it. Some of the statements contradict what is shown on the graph. Write **Contradictory** or **Not contradictory** for each statement.

TREE WIDTH AND TREE AGE

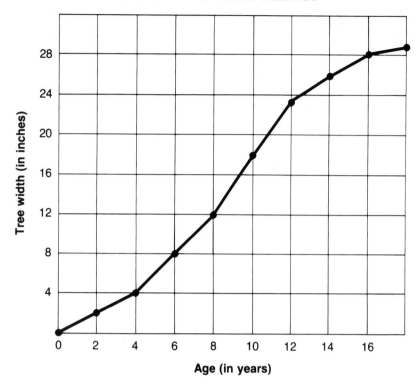

1. Older trees are narrower.
2. When a tree is twelve years old, it is twelve inches wide.
3. When a tree is nine months old, it is eight inches wide.
4. A fifteen-year-old tree is wider than a twelve-year-old tree.
5. Sixteen-year-old trees are twenty-eight inches wide.

PART G   Arguments

Here's a rule: *Just because two events happen around the same time doesn't mean one event causes the other event.*

The following argument breaks the rule.

"Sometimes I ride my bike to school and sometimes I take the bus. But it seems like every time I ride the bus, we have a surprise test in our math class. I'm going to start riding my bike tomorrow."

1. What two events happen around the same time?
2. What event does the writer think causes the surprise test?

PART H   Review Items

Write which story occurred in each place. Choose from *The Spider, the Cave, and the Pottery Bowl, Sara Crewe, The Necklace, Persephone, Harriet Tubman, The Cruise of the Dazzler, Tom Sawyer,* or *The Last Leaf.*

1. Saint Petersburg
2. London, England
3. On a mesa
4. Near San Francisco
5. In Maryland and Pennsylvania
6. Greenwich Village

PART I   Writing Assignment

Do you think that Tom and Huck will keep their oath? Write a paragraph that explains your answer.

Make your paragraph at least **six** sentences long.

Lesson 106

PART A   Word Lists

1
climax
haggard
trifle
verdict
confidentially

2
wretched
wretchedness
detective
interfere

3
Vocabulary words
give a verdict
haggard
climax
trifle
immortal
insecure

PART B   New Vocabulary

1. **give a verdict**—When a court decides whether a person is guilty or innocent of a crime, the court **gives a verdict.**
   - What does a court do when it decides whether a person is guilty or innocent of a crime?*

2. **haggard**—When somebody is very tired or weary, that person is **haggard.**
   a. What's another way of saying **She looked very weary?***
   b. What's another way of saying **After staying up all night, he felt weary?***

3. **climax**—When something builds up, the highest point that it reaches is called the **climax.** When a story builds up and builds up, the highest point that it reaches is the **climax** of the story.
   - What is the highest point of a story that builds up and builds up?*

4. **trifle**—Something that is slightly different is a **trifle** different.
   a. What's another way of saying **She was slightly faster?***
   b. What's another way of saying **Would you talk slightly louder?***

5. **immortal**—Something that is **immortal** lives on forever. A book that lives on forever is an **immortal** book.
   a. What would we call a person who lives on forever?*
   b. What would we call a legend that lives on forever?*

6. **insecure**—Things that are **insecure** are uncertain.
   a. What's another way of saying **She felt very uncertain?***
   b. What's another way of saying **The planks on the bridge were uncertain?***

PART C   Vocabulary Review

1	2	3
topic	isolated	flustered
diary	villain	abuse
atmosphere	sensation	indifferent

1. When you treat something badly, you _____ it.
2. A subject that people discuss is a _____.
3. The mood that surrounds a setting is the _____ of that setting.
4. Things that are not close to other things are _____.
5. When you don't care about things, you are _____ about those things.
6. Another word for **embarrassed and bewildered** is _____.

PART D   Story Items

1. **a.** What event began at the beginning of this chapter?
   b. What crime was this character accused of committing?
2. **a.** At first, did Potter's lawyer do a **good job** or a **bad job** of showing that Potter was innocent?
   b. How many questions did Potter's lawyer ask the first witnesses?
      • Many   • Some   • None
   c. After the lawyer who was against Potter finished his case, who did the other lawyer call to the stand as a surprise witness?
3. The lawyer asked that witness some questions. Answer each question:
   a. Where were you on the seventeenth of June, about the hour of midnight?
   b. Were you anywhere near Horse Williams's grave?
   c. Where were you hiding?
   d. What did you take there with you?
4. **a.** Just as Tom was preparing to tell what _____ did, a commotion occurred in the courtroom.
   b. Which character created the commotion?
5. **a.** How had Muff Potter's lawyer found out the truth of what had happened in the graveyard?
   b. The lawyer had promised not to tell anybody about _____.
      • Huck   • Tom   • Outlaw Joe
   c. Who was afraid that the lawyer would not keep his promise?
   d. That person was upset because Tom had broken the _____.
6. **a.** Tom was afraid _____.
      • at night   • during the day
   b. Tom felt like a town hero _____.
      • at night   • during the day
   c. Did Outlaw Joe escape?

PART E   Arguments

Here's a rule: *Just because a person is an expert in one field doesn't mean the person is an expert in another field.*

The following argument breaks the rule.

"Hi, my name is Francis Viceroy. I'm sure you've heard my records on the radio, including my famous, 'You Ain't Nothing But a Possum.' You know, singing is a full time business, and I really can't worry about much else, like worrying about whether my car will perform well. That's why I recommend Fritz Automobiles. They're well-made, and they're trouble-free. Take it from me: Buy a Fritz."

1. Who is the expert in the argument?
2. In which field is that person an expert?
3. That person makes a statement about another field. Which other field?
4. Does the argument show that the person is an expert in this other field?

PART F   Arguments

Here's a rule: *Just because the writer presents some choices doesn't mean that there are no other choices.*

The following argument breaks the rule.

"We have really been lucky with our garden, but this year is different. We're actually too lucky. We planted some corn, and now we have bushels and bushels of corn. There is far more than we can eat. If we just leave the corn in the garden, it will rot. So we have to either burn the corn or throw it away."

1. Which two choices does the writer present?
2. Name another choice that could be possible.

PART G   Writing Assignment

The lawyer asked Tom to tell the story of what happened that night. Write the story as Tom would have told it.

Make your story at least **eight** sentences long.

Lesson 107

PART A   Word Lists

1
bay
wretchedness
baying
anatomy

2
Vocabulary words
confidentially
interfere
pick

PART B   New Vocabulary

1. **confidentially**—Things that are told **confidentially** are told as secrets.
   a. What's another way of saying **Tom told her things as secrets?***
   b. What's another way of saying **Huck expressed his feelings as secrets?***

2. **interfere**—Something **interferes** with things if it gets in the way of those things. Here's another way of saying **Fernando would not get in the way of the party: Fernando would not interfere with the party.**
   a. What's another way of saying **Fernando would not get in the way of the party?***
   b. What's another way of saying **Huck didn't want to get in the way of the trial?***

3. **pick**—A **pick** is a long-handled tool with a large, pointed head. You use a **pick** for digging. You swing it and strike the ground with the pointed head.

PART C   Vocabulary Review

1	2
climax	immortal
gives a verdict	trifle
insecure	flustered
haggard	

1. When a court decides whether a person is guilty or innocent of a crime, the court _____.
2. Things that are uncertain are _____.
3. When something builds up, the highest point that it reaches is called the _____.
4. Another word for **embarrassed and bewildered** is _____.
5. When somebody is very tired or weary, that person is _____.
6. Something that is slightly different is a _____ different.
7. Something that lives on forever is _____.

PART D   Story Items

1. During the summer, Tom developed an urge to find something.
   a. What was that?
   b. Who did he talk to about working with him?
   c. Tom told where they might look. Name at least **two** places that he mentioned.
   d. Huck wanted the hundred dollars if they found it. But he didn't want any _____.
2. a. At which place did they decide to look first?
   b. How far away was that?
3. a. How much of his share did Huck plan to save?
   b. What did Huck say would happen if he didn't spend it fast?
   c. What kinds of things did Huck plan to do with his share?
   d. Name at least **two** things that Tom would do with his share.
   e. Did Tom tell the name of the person he planned to marry?

4. **a.** What results did Tom and Huck have at their first digging site?
   b. Where did they dig next?
   c. What results did they have at that site?
5. **a.** At last Tom realized that they had to dig where the limb's _____ falls at _____.
   b. So, when did they plan to resume their digging?
   c. How was Huck to signal Tom that it was time to go to their digging site?

PART E Arguments

Here's a rule: *Just because a person is an expert in one field doesn't mean that person is an expert in another field.*

The following argument breaks the rule.

"Professor Johnson has been with the University of New York for twelve years and is chairperson of the history department. Professor Johnson is urging that the city should close four junior high schools. Surely it is foolish to ignore the wisdom this man is offering us."

1. Who is the expert in this argument?
2. In which field is that person an expert?
3. That person makes a statement about another field. Which other field?
4. Does the argument show that the person is an expert in this other field?

PART F Metaphors

Here's a metaphor: *A faint wind moaned through the trees.*
1. So, the wind was like something that _____.
2. What could that something be?
3. Use accurate language to tell how the wind's noise and a _____'s noise could be the same.

PART G Arguments

Here's a rule: *Just because the writer presents some choices doesn't mean that there are no other choices.*

The following argument breaks the rule.

"I tell you, these football players are a real problem at our high school. None of them gets good grades, and they really slow up the classes. It's obvious that football takes up too much of their time. If they don't stop playing football, they'll continue to get poor grades."

1. Which choices does the writer present?
2. Name another choice that could be possible.

PART H Review Items

Tom and Huck are alike in some ways, and different in other ways. Write whether each statement describes **Tom, Huck,** or **Both.**
1. _____ wanted to get married.
2. _____ knew how to find treasure.
3. _____ didn't trust girls.
4. _____ had superstitious beliefs.
5. _____ feared Outlaw Joe.

PART I Writing Assignment

What would you do if you found a buried treasure? Write a paragraph that explains your answer.

Make your paragraph at least **six** sentences long.

Lesson 108

PART A   Word Lists

1
whiten
whitening
mute
unearth

2
Vocabulary words
baying
utterly
intruder

PART B   New Vocabulary

1. **baying**—Baying is another word for howling.
   a. What's another way of saying **The hounds howled at night?***
   b. What's another way of saying **The strong wind seemed to howl through the trees?***

2. **utterly**—Another word for **completely** is **utterly**.
   a. What's another way of saying **She was completely shocked?***
   b. What's another way of saying **The cabin was completely isolated?***

3. **intruder**—Somebody who is not invited but goes into a situation is an **intruder** in that situation. If you go to a party you are not invited to, you are an intruder at the party.
   ● What are you called if you enter into a conversation you're not invited to be in?

PART C   Vocabulary Review

1	2
immortal	pick
atmosphere	confidentially
trifle	haggard
interferes	climax
isolated	

1. Something that gets in the way of things _____ with those things.
2. A long-handled tool with a large, pointed head that is used for digging is a _____.
3. Things that are not close to other things are _____.
4. Things that are told as secrets are told _____.
5. Something that lives on forever is _____.
6. The mood that surrounds a setting is the _____ of that setting.

PART D   Arguments

Here's a rule: *Just because you know about the whole thing doesn't mean you know about every part.*

The following argument breaks the rule.

"The Googblat Company is very well known and highly respected. There is no way that their treasurer, Mr. Gomadon, could be a crook."

1. Which is the whole in this argument?Ⓐ
2. Which is the part?Ⓑ
3. What conclusion does the writer draw about the part?Ⓒ

PART E   Story Items

1. a. Around what time did Huck and Tom start to dig at the tree?
   b. What marked the place where they started digging?
   c. What did the boys decide about that site after they had dug a large hole?
   d. Tom observed that they only guessed at the time. The hour may not have been exactly _____.

2. a. What was the next place they decided to try?
   b. They would go there in the _____.
      ● daytime   ● nighttime

c. What did the boys think caused the blue light inside that place?

3. a. At noon the next day, Huck pointed out a problem with their plans to dig at the new site. What was that problem?

b. Huck told about another bad sign. He had a dream about _____.

4. a. That afternoon the boys decided to play _____.

b. Tom described that person, but he exaggerated. Name **one** thing he exaggerated about.

5. a. On which day did they return to the new site?

b. What part of the house did they explore first?

c. What part of the house did they explore next?

d. What happened while they were upstairs?

e. How did Tom and Huck see the approaching strangers?

PART F Exaggeration

Here's an example of exaggeration: *Each day was a day of splendor, but each night was a season of horror.*

1. How long does the statement say each night lasted?

2. Write an accurate statement that tells how long each night lasted.

PART G Arguments

Here's a rule: *Just because the writer presents some choices doesn't mean that there are no other choices.*

The following argument breaks the rule.

"Many runners have problems with their knees and ankles when they run on hard surfaces. These injuries may be so bad that the runner must have surgery. If these runners don't stop running, they will continue to have these injuries."

1. Which choices does the writer present?

2. Name another choice that could be possible.

PART H Review Items

1. Here are some things that Tom and Huck believed. Write whether each belief is **Superstitious** or **Not superstitious.**

a. Friday is an unlucky day.

b. There were ghosts in the haunted house.

c. Robin Hood was a great man.

d. A dead man might say something.

2. Write which story each sentence comes from. Choose from *The Doughnuts; The Necklace; The Voyage of the Northern Light; A White Heron; The Star;* or *Mrs. Dunn's Lovely, Lovely Farm.*

a. The astronomer's warning was already known all over the world, and had been translated into a thousand languages.

b. One day the terrible, horrible landlord came to collect the rents.

c. "I shoot the birds and then they're stuffed and preserved."

d. Sometimes, she sat down near the window, and thought of that gay evening of long ago.

PART I Writing Assignment

Tom admired Robin Hood. Which person from history do you admire? Write a paragraph that explains your answer.

Make your paragraph at least **six** sentences long.

Lesson 109

PART A   Word Lists

1
eternity
distinct
amid
slaughter

2
shanty
infernal
hideous
exaggeration
charter

3
Vocabulary words
mute
distinct
eternity
unearth
blissful

PART B   New Vocabulary

1. **mute**—A **mute** is a person who cannot speak.
   - What do we call a person who cannot speak?*

2. **distinct**—Something that is easily recognized is **distinct.**
   a. What's another way of saying **Her words were easily recognized?***
   b. What's another way of saying **He saw an easily recognized figure on the hill?***

3. **eternity**—Things that last for an **eternity** last forever.
   a. What's another way of saying **Nothing on earth lasts forever?***

   b. What's another way of saying **It seemed that the meeting lasted forever?***

4. **unearth**—When something is dug up or discovered, it is **unearthed.**
   a. What's another way of saying **The box was dug up?***
   b. What's another way of saying **The detective discovered the evidence?***

5. **blissful**—Another word for **great joy** is **bliss.** Things that create great joy are **blissful.** A **blissful** morning is a morning that creates great joy.
   - What would we call a party that creates great joy?*

PART C   Vocabulary Review

1	2
intruder	baying
isolated	utterly
pick	immortal
trifle	insecure

1. Another word for **howling** is
   _____.

2. Somebody who is not invited but goes into a situation is an _____ in that situation.

3. Something that is slightly different is a _____ different.

4. Another word for **completely** is
   _____.

5. A long-handled tool with a large, pointed head that is used for digging is a _____.

PART D   Arguments

Here's a rule: *Just because you know about the whole thing doesn't mean you know about every part.*

The following argument breaks the rule.

"The soccer team took first place in a city-wide tournament. Ginny is on that team, so she must be the best soccer player in the city."

1. Which is the whole in this argument?Ⓐ
2. Which is the part?Ⓑ
3. What conclusion does the writer draw about the part?Ⓒ

PART E   Story Items

1. **a.** How many men entered the house?
   b. The boys had seen one of them once or twice before. What handicaps did that man appear to have?
   c. Had the boys seen the other man before?
   d. Was one of the men really deaf and mute?
   e. Who was the man who appeared to be handicapped?
2. **a.** One of the men was complaining that their plan was dangerous. Which man?
   b. The other man pointed out that the plan was no more dangerous than another one they had carried out. Which man made that observation?
   c. The men were using the house as a
   _____.
3. The men were planning a dangerous job.
   a. Where was the dangerous job to take place?
   b. Where did the men plan to go after that job?
4. **a.** Which man went to sleep first?
   b. What was the other man supposed to do?
   c. What did that man do after a while?
5. **a.** What evidence did Tom and Huck have that the men were asleep?
   b. When the men were asleep, Tom started to leave. What stopped him?
   c. So, what did the boys do?
6. The men came into the house to bury something.
   a. What were they going to bury?
   b. How had they acquired that material?
   c. As the men dug, they discovered something. What was that?
   d. Their discovery was worth
   _____ dollars.
   - thousands of   - one hundred
   - millions of

7. **a.** What were the men going to do with the treasure at first?
   b. What made them change their minds?
   c. Who had brought the tools to the house?

PART F   Map Skills

Assume that the map below is accurate. Examine the map carefully, and then read the statements below it. Some of the statements contradict what is shown on the map. Write **Contradictory** or **Not contradictory** for each statement.

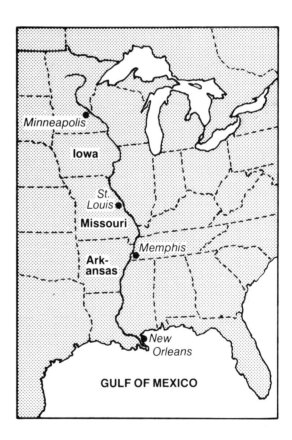

1. New Orleans is south of Memphis.
2. The Mississippi flows into the Gulf of Mexico.
3. Saint Louis is in the state of Missouri.
4. The Mississippi touches twelve states.
5. Arkansas is north of Iowa.

PART G   Arguments

Here's a rule: *Just because you know about a part doesn't mean you know about the whole thing.*

The following argument breaks the rule.

"My friend Minnie loves cats. She has a black cat that drives me nuts. It meows so loudly you can't hear. I think that all black animals must meow loudly."

1. Which thing in this argument is the part?
2. Which thing is the whole?
3. What conclusion does the writer draw about the whole?

PART H   Writing Assignment

Every time Tom and Huck do something that involves superstitions, their beliefs seem to come true. Write a paragraph about one of their adventures. Explain what they thought would happen, then tell what actually happened.

Make your paragraph at least **six** sentences long.

Lesson 110

PART A   Word Lists

1
profound
resemble
slaughterhouse
rollick
throng

2
Vocabulary words
amid
cluttered
spade
slaughterhouse
charter
throng
reflect

PART B   New Vocabulary

1. **amid**—Amid means **in the middle of.** Something that is **amid** the ruins is in the middle of the ruins.
   ● What's another way of saying **In the middle of her friends?***
2. **cluttered**—If something is not orderly and neat, it is **cluttered.**
   a. What's another way of saying **His desk was not neat and orderly?***

   b. What's another way of saying **Her room was not neat and orderly?***

3. **spade**—A **spade** is a shovel designed for digging down, not for scooping.
   ● What do we call a shovel designed for digging down, not for scooping?***
4. **slaughterhouse**—A **slaughterhouse** is a place where people kill animals and prepare them for market.
5. **charter**—When you **charter** a vehicle, you rent the vehicle for a special tour.
6. **throng**—A large group of people is a **throng** of people.
   ● What's a large group of children?***
7. **reflect**—When you ponder or contemplate, you **reflect.**
   ● What's another way of saying **She contemplated for a moment?***

PART C　Vocabulary Review

1	2
unearthed	eternity
trifle	pick
blissful	baying
distinct	

1. Things that last forever last for an
_____.

2. Something that is easily recognized is
_____.

3. When something is dug up or
discovered, it is _____.

4. Things that create great joy are
_____.

PART D　Arguments

Below are three rules about arguments.

● Rule 1: *Just because two events happen
around the same time doesn't mean
one event causes the other event.*

● Rule 2: *Just because you know about a
part doesn't mean you know about the
whole thing.*

● Rule 3: *Just because a person is an
expert in one field doesn't mean the
person is an expert in another field.*

1. The following argument breaks one of
the rules.

   "We live on a farm, and the sun
   always rises after the rooster crows.
   But today our rooster got sick. I guess
   the sun won't rise tomorrow."

● Which rule does the argument
break?Ⓐ

2. The following argument breaks one of
the rules.

   "Veronica James is a highly skilled
   banker. She knows all about the
   different accounts and how to figure
   interest payments. So when she tells
   me which car to buy, I listen."

● Which rule does the argument
break?Ⓑ

PART E　Story Items

1. a. Outlaw Joe was suspicious of the
pick because it had _____
on it.
   b. Where did Joe decide to look?
   c. As he started up the stairs,
   something happened to save the
   boys. What was that?
   d. Joe's comrade argued that if
   anybody else was upstairs,
   something would have happened to
   them. What?
   e. The men went with their treasure
   to hiding place _____.

2. a. Did Huck and Tom follow the men?
   b. Who did Tom think Joe was after
   for his revenge?

3. Tom wasn't sure whether the
adventure in the haunted house had
actually happened.
   a. To find out whether the adventure
   had actually taken place, who did
   Tom visit the next day?
   b. Why didn't Tom mention the
   adventure to that person?

4. Tom suggested that the number of the
hiding place referred to a house
number.
   a. What was wrong with that idea?
   b. What was the number of the
   hiding place the men went to?
   c. What did the boys next think that
   the number of the hiding place
   referred to?

5. a. Who went to town to investigate?
   b. He discovered that there was a
   strange room in the _____
   hotel.
   ● best　● not-so-fancy
   c. What kind of passageway led up to
   the back of the room?

6. a. Who were the boys going to observe
   before they tried to get
   into the room?
   b. How were they going to try to open
   the door?
   c. At the end of the chapter, both
   boys agreed to _____
   Outlaw Joe.

PART F Conversations

Below is a conversation between Huck and Tom. Write which person makes each statement.

"Here's how I cure warts with stump water, Huck," Tom said. ①

"How's that?" ②

"I put my hand in a stump just as it's midnight and I say, 'Barley-corn, barley-corn, Injun-meal shorts; Stump water, stump water, swallow these warts.' ③ Then I walk away quick, with my eyes shut." ④

"Well, that sounds like a good way, but that ain't what Bob Tanner did." ⑤

PART G Arguments

Here's a rule: *Just because you know about the whole thing doesn't mean you know about every part.*

The following argument breaks the rule.

"The Comets are the best baseball team in the country. Fernando Miranda plays first base for the Comets. Therefore, Fernando must be the best first baseman in the country."

1. Which is the whole in this argument?
2. Which is the part?
3. What conclusion does the writer draw about the part?

PART H Writing Assignment

Do you think that the hiding place is hotel room Number Two? Write a paragraph that explains your answer.

Make your paragraph at least **six** sentences long.

Lesson 111

PART A   Word Lists

1	2	3
catastrophe	gravel	**Vocabulary words**
sentry	outweigh	resemble
inlet	hayloft	profound
elude	yield	catastrophe
tolerant		sentry
intricate		consent
		rollick

PART B   New Vocabulary

1. **resemble**—Something that **resembles** another thing looks like that thing. Here's another way of saying **Henry looked like John: Henry resembled John.**
   a. What's another way of saying **Henry looked like John?***
   b. What's another way of saying **The pictures did not look like each other?***

2. **profound**—Something that is very great or deep is **profound.**
   a. What's another way of saying **His thoughts were very great?***
   b. What's another way of saying **The stillness was very deep?***

3. **catastrophe**—Another word for **disaster** is **catastrophe.**
   a. What's another way of saying **The hurricane created a disaster?***
   b. What's another way of saying **There was a great disaster in California?***

4. **sentry**—A **sentry** is a guard.
   ● What's another way of saying **There were four guards outside the gate?***

5. **consent**—When you **consent** to do something, you agree to do it.
   a. What's another way of saying **He agreed to take his brother to the park?***
   b. What's another way of saying **The widow would not agree to the contract?***

6. **rollick**—When you **rollick,** you play and make a lot of noise.
   a. What's another way of saying **The children were playing and making a lot of noise outside the window?***
   b. What's another way of saying **They played and made noise at the picnic?***

PART C   Vocabulary Review

1	2
cluttered	blissful
intruder	spade
throng	immortal
amid	unearthed
distinct	reflect

1. Something that is easily recognized is _____.

2. If something is not orderly and neat it is _____.

3. Another word for **in the middle of** is _____.

4. Something that lives on forever is _____.

5. A shovel designed for digging down, not for scooping, is a _____.

6. When you ponder or contemplate, you _____.

7. A large group of people is a _____ of people.

8. Things that create great joy are _____.

PART D Arguments

Below are three rules about arguments.

- Rule 1: *Just because two events happen around the same time doesn't mean one event causes the other event.*

- Rule 2: *Just because a person is an expert in one field doesn't mean the person is an expert in another field.*

- Rule 3: *Just because you know about the whole thing doesn't mean you know about every part.*

1. The following argument breaks one of the rules.

   "The Bashers have the best basketball team in the league. They haven't lost a game all season. I'm sure they must have the best center in the league."

   - Which rule does the argument break?Ⓐ

2. The following argument breaks one of the rules.

   "Sylvester Prince is one of the finest architects in the world today. He has designed several skyscrapers and countless homes. He recommends using Pummel soap, so that's what I use."

   - Which rule does the argument break?Ⓑ

PART E Story Items

1. **a.** Which two parts of the hotel did the boys watch?
   b. On Monday, did anybody resembling Outlaw Joe enter the hotel?
   c. On Tuesday, did anybody resembling Outlaw Joe enter the hotel?
   d. On which night did the boys have better luck?
2. **a.** Where did Huck sleep?
   b. Who stood on guard as the other tried to get into the room?
   c. Did the other person go **in the front door** or **into the alley**?

   d. What did Tom tell Huck to do as Tom left the alley?
   e. Where did the boys go?
3. **a.** Tom explained that the door was _____.
   b. Who was inside the room?
   c. What was that person doing?
   d. What did Tom remember to pick up before leaving the room?
   e. Did Tom see the treasure box?
4. The boys agreed on a plan.
   a. Who said that he would watch all night long?
   b. Who said that he would snatch the box?
5. **a.** Who returned to the village on Friday?
   b. On which day did that person plan to have a picnic?
   c. The picnic was to take place south of town, near the _____.
   d. How did the children get to the picnic site?
6. **a.** Where did Tom and Becky plan to spend the night after the picnic?
   b. The picnic presented a problem for Tom because _____ might try to signal him that night.
   c. After Tom thought about this problem, what did he decide to do?
   - Have fun   • Wait for Huck
   - Play with Sid

PART F Irony

Below is an example of irony from *Tom Sawyer*.

1. When Tom and Huck started to look for buried treasure, they had a mistaken belief about where they would find the treasure. What was that?
2. Tom and Huck did something that was based on the belief. What did they do?
3. What would Tom and Huck have done if they had known the truth about the treasure?

PART G   Arguments

Here's a rule: *Just because you know about the whole thing doesn't mean you know about every part.*

The following argument breaks the rule.

"Wholesome Heights is the richest part of this city. Hugh comes from Wholesome Heights. He must be pretty rich."

1. Which is the whole in this argument?
2. Which is the part?
3. What conclusion does the writer draw about the part?

PART H   Writing Assignment

Tom and Becky are really looking forward to the picnic. Write a paragraph that describes the kind of picnic you would like to go on. Tell where you would go, what you would eat, and what games you would play.

Make your paragraph at least **six** sentences long.

Lesson 112

PART A Word Lists

1	2
romantic	**Vocabulary words**
estate	inlet
horsewhipped	romp
murder	intricate
murderous	elude
scoundrel	flinch

PART B New Vocabulary

1. **inlet**—An **inlet** is a place where the shore forms a small bay or cove.

2. **romp**—Another word for **rollick** is **romp**.
   a. What's another way of saying **They rollicked around the playground?***

   b. What's another way of saying **Stop all that rollicking?***

3. **intricate**—Something that is very delicate and detailed is **intricate.**
   a. What's another way of saying **He had a very detailed plan?***
   b. What's another way of saying **The spider wove a delicate web?***

4. **elude**—When you **elude** a person, you hide from the person or avoid that person.
   a. What's another way of saying **They avoided the pirates?***
   b. What's another way of saying **I can't catch her because she keeps avoiding me?***

5. **flinch**—When you **flinch,** you jump when somebody startles you.

PART C Vocabulary Review

1	2
catastrophe	rollick
resembles	sentry
immortal	reflect
blissful	verdict
profound	consent

1. Something that looks like another thing _____ that thing.
2. When you agree to do something, you _____ to do it.
3. When you ponder or contemplate, you _____.
4. Another word for **disaster** is _____.
5. Something that is very great or deep is _____.
6. When you play and make a lot of noise, you _____.
7. A guard is a _____.

PART D Arguments

Here's a rule: *Just because two words sound the same doesn't mean they have the same meaning.*

The following argument breaks the rule.

"Bob said that he would give me a ring on Thursday, and all he did was call me on the phone. I wonder if I should ever see him again."

1. Which word has two meanings in this argument?**Ⓐ**
2. What does the writer think that word means?**Ⓑ**
3. What does the word actually mean?**Ⓒ**

PART E   Story Items

1. **a.** Where did Tom and Becky plan to spend the night after the picnic?
   b. How did the children get to the picnic site?
   c. Where did the children go after they ate?
   d. The mouth of the cave was shaped like the letter _____.
   e. How many people "knew" the entire cave?
   f. Which boy knew as much of the cave as anyone?
2. **a.** When most of the children returned to the mouth of the cave, what time was it?
   b. What signal had been blowing for over half an hour?
3. **a.** What was Huck doing as the steamboat returned to Saint Petersburg?
   b. Huck was about ready to give up when he observed something. What was that?
   c. To whose place did Huck follow them?
4. **a.** Who was Outlaw Joe going after for his revenge?
   b. Why did Outlaw Joe want revenge on that person?
   c. Which man didn't want to carry out the plan?
   d. What did Outlaw Joe say he would do to that person if he didn't help?
5. **a.** As Huck was backing up, what happened to make a noise?
   b. The first time Huck ran away from the Widow Douglas's place, he went to the _____'s house.
   c. Why did he run away from the Widow Douglas's place a second time?

PART F   Arguments

Here's a rule: *Just because you know about the whole thing doesn't mean you know about every part.*

The following argument breaks the rule.

"Swan Bicycles is a very dishonest company. My friend Leroy works on the assembly line for Swan Bicycles. It just occurred to me that Leroy must be very dishonest too."

1. Which is the whole in this argument?
2. Which is the part?
3. What conclusion does the writer draw about the part?

PART G   Review Items

Here are some pairs of story events. The events in some of the pairs happened at the same time. Write **Same time** for those events. The events in other pairs happened at different times. Write **Different times** for those events.
1. The steamboat went past the wharf. Huck was still watching the hotel.
2. The children played in the cave. Huck followed the two men.
3. Outlaw Joe stood outside the Widow Douglas's gate. Huck went to warn the Welshman.

PART H   Writing Assignment

The novel said that when Huck stood outside the widow's gate, "his heart shot into his throat, but he swallowed it again." What do you think that sentence means? Write a paragraph that explains your answer.

Make your paragraph at least **five** sentences long.

Lesson 113

PART A Word Lists

1
deputy
relic
lavish

2
pleasantest
burglar
murderous
tolerant
intolerant

3
Vocabulary words
scoundrels
deputy
bore

PART B New Vocabulary

1. **scoundrels**—Another word for **villains** is **scoundrels**.
   a. What's another way of saying **There was a band of villains in town?***
   b. What's another way of saying **He was a liar and a villain?***

2. **deputy**—A **deputy** is a lawman who is not high ranking.

3. **bore**—When something makes a hole, it **bores**.
   a. What's another way of saying **The drill made a hole through the wood?***
   b. What's another way of saying **His eyes made a hole into my mind?***

PART C Vocabulary Review

1	2	3
intricate	sentry	baying
romp	profound	elude
cluttered	consent	amid

1. Another word for **in the middle of** is _____.
2. Something that is very delicate and detailed is _____.
3. When you hide from a person or avoid the person, you _____ that person.
4. Another word for **rollick** is _____.
5. Something that is very great or deep is _____.
6. When you agree to do something, you _____ to do it.

PART D Arguments

Here's a rule: *Just because two words sound the same doesn't mean they have the same meaning.*

The following argument breaks the rule.

"The description of the robber said he was carrying arms. Since most people have arms, I don't think it was a very good description."

1. Which word has two meanings in this argument?**Ⓐ**
2. What does the writer think this word means?**Ⓑ**
3. What does the word actually mean?**Ⓒ**

PART E Story items

1. **a.** Where did Huck go on Sunday morning?
   b. How did the Welshman greet Huck?
   c. What did the Welshman offer Huck after he came in?
   d. The Welshman treated Huck well because he had saved _____.
2. The Welshman told his story.
   a. What happened to him when he was fifteen feet from the villains?
   b. What did the villains do then?
   c. Who were the villains?
3. Huck pleaded with the Welshman and his sons not to do something. What was that?
4. Huck told a lie about what had happened.
   a. According to his story, why was he standing by the brick wall?
   b. What made it possible for him to see the faces of the men?
   c. Huck made another mistake when he told his story. What did he say that couldn't be possible?
   d. At last, Huck told the truth about something. What was that?
5. **a.** What was in the bundle the villains left behind?
   b. What did Huck fear the villains had left behind?
   c. When the Welshman asked Huck what he thought was in the bundle, Huck said _____.
   d. Huck felt relieved when he figured out that the treasure was in

   _____.

   e. What did Huck plan to do that night?

PART F Arguments

Below are three rules about arguments.

- Rule 1: *Just because two events happen around the same time doesn't mean one event causes the other event.*

- Rule 2: *Just because a person is an expert in one field doesn't mean the person is an expert in another field.*

- Rule 3: *Just because you know about the whole thing doesn't mean you know about every part.*

1. The following argument breaks one of the rules.

   "The last time I turned on the radio, I heard a news bulletin about a terrible accident. I'd better not turn on the radio again, or another accident will occur."
   - Which rule does the argument break?

2. The following argument breaks one of the rules.

   "Sunset Hills has the highest average income in the country. Peggy James comes from Sunset Hills, so she must have a high income."
   - Which rule does the argument break?

PART G   Inference

Read the passage below and answer each question. Write **Words** if the question is answered by words in the passage. Write **Deduction** if the question is answered by a deduction.

Tolerant and Intolerant Trees

*Some trees do not need much sunlight to survive. These trees are called **tolerant**. A tolerant tree is tolerant of shade, which means it can get along in shade. Trees that are not tolerant can't survive in shade. They are called **intolerant**. The top of an intolerant tree must be in full sunlight.*

Find a tree whose lower branches are always shaded by its upper ones. If the lower branches are bare and the upper leaves are dense, the tree is probably intolerant. On an intolerant tree, leaves that are always shaded die.

Intolerant trees are usually fast growers. They have to grow fast to survive. If seeds from different trees fall on the bank of a river, the fastest-growing trees are going to get the sunlight. The slower-growing trees will be shaded by the faster-growing trees. If the intolerant trees were slow growers, they would be shaded and then die. Just as intolerant trees are usually fast growers, tolerant trees are usually slow growers. They can survive in the shade; therefore, they don't have to grow fast and be the first to reach for the sunlight.

1. a. A Douglas fir is a very intolerant tree. Is it probably a **fast-growing tree** or a **slow-growing one**?
    b. Is that question answered by **Words** or by a **Deduction**?
2. a. What are trees called that can't survive in shade?
    b. **Words** or **Deduction**?
3. a. What are trees called that can survive in shade?
    b. **Words** or **Deduction**?
4. a. You can find young white oak trees growing beneath Douglas fir trees. What do you know about those white oaks?
    b. **Words** or **Deduction**?

PART H   Writing Assignment

Tom Sawyer was very good at lying. Pretend that Tom had followed the men to the Widow Douglas's place. Write a paragraph that tells the lie he might have told to the Welshman. Try to make your writing sound like Tom.

Make your paragraph at least **eight** sentences long.

Lesson 114

PART A   Word Lists

1
crazed
homeward
revive

2
Vocabulary words
lavish
relic
whiskey

PART B   New Vocabulary

1. **lavish**—Something that is very showy and excessive is **lavish**.
   a. What's another way of saying **They ate a very showy and excessive dinner?***

b. What's another way of saying **Her praise was very showy and excessive?***

2. **relic**—Something that is left over from the past is a **relic**.
   • What's another way of saying **They found many things left over from the past?***

3. **whiskey**—**Whiskey** is a strong, alcoholic drink.

PART C   Vocabulary Review

1	2
bores	profound
reflect	lull
sentry	catastrophe
scoundrels	resembles
consent	intricate

1. When you ponder or contemplate, you _____.
2. When something makes a hole, it _____.
3. Another word for **villains** is _____.
4. Something that is very great or deep is _____.
5. When you agree to do something, you _____ to do it.
6. Something that is very delicate and detailed is _____.
7. Something that looks like another thing _____ that thing.

PART D   Story Items

1. a. Becky was supposed to spend the night at _____'s house.
   b. But she secretly planned to eat ice cream at _____'s house.

2. a. Where was Huck at the beginning of this chapter?
   b. Who was among the people who came to the house?
   c. What emotion did that person express?
      • Anger   • Gratitude   • Sorrow
   d. Did the Welshman tell who was really responsible for rescuing the Widow Douglas?

3. a. At church, who did Mrs. Thatcher ask about?
   b. She thought that person had spent the night at _____'s house.
   c. Who else was missing that morning?
   d. In which place had the two missing persons last been seen?
   e. Where did the men from town go when they realized those two people were missing?

4. List two clues of Tom and Becky that the searchers found in the cave by Monday morning.

5. a. What condition was Huck in as the searchers hunted for the others?
   b. Who was taking care of him?
   c. Did Huck know that Tom was missing?
   d. The Widow Douglas told Huck what had been found at the hotel. What had been found?

6. Write where each character was at the end of this chapter. Choose from **the Welshman's house, The cave,** or **Tom Sawyer's house.** If the chapter did not tell where a character was, write **Missing** for that character.
   a. Huck
   b. Tom
   c. Aunt Polly
   d. Outlaw Joe
   e. Becky
   f. The Widow Douglas

PART E   Arguments

Here's a rule: *Just because two words sound the same doesn't mean they have the same meaning.*

The following argument breaks the rule.

"My friends said that the baker had a lot of dough. But when I went over to the baker's house, all I saw was a bunch of flour. I don't think the baker is rich, after all."

1. Which word has two meanings in this argument?
2. What does the writer think this word means?
3. What does the word actually mean?

PART F   Arguments

Below are three rules about arguments.

● Rule 1: *Just because you know about a part doesn't mean you know about the whole thing.*

● Rule 2: *Just because a person is an expert in one field doesn't mean the person is an expert in another field.*

● Rule 3: *Just because the writer presents some choices doesn't mean that there are no other choices.*

1. The argument in the next column breaks one of the rules.

"As your president, I must make difficult choices every day. At the moment, our economy is in a mess. We must either have high inflation or high unemployment. Which would you prefer?"
● Which rule does the argument break?

2. The following argument breaks one of the rules.

"Lloyd Lucas was one of the first people to walk on the moon. He is an expert on rocket design and on all aspects of space travel. He would make an excellent governor."
● Which rule does the argument break?

PART G   Review Items

1. On which island did Odysseus live?
2. In which bay did *The Cruise of the Dazzler* take place?
3. Along which river is Saint Petersburg located?
4. In which city did Sara Crewe live?

PART H   Writing Assignment

Sometimes news stories get changed as the news spreads. Pretend one villager is telling another villager about what has happened to Outlaw Joe and to Tom and Becky. Change some of the facts, and introduce new facts.

Make your story at least **six** sentences long.

Lesson 115

PART A   Word Lists

1
stalagmites
stalactites
apprehensive
paralyze

2
reference
bygone
famished
clam
clammy

3
Vocabulary words
stalactites
stalagmites
apprehensive
revive

PART B   New Vocabulary

1. **stalactites**—**Stalactites** are long columns of rock that hang down from the top of a cave.
   stalagmites—**Stalagmites** are columns of rock on the floor of a cave that pile up below stalactites.
   Here's how to remember the difference: **Stalactites** hang on **tight.**

2. **apprehensive**—When you're **apprehensive,** you're uncertain and afraid.
   a. What's another way of saying **Becky grew uncertain and afraid?***

   b. What's another way of saying **Tom was uncertain and afraid as he entered the cave?***

3. **revive**—When something **revives,** it comes back to life or to a healthy state. If the water brought the plant back to life, the water revived the plant.
   a. What happens if the water brought the plant back to life?*
   b. What happens if the doctors brought the man back to a healthy state?*

PART C   Vocabulary Review

1	2
throng	immortal
haggard	elude
profound	lavish
intricate	

1. Something that is very delicate and detailed is _____.
2. When you hide from a person or avoid the person, you _____ that person.
3. A large group of people is a _____ of people.
4. Something that is very showy and excessive is _____.

PART D   Story Items

1. What game did Tom and Becky play inside the cave with the other children?
2. a. Tom and Becky found a secret stairway behind a _____.
   b. When Tom and Becky came to a large cavern, what animals covered the ceiling?
   c. What irritated those animals?
   d. What did Tom and Becky do when the animals became irritated?
3. a. Did Tom want to return the way he and Becky had come?
   b. What was Tom afraid of if he and Becky returned to the large cavern?
   c. What did Tom do to try to attract the attention of the others?
   d. At last, Tom and Becky realized that they were hopelessly _____.

4.
  a. What did Tom do to make sure that they would have some light even if they were in the cave for a long time?
  b. What did Becky fear would happen to Tom and her?

PART E Combined Sentences

Below is a combined sentence that presents a new word and tells what the new word means. The new word is not underlined.

The emu, a large bird that cannot fly, is related to the ostrich.

1. What is the new word?
2. What does the new word mean?
3. What else does the sentence tell about the new word?

PART F Arguments

Here's a rule: *Just because two words sound the same doesn't mean they have the same meaning.*

The following argument breaks the rule.

"I read in our textbook that Homer used a lyre. That surprised me. I couldn't understand why he'd want to use someone who is dishonest."

1. Which word has two meanings in this argument?
2. What does the writer think this word means?
3. What does the word actually mean?

PART G Arguments

Below are three rules about arguments.

- Rule 1: *Just because you know about a part doesn't mean you know about the whole thing.*

- Rule 2: *Just because you know about the whole thing doesn't mean you know about every part.*

- Rule 3: *Just because two words sound the same doesn't mean they have the same meaning.*

1. The following argument breaks one of the rules.

  "I wanted to buy ten tickets for the movies. But when I went up to the ticket window, the man said he could only sell me a pair. I told the man that I wanted tickets, not fruit."
- Which rule does the argument break?

2. The following argument breaks one of the rules.

  "I bought a box of Ruts crackers the other day. The first cracker I pulled out of the box was burned. I didn't pull any more out. I was sure they were all burned."
- Which rule does the argument break?

PART H Review Items

Tell which poem each line comes from. Choose from *Casey at the Bat; Miracles; The Tide Rises, the Tide Falls;* or *Written in March*.
1. "The little waves, with their soft white hands."
2. "To me the sea is a continual miracle."
3. "Or the exquisite, delicate thin curve of the new moon in spring."
4. "From the benches, black with people, there went up a muffled roar."
5. "There's joy in the fountains."

PART I Graph Skills

Assume that the graph on the next page is accurate. Examine the graph carefully, and then read the statements below it. Some of the statements contradict what is shown on the graph. Write **Contradictory** or **Not contradictory** for each statement.

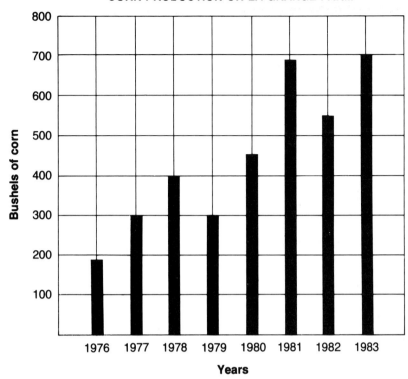

CORN PRODUCTION ON LA GRANGE FARM

1. 1979 was the least productive year for corn.
2. The farm produced more corn in 1981 than it did in 1976.
3. Four hundred barrels of corn were produced in 1978.
4. Corn production decreased from 1979 to 1981.
5. Corn production increased from 1976 to 1978.

PART J   Writing Assignment

Write a paragraph that describes the beautiful country that Becky saw in her dream.

Make your paragraph at least **six** sentences long.

PART K   Special Projects

1. (Individual Project) There are only five chapters left in *Tom Sawyer*. Without reading ahead, make up your own ending for the novel. Tell what happens to Tom, Becky, Huck, and Outlaw Joe.

   Make your ending at least **three** pages long. Then turn your ending in to the teacher. The teacher will read the endings out loud after the class finishes the novel.

2. (Group Project) Draw a large map of the Mississippi River. Show all the large cities along the river. Also show the rivers that feed into the Mississippi. Put labels on the map. Next to the labels, write facts about each state, city, or river. Make each state a different color. Finally, put Hannibal on the map.

Lesson 116

PART A   Word Lists

1
to estimate
tedious
funeral
foundry

2
portion
paralyzed
provisions

3
Vocabulary words
estimate
pitfall
famished
tedious

PART B   New Vocabulary

1. **estimate**—When you **estimate** something, you make an intelligent guess about that thing.
   a. What's another way of saying **He made an intelligent guess about the time?***
   b. What's another way of saying **She made an intelligent guess about the answer to the problem?***

2. **pitfall**—A **pitfall** is a large hole.

3. **famished**—When you are **famished**, you are very, very hungry.
   a. What's another way of saying **Mark was very, very hungry?***
   b. What's another way of saying **After all the romping, the children were very, very hungry?***

4. **tedious**—Something that is very boring is **tedious**.
   a. What's another way of saying **They had a very boring experience?***
   b. What's another way of saying **The boring activity lasted for hours?***

PART C   Vocabulary Review

1	2
revives	cluttered
bores	resembles
apprehensive	sentry
amid	

1. When you're uncertain and afraid, you are _____.
2. When something comes back to life or to a healthy state, it _____.
3. A guard is a _____.
4. When something makes a hole, it _____.

PART D   Arguments

Here's a rule: *Just because you know about one part doesn't mean you know about another part.*

The following argument breaks the rule.

"I can prove that this bicycle has the best handlebars of any bike on the road. Here's the proof: This bike has the very best seat of any bike made. So you know that the handlebars must be the very best."

1. The argument tells about two parts and a whole.
   a. Name the whole. Ⓐ
   b. Name the two parts. Ⓑ
2. Which part do you know something about? Ⓒ
3. Which part does the writer draw a conclusion about? Ⓓ
4. What does the writer conclude about that part? Ⓔ

PART E Story Items

1. **a.** What food did Tom offer Becky?
   b. When did he get that food?
   c. Tom realized that Becky's mother would not miss her until

   _____.

   d. Why wouldn't Becky's mother miss her sooner?
2. **a.** Tom wanted to stay by the spring. Why?
   b. After they had eaten, what happened to the last candle?
3. Later, something gave hope to the two captives.
   a. What was that?
   b. How did Tom signal to indicate where he and Becky were?
   c. In the darkness, Tom and Becky came to a place they did not dare to cross. Why?
4. **a.** As Tom explored in the darkness, what did he use to mark the route?
   b. Where did Becky remain?
   c. When Tom had gone as far as he could go, he saw something about twenty yards ahead of him. What was that?
   d. Who did the hand belong to?
   e. When Tom shouted, that person

   _____.

   - shouted back
   - threw something
   - ran away
5. **a.** Did Tom tell Becky who he had seen?
   b. What did Becky fear would happen to her at the end of this chapter?
   c. What did Tom set off to do?

PART F Outlining

Make up an outline for the following passage. Write a main idea for each paragraph; then write three supporting details under each main idea. Use complete sentences to write the main idea and supporting details.

Saturday morning came, and all the summer world was bright and fresh, and brimming with life. There was a song in every heart; there was cheer in every face and a spring in every step. The locust trees were in bloom and the fragrance of the blossoms filled the air.

Tom appeared on the sidewalk with a bucket of whitewash and a long-handled brush. He viewed the fence. All gladness left him and a deep melancholy settled down on his spirit. He had to whitewash thirty yards of board fence nine feet high. Life to him seemed hollow, and living just a burden.

PART G Arguments

Here's a rule: _Just because two words sound the same doesn't mean they have the same meaning._

The following argument breaks the rule.

"There is really no reason to install new lights in the library. All of the people who use the library are very bright. It would be silly to put more light into the rooms."

1. Which word has two meanings in this argument?
2. What does the writer think this word means?
3. What does the word actually mean?

PART H Arguments

Below are three rules about arguments.

- Rule 1: *Just because two events happen around the same time doesn't mean one event causes the other event.*

- Rule 2: *Just because the writer presents some choices doesn't mean that there are no other choices.*

- Rule 3: *Just because two words sound the same doesn't mean they have the same meaning.*

1. The following argument breaks one of the rules:

   "We planted tomatoes in our vegetable garden. Pretty soon, the tomato plants were covered with bugs. I tried to pick the bugs off with my hands, but they came back the next day. I guess I'll have to dig up the plants and throw them away."
   - Which rule does the argument break?

2. The following argument breaks one of the rules.

   "The dog next door used to bark every evening when the sun went down. But our neighbors took the dog on vacation this morning. I guess the sun won't go down this evening."
   - Which rule does the argument break?

PART I Writing Assignment

Imagine what it would be like to be in a place that was completely dark and isolated. Write a paragraph that describes what you would think and feel in such a place.

Make your paragraph at least **six** sentences long.

Lesson 117

PART A   Word Lists

1
secure
security
stalagmite
foundry
groped
stalactite

2
Vocabulary words
peal
clad
hamlet
provisions
fret
bluff

PART B   New Vocabulary

1. **peal**—When bells ring, they **peal**.
   - What's another way of saying
     He heard the bells ring?*

2. **clad**—Clad means **dressed**.
   a. What's another way of saying
      He was dressed in a swimsuit?*
   b. What's another way of saying
      They were half dressed?*

3. **hamlet**—A small town is a **hamlet**.
   - What's another way of saying
     They lived in a small town?*

4. **provisions**—The supplies that you
   take with you on a trip are
   provisions.
   a. What's another way of saying
      **They loaded their supplies into
      the ship?***
   b. What's another way of saying
      **We will need many supplies for
      this venture?***

5. **fret**—When you worry about
   something, you **fret** about that thing.
   a. What's another way of saying
      **He worried about his
      appearance?***
   b. What's another way of saying
      **They worried about Tom and
      Becky?***

6. **bluff**—A large, rounded hill is a
   bluff.

PART C   Vocabulary Review

1	2	3
famished	estimate	rollicked
lavish	bores	scoundrel
tedious		

1. Something that is very showy and
   excessive is _____.
2. When you are very, very hungry, you
   are _____.
3. Something that is very boring is
   _____.
4. When you make an intelligent guess
   about something, you _____
   that thing.

PART D   Arguments

Here's a rule: *Just because you know
about one part doesn't mean you know
about another part.*

The following argument breaks the rule.

"My friend Manuel is very honest. He
belongs to the Star Society, which meets
twice a week. Yesterday I met a girl
named Rosa. It turned out that she also
belongs to the Star Society. She must be
very honest too."

1. The argument tells about two parts
   and a whole.
   a. Name the whole.Ⓐ
   b. Name the two parts.Ⓑ
2. Which part do you know something
   about?Ⓒ
3. Which part does the writer draw a
   conclusion about?Ⓓ
4. What does the writer conclude about
   that part?Ⓔ

PART E   Story Items

1. **a.** On which night did the village celebrate?
   b. Why?
   c. Tom did not tell about someone that he had seen in the cave. Who was that?
2. Tom told how he had escaped.
   a. What did he use to mark his path?
   b. When he had gone as far as he could, what did he notice?
   c. When he peeped out, what did he see?
   d. Tom and Becky came out _____ miles from the cave entrance.
3. **a.** Which of the two children recovered first from the experience in the cave?
   b. On what day was that person nearly completely well?
   c. In what condition was the other person at that time?
   d. When did Becky finally leave her room?
4. **a.** Who did Tom try to visit?
   b. Tom had heard about Outlaw Joe's companion. What had happened to him?
5. **a.** Judge Thatcher said that nobody would be lost _____ anymore.
   b. Why?
   c. Tom turned pale because he knew something about the cave. What was that?
6. **a.** In what condition was Outlaw Joe?
   b. When the cave door was unlocked, where was Outlaw Joe lying?
   c. Why were there no candle bits in the cave near Joe?
   d. What animals had Joe eaten?
   e. Where was Joe buried?
   f. The people confessed that the time they had at the funeral was almost as satisfactory as a _____ would have been.

PART F   Arguments

Below are three rules about arguments.

- Rule 1: *Just because you know about a part doesn't mean you know about the whole thing.*

- Rule 2: *Just because a person is an expert in one field doesn't mean that person is an expert in another field.*

- Rule 3: *Just because you know about the whole thing doesn't mean you know about every part.*

1. The following argument breaks one of the rules.

   "June LaRue is one of the finest figure skaters in the world. She has won five gold medals and countless other prizes. So when she recommends using the Robbers' Bank, you know she's right."
   - Which rule does the argument break?

2. The following argument breaks one of the rules.

   "The Cunning Candy Corporation has a very good reputation. Felipe Lopez works for that corporation. He must have a very good reputation also."
   - Which rule does the argument break?

PART G   Review Items

1. Write which story each character appeared in. Choose from *Harriet Tubman; Sara Crewe; The Last Leaf; The Necklace; Mrs. Dunn's Lovely, Lovely Farm; The White Heron;* or *The Red Room.*
   a. An Irish woman who tricked her landlord
   b. A former slave who worked for the Underground Railroad
   c. A country girl who saved a bird's life
   d. An artist who thought she was going to die

2. Tell which story occurred in each location. Choose from *Sara Crewe; Tom Sawyer; The Red Room; The Odyssey; Casey at the Bat; Harriet Tubman;* or *The Voyage of the Northern Light.*

   a. The sea near Nova Scotia

   b. Mudville

   c. Saint Petersburg

   d. Ithaca

PART H   Writing Assignment

Do you feel sorry for what happened to Outlaw Joe? Write a paragraph that explains your answer.

Make your paragraph at least **six** sentences long.

Lesson 118

PART A   Word Lists

1
landslide
ransom
adopt
furnish

2
Vocabulary words
gloat over
loft
foundry
adopt
impact
quench
furnish

PART B   New Vocabulary

1. **gloat over**—When you act very smug about something that happened, you **gloat over** that thing.
   a. What's another way of saying **She was very smug over her victory?***
   b. What's another way of saying **Stop being smug over your good report card?***

2. **loft**—A **loft** of a barn is the second floor, where things are stored.

3. **foundry**—A **foundry** is a place that melts down metal things and makes them into large blocks.

4. **adopt**—When people **adopt** a child, they agree to raise that child as their own.

5. **impact**—If something creates a great impression, it has **impact**. Here's another way of saying **His words made a great impression on me: His words had a great impact on me.**
   ● What's another way of saying **The experience made a great impression on me?***

6. **quench**—When a need is satisfied, that need is **quenched**.
   a. What's another way of saying **His thirst was satisfied?***
   b. What's another way of saying **His dreams were satisfied?***

7. **furnish**—When you supply something, you **furnish** it.
   a. What's another way of saying **Tom could supply the shovels?***
   b. What's another way of saying **Huck supplied an explanation?***

PART C   Vocabulary Review

1	2
provisions	fret
apprehensive	clad
tedious	famished
peal	revives
lavish	

1. When you're uncertain and afraid, you are _____.
2. When something comes back to life or to a healthy state, it _____.
3. The supplies that you take with you on a trip are _____.
4. When bells ring, they _____.
5. Another word for **dressed** is _____.
6. When you worry about something, you _____ about that thing.

PART D   Story Items

1. a. At the beginning of this chapter, Tom and Huck talked about _____.
   b. Huck reported that the only thing that had been found at the hotel was _____.
   c. Tom made an important announcement to Huck about the treasure. What was that?
   d. How far was the treasure from the cave entrance?

2. a. Outlaw Joe had run from the sound of Tom's voice. Would he really be afraid of Tom?
   b. Possibly, Outlaw Joe didn't want anybody to see what he was doing in that cave. What secret thing could he be doing?

3. **a.** What vehicle did Tom and Huck use to get to the secret entrance?
   b. What marked the secret entrance?
   c. What game did Tom want to play in the cave?
   d. What was the name of the gang that Tom wanted to form?
   e. Where had Tom found out about robbers and how they behave?
4. **a.** What sign made in candle smoke did Tom lead Huck to?
   b. Where had Tom and Huck been when they heard about that sign?
   c. Tom pointed out that Outlaw Joe's ghost would not come around where there was a _____.

PART E Arguments

Below are three rules about arguments.

- Rule 1: *Just because you know about a part doesn't mean you know about the whole thing.*

- Rule 2: *Just because you know about the whole thing doesn't mean you know about every part.*

- Rule 3: *Just because two words sound the same doesn't mean they have the same meaning.*

1. The following argument breaks one of the rules.

   "That creep Roger Tolbert is from the north side of town. He is really an unpleasant character. I guess all of the people from the north side are like Roger."
   - Which rule does the argument break?

2. The following argument breaks one of the rules.

   "That tennis player Brad Braggart sure must have a lot of trouble with the law. I read that he spends most of his time in the courts."
   - Which rule does the argument break?

PART F Arguments

Here's a rule: *Just because you know about one part doesn't mean you know about another part.*

The following argument breaks the rule.

"We are reading poems by Walt Whitman in our English class. Last week, we read a poem of his called "Miracles." That poem didn't rhyme. Next week, we'll read another poem of his, "Oh Captain! My Captain!" I'm sure that won't rhyme either."

1. The argument tells about two parts and a whole.
   a. Name the whole.
   b. Name the two parts.
2. Which part do you know something about?
3. Which part does the writer draw a conclusion about?
4. What does the writer conclude about that part?

PART G Review Items

1. Tell whether each statement describes **Tom, Huck,** or **Both.**
   a. _____ knew about things by reading books.
   b. _____ had been staying at the Welshman's house.
   c. _____ had superstitious beliefs.
   d. _____ wanted to find the treasure.
2. Write whether each item is **a novel, a short story, a poem,** or **a play.**
   a. *Mystery Yarn*
   b. *All in Favor*
   c. *Written in March*
   d. *The Red Room*
   e. *Tom Sawyer*
   f. *Casey at the Bat*

PART H   Writing Assignment

Do you think that Tom Sawyer's gang
will really rob people and raise ransoms?
Write a paragraph that describes what
you think they will really do.

Make your paragraph at least **six**
sentences long.

Lesson 119

PART A   Word Lists

1
initiation
rind
moccasins
biographical

2
gnawed
rubbish
edit
editor
quench

PART B   Vocabulary Review

1	**2**
fret	gloat over
revives	tedious
impact	clad
furnish	quenched
lavish	famished

1. When you supply something, you _____ it.
2. When you worry about something, you _____ about that thing.
3. When you are very, very hungry, you are _____.
4. Something that is very boring is _____.
5. When a need is satisfied, that need is _____.
6. If something creates a great impression, it has _____.
7. When you act very smug about something that happened, you _____ that thing.

PART C   Story Items

1. **a.** Hiding place Number Two was supposed to be under a

   _____.
   • cloud   • cross   • tree
   b. Could the boys find the hiding place at first?
   c. What tool did Tom use to uncover it?
   d. Did Tom see the box at first?
   e. Who led the way toward the treasure?

2. **a.** About how much did the box weigh?
   b. What was it filled with?
   c. Why didn't the boys take the box out of the cave?
   d. The boys put the contents of the box into _____.

3. **a.** When the boys returned to town, they put the bags in a

   _____.
   b. Tom and Huck stopped to rest in front of the _____ house.
   c. Who came out and offered to haul the wagon for them?
   d. Whose house did the Welshman lead Tom and Huck to?

4. **a.** Who was going to make an announcement at that place?
   b. What was that announcement?
   c. What did the Widow Douglas direct the boys to do before the announcement?

5. **a.** What surprise comment did Tom make about Huck after the Widow Douglas made her announcement?
   b. About how much money was there all together?
   c. About how much was Huck to get?

PART D   Arguments

Here's a rule: *Just because you know about one part doesn't mean you know about another part.*

The following argument breaks the rule.

"My job is to inspect cars. When I bring a car into my shop, I always look at the headlights. If the headlights are good, then I know that the brakes must also be good."

1. The argument tells about two parts and a whole.
   a. Name the whole.
   b. Name the two parts.
2. Which part do you know something about?
3. Which part does the writer draw a conclusion about?
4. What does the writer conclude about that part?

PART E   Arguments

Below are three rules about arguments.

- Rule 1: *Just because two events happen around the same time doesn't mean one event causes the other event.*

- Rule 2: *Just because you know about a part doesn't mean you know about the whole thing.*

- Rule 3: *Just because you know about one part doesn't mean you know about another part.*

1. The following argument breaks one of the rules.

   "I started reading a book of short stories yesterday. The first story was about a boy who made doughnuts. I'm sure the next story also will be about doughnuts."
- Which rule does the argument break?

2. The following argument breaks one of the rules.

   "About a month ago, I went into a bookstore and it started raining. Then a couple of weeks ago, I went into another bookstore and it started raining. I don't think I'll go into any bookstores today because I didn't bring my umbrella."
- Which rule does the argument break?

PART F   Writing Assignment

Tom told the story of the treasure. Tell the story in your own words, beginning with the scene in the haunted house.

Make your story at least **ten** sentences long.

Lesson 120

PART A   Word Lists

1
glorified
initiation
tranquil
respectable

2
Vocabulary words
biographical sketch

PART B   New Vocabulary

1. **biographical sketch**—A **biographical sketch** is a short biography.

PART C   Vocabulary Review

1	**2**
impact	quenched
tedious	gloat over
fret	peal
clad	

1. When you act very smug about something that happened, you _____ that thing.
2. If something creates a great impression, it has _____.
3. When bells ring, they _____.
4. When a need is satisfied, that need is _____.

PART D   Story Items

1. **a.** What did the Widow Douglas do with Huck's share of the treasure?
   b. Where did Tom's half go?
   c. How much income did Tom have every day of the year?
2. Huck's life changed a great deal.
   a. How did he feel about his new life?
   b. Name **two** things that he now had to do.
   c. Name **two** things that he couldn't do while he lived with the widow.
3. **a.** After three weeks of that new life, what did Huck do?
   b. Where did Tom find him?
   c. Describe how Huck looked.
4. **a.** Tom said that he still wanted to be a _____ even though he was rich.
   b. Tom tricked Huck into going back home by telling Huck that he couldn't be in _____ unless he was respectable.
   c. So, what did Huck finally promise to do?
5. **a.** Why couldn't the boys have their initiation ceremonies in a haunted house?
   b. At what time did the boys plan to have the initiations?
   c. What did Huck think might make the Widow Douglas proud of him?

PART E Outlining

Make up an outline for the following passage. Write a main idea for each paragraph; then write three supporting details under each main idea. Use complete sentences to write the main idea and supporting details.

The Widow Douglas introduced Huck into society, and his sufferings were almost more than he could bear. The widow's servants kept him clean and neat, combed and brushed. They put him to bed nightly in sheets that had not one little spot or stain. He had to eat with a knife and a fork, and he had to go to church. Wherever he turned, civilization shut him in and bound him hand and foot.

He bravely endured his miseries for three weeks, and then one day turned up missing. For forty-eight hours the widow hunted for him everywhere in great distress. The public were profoundly concerned—they searched high and low, they dragged the river for his body. Early the third morning, Tom Sawyer wisely went poking among some old empty barrels down behind the slaughterhouse, and he found Huck in one of them.

PART F Arguments

Here's a rule: *Just because you know about one part doesn't mean you know about another part.*

The following argument breaks the rule.

"Frank's house is in Danville. His house is painted blue. Debby's house is also in Danville. Her house must also be painted blue."

1. The argument tells about two parts and a whole.
   a. Name the whole.
   b. Name the two parts.
2. Which part do you know something about?

3. Which part does the writer draw a conclusion about?
4. What does the writer conclude about that part?

PART G Arguments

Below are three rules about arguments.

- Rule 1: *Just because the writer presents some choices doesn't mean that there are no other choices.*

- Rule 2: *Just because you know about the whole thing doesn't mean you know about every part.*

- Rule 3: *Just because you know about one part doesn't mean you know about another part.*

1. The following argument breaks one of the rules.

   "We got our report cards yesterday. My sister got a B in English. She must have gotten a B in Social Studies also."
- Which rule does the argument break?

2. The following argument breaks one of the rules.

   "The west side of town is pretty dumpy. Mr. Brown's house is on the west side. His house must be pretty dumpy."
- Which rule does the argument break?

PART H Writing Assignment

What do you think is going to happen to Tom and Huck? Write a paragraph about each character. Use evidence from the story to support your answer.

Make each paragraph at least **five** sentences long.